"GET IT":

"An immersive and informative memoir of a girlhood in Samburu County." -*Kirkus Reviews*

See what readers have to say about *Daughter of the Leopard*:

"Beautifully written and inspiring book: Little Monique invites the reader into her world and once you've stepped in, you are at her side, a witness, for the duration. Written in vivid detail, the effect is almost cinematic."

"Magical stories—a fantastic read: I absolutely loved this book! It tells the most incredible stories about a young girl named Monique as she grows up in rural Kenya. ... The characters are rich and well-developed, and Monique's father is truly larger than life. ... The author did a fabulous job bringing these stories to life, portraying a childhood that was both idyllic and incredibly challenging. ... This book was a real page-turner—I couldn't wait to see what would happen next."

"Skillfully written, this winsome volume transports the reader to magnificent Kenya. Young Monique is brave and steadfast in her adventures with an understated tone of protest."

"Fun, interesting, and easy to read"

"What an incredible book telling stories of growing up in a Maasai community in Kenya. It was so good I bought a 2nd copy for my sister who loves to hear about strong women."

"I am so glad my book group read this book! It described a land and culture and people that I had no knowledge of and what a beautiful story it is! ... Highly recommend!"

"A true story of strength and resilience: ... Left me anxiously waiting for the next book & completely rooting for this strong little girl who repeatedly defies the odds."

"I especially enjoyed the recounting of native, natural healing methods used in rural Kenya. Very much looking forward to the next installment."

Daughter OF THE Leopard

Daughter OF THE Leopard

True Stories From
A Samburu Maasai Girlhood

Monique N. Leparleen · Ann Hendricks

Swallow and Quill Literary

To request permission for using passages from this book, or to arrange author speaking or interviews, please visit the website daughteroftheleopard.com

No AI was used in the writing or design of this book.

Published by Swallow and Quill Literary, Bellevue, Washington, USA
Printed in the United States of America

ISBN 979-8-9924929-0-3
Library of Congress Control Number 2025902837

For image credits, please see back pages. Cover design by Ann Hendricks

Publisher's Cataloging-in-Publication
(Provided by Cassidy Cataloguing Services, Inc.)
Names: Leparleen, Monique N., author. | Hendricks, Ann (Ann Elizabeth), author.
Title: Daughter of the leopard : true stories from a Samburu Maasai girlhood / Monique N. Leparleen [and] Ann Hendricks.
Description: Bellevue, Washington, USA : Swallow and Quill Literary, [2025] | Series: Daughter of the Leopard ; [book 1] | Includes bibliographical references.
Identifiers: ISBN: 979-8-9924929-0-3 (softcover) | 979-8-9924929-1-0 (Kindle) | 979-8-9924929-2-7 (ePub) | LCCN: 2025902837
Subjects: LCSH: Leparleen, Monique N.--Childhood and youth. | Children--Kenya--Samburu-- Biography. | Samburu (African people)--Kenya--Social conditions. | Women--Kenya-- Samburu--Social conditions. | Social change--Kenya--Samburu. | Country life--Kenya-- Samburu. | Kenya-- Biography. | LCGFT: Autobiographies. | BISAC: BIOGRAPHY & AUTOBIOGRAPHY / Cultural & Regional. | BIOGRAPHY & AUTOBIOGRAPHY / Memoirs. | BIOGRAPHY & AUTOBIOGRAPHY / Historical.
Classification: LCC: DT433.545.S26 L46 2025 | DDC: 306.089965--dc23

For Akuyia

and Esther and Rose

and Papa

and for all the children
who have questions for the sun

Contents

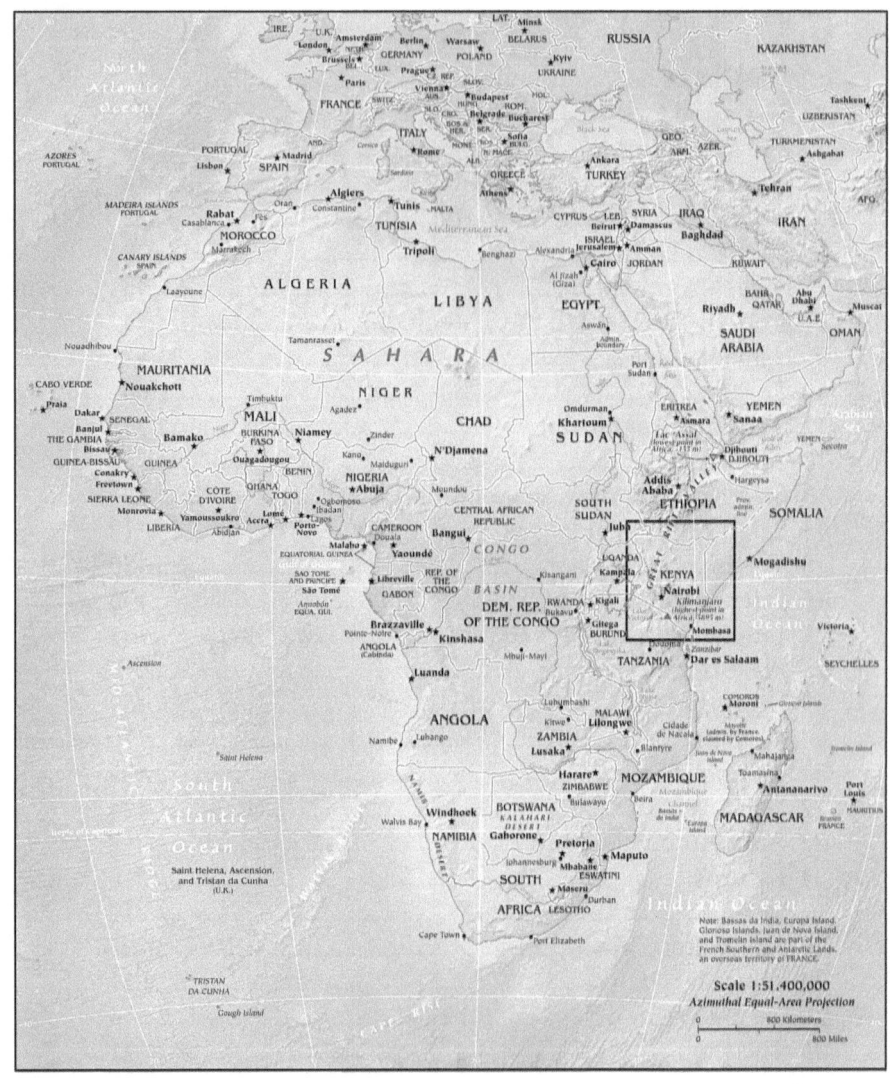

Africa and its neighbors. Kenya is boxed.

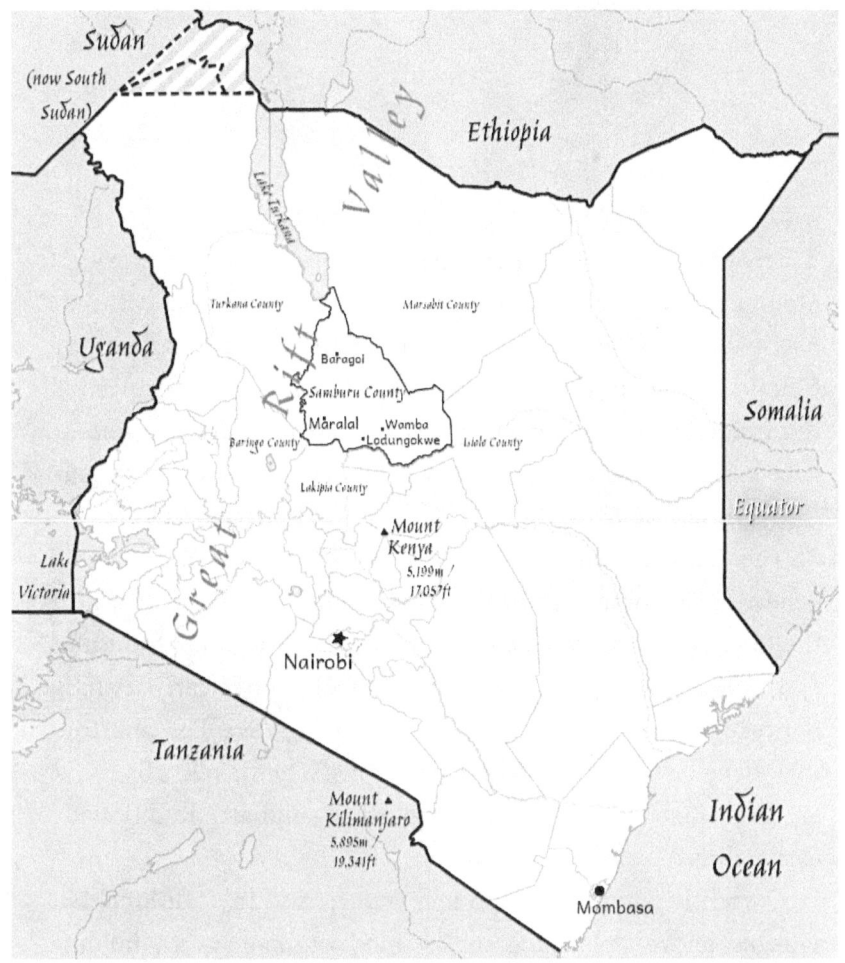

Kenya and its neighbors. Samburu County and places of interest in the book and Monique's life are marked. Solid lines are county borders, dashed are rivers.

The 47 Kenyan counties resemble US states. Each has a governor, and they are fairly large, ranging in size between Washington DC and Indiana. Samburu County is one of the largest, roughly the size of Massachusetts.

Preface

This book has a few purposes. It's primarily the story of Monique Ntorisian Leparleen's remarkable girlhood, with its massive interest and drama and her incredible grit, in Samburu County, Kenya, in the 1970s and 80s. Her childhood occurred at the inflection point when modernity had just met her remote tribe's ancient ways, and she and her family had to navigate through the competing pushes and pulls of both ways of life.

The Samburu are a group of the Maasai (Maa-speaking) tribes. Their home is in Kenya's cool northwest highlands, near the Great Rift Valley. They take much pride in their traditions and culture: Samburu culture is ancient, and clearly rich in heritage and skill for surviving via the Old Ways. For centuries they have been quasi-nomadic pastoralists: herdsfolk who move around when it's useful to help their animals, traditionally cattle, thrive.

Currently Samburu live in many ways: still in traditional hut villages and shepherding, or in modern homes and holding every type of job from casual labor to high government positions. Monique's childhood was at a unique transition point, but the issues she struggled with are still challenging in a great many families. This is especially so for the most remote and the poorest, and for women and girls, who often still face enormous misogyny, abuse, FGM, and forced marriage. Traditional society is rigidly organized, with roles set by age and gender. It strictly controls women and girls, seeing them as mainly supports—or commodities—for men, and for raising children and doing most of the village labor. Samburu women and girls have often faced great difficulty if they aspire to a different path, such as many of Kenya's other women pursue.

Ironically it is the long-considered-unmovable traditional path that is now finding itself the most threatened. The forces of modernity and climate change have placed additional strain on the already-difficult highland pastoralist life. The culture is transforming rapidly in response. The ancient manyatta-based cattle-keeping ways and the traditional medicine practiced by Monique's grandfather, for instance, may not last much longer. So we hope her stories are also a useful record of some of those rapidly-vanishing ways, seen through her eyes; and a record of what it was like to live—as a girl—at the point when the hammer hit the anvil: when great change came for a culture that had long been seen as, and indeed regarded itself as, unchangeable.

Her stories also raised for us several big questions that perhaps many people can relate to.

• *Do we have to follow what our culture has planned for us, just because it has long been upheld as excellent?*

• *What do we do when the multiple aspects of our identities— ethnic/tribal, national, religious, gender, human—place conflicting demands on us and our rights and desires?*

• *How do children who face great difficulty and lack of support survive? How much can they thrive without that full support?*

• *How do you face intolerable control, hostility, and prejudice and escape to build your own life?*

We hope you enjoy these stories of her young rural life. As women born across the world from each other but destined to become great friends, we worked very hard over many years to bring the stories faithfully to the page. We hope to soon get the sequel out, as well as excerpted age-appropriate children's stories. You can read more about our writing process in the "Notes on the Collaboration" section in the back, or at our website, daughteroftheleopard.com.

As far as we can attest, the stories in this book are generally told as Monique remembers experiencing them, with a few small caveats:

• Memory is wonky. Monique tried her best. We had to reconstruct scenes and dialogue, and several small details are likely different from "what happened." These are within the norms of memoir and creative nonfiction: we believe nothing significant was different.

• This is a collaboration, and while the story came, often verbatim, from Monique's interviews and transcripts and she checked everything, Ann wrote it. Two minds involved inherently risks a bit more deviation from "what happened." (Although it also likely provided clearer insight!)

• We changed several people's names, for their privacy.

We wish to thank everyone who reads this story, and everyone who showed patience and encouragement with us throughout our lives and while writing: and God for His unfailing support. We are both fairly cynical and foul-mouthed, but also devout—Monique a Christian and Ann a Bahá'í—and we have great thanks for the Faith and Love that sustained us both on our rocky paths.

Daughter OF THE Leopard

1

The Girl of Leopards and Chalk

In imagination, Africa is dry golden savanna and heat waves rising around panting animals; or perhaps dank sweltering jungle, machetes slicing paths like scythes through a harvest. In reality, it is nearly everything. The vast continent undulates and transforms in perpetual variety, everywhere distinct yet linked, as the lives of its peoples. White sand beaches shift to scrublands and forests, then enormous lakes and snow-capped peaks and ranges. Cliffs and waterfalls plunge, fish multitudes chortle deep in rivers, desert realms drown life in oceans of sand, and crops quietly luxuriate in tended fields.

Our story, of a little girl among a remarkable remote tribe, takes place to the east, in the land now called Kenya.

To get to her home, start at the torrid coast, where mangoes ripen fat and sweet and sea-traders' boots have for millennia landed on the sand. Turn from the sunrise and travel inland. Pass the large jumbling cities and the estates of the wealthy, and continue northwest, through the hot lowland savannas and forests. You will find that the land begins to climb, and climb, and climb: as though in aspiration to escape the earth and join the stars. A mile plus a thousand feet above sea level—if you can continue that high—you find yourself on a vast highland plateau, just east of the lush plummet of the Great Rift Valley, the crevice of humanity's birth.

This plateau is a triumphant land, that rose determinedly above the Equator's heat to provide ideal, temperate conditions for those who climbed and found its blessings. The sun reigns daily across its full twelve hours, but much of its heat rolls away down the hillsides, leaving the highlands fresh and luminous. Animals graze on dawn pastures decked with dewdrops; cool breezes blow; and nights fall crystalline cold, the sky richly knit with bright stars, innumerable as blades of grass, as Great Creator *Nkai*'s herds. The elevation cleaves time as well as space and temperature from the goings-on below: above, life unfolds as it has for millennia, untouched by lowland hubbub. The stars of lives are born, burn, die out, and sink without trace into the silent sea of time, their stories untold. Especially those of women and girls.

Here, not so very long ago, when the modern age was just creeping its edge toward the heart of the ancient ways, a stubborn little Samburu girl lived. She lived despite her mother's best attempts that she wouldn't; and her story will not be untold. Her name was Monique.

The Samburu have long lived in and fought over the lands around the Lorroki Plateau. They are a group of Maasai people, and speak Maa, and also often Swahili, English, and anything else they have picked up.[1] From time immemorial their life has been highly organized around raising cattle and other livestock, fending off raids from nearby tribes, and raiding those tribes of

---

[1] The famous southern Maasai and the Samburu have a long rivalry over who are the most authentic "real Maasai." The Samburu are less well-known, as their homeland was walled off for decades by the British colonial government, within the Northern Frontier District. No one, Kenyan or otherwise, could go in or out without serious approval. The British felt the ancient, constant warring between the northern and southern tribes would be no match for

their animals. They traditionally need nothing from the outside world: they can obtain everything from their lands, their herds, and their ways. And they are loath to change their ways, and take much pride in their traditions, for they have from antiquity survived and thrived where others did not.

Copious fresh milk, wild honey, and clear air under a benevolent sun grew Monique's people tall and beautiful and strong, with skin in tones from light mahogany to near ebony. The eyes she looked into ranged from a rare gold, or silver-grey as Papa's were, to a more common dark, warm brown. Everyone's black hair was usually shaved or curled tight against their heads, unless it was long and twisted and ochred into beautiful patterns, as she saw the male warriors, the *moran*, do. Papa had long adopted western clothing, favoring safari khakis, but the rest of her community bedecked themselves with a rich palette of bright cloths and ornaments made from beads and feathers, metal and wood, and shell and bone. These all told stories about the wearer and their station. Everyone's roles in society were clear and pre-determined by their gender and their age: child, warrior, wife, father, mother, elder. These were as they had been since time out of memory, without exception.

Until modernity finally made it up the hills.

Papa and his children were raised in the way of all Samburu: in a tradition-bound, ancient way of life full of roles, stations, expectations and taboos, ceremonies, beads and cattle and fetching water and fire and knives and dew on the grass and starlight. But Papa had also been the first of his huge family and clan to be sent for a modern Kenyan education, priests rapping

---

proper administration. They simply put the whole troublesome northern region in a giant Time Out: you stay on this side of the line, and you on the other. In result, the Samburu thrived, and remained more isolated and traditional than southern Maasai, which suited them fine. The region only began opening to the outside world with Kenya's independence in 1963.

out new ways with chalk and rulers. This education and his talents brought him and his family and tribe great success and wealth. It also brought them new ways to live. Life suddenly became constant negotiation and tension between old ways and new possibilities.

This was especially so for girls and women, who previously had no choice in their lives. They would be sold off in young marriage to an unknown old man, consent irrelevant, and spend their lives working in the village of his mother and raising his children. They would hope he was not cruel. But it wouldn't matter much to anyone but them if he was. They had little recourse. It had been this way for time out of memory. They had seen no alternative; they often could not even imagine one. After the Frontier District opened, however, women's varied lives and possibilities in wider Kenya became visible.

And so because of who her father was within this community, and the time she was born, a scant decade after her homeland began opening to the outside world, Monique's life was lived at the inflection point. She toed an extremely dodgy wobble along a rough, bucking tightwire connecting the ancient and the modern. Behind, the traditional ways that her tribe insisted upon for her as a Samburu. Ahead, the possibility to determine her own life, as other Kenyan women could. (*And am I not also Kenyan?* she reflected.) Below, an abyss.

Change is not full and instant, and the Maasai male wanderlust and compulsion towards small, personal empire— usually expressed in keeping several wives and homes and livestock holdings—would not be quenched in her father's generation or hers. So Monique grew up in many homes near the small scrubby outpost capital of Maralal in Samburu County. With her grandmother, home was a traditional little round hut in a big round, bustling village. During schooldays, home was a boarding school in town run by strict and often terrifying Italian nuns. Otherwise in her earliest life, home was a colonial farmhouse built beautifully on a hill by the British Army and then left behind when they departed, just outside Maralal town.

As all traditional Samburu thought was right, Papa's daughters would never be as well-favored as his male relatives, even the far-flung nephews. But Papa insisted they too receive a modern education in addition to being raised in the old ways.

And so Monique was raised in the way of all girl Samburus through all their history. But she was also raised with more. She was a girl of two often-warring worlds: ancient and modern; a girl of leopards and chalk.

2

Beads and Cattle

The Samburu are called "the butterfly people" of Kenya, due to the rich, vivid dress and ornamentation worn by both men and women. A Samburu in full regalia—even the everyday-wear version—is resplendent. From afar we first see their colorful *shukas*: the large, thin cotton shawls they wear as an all-purpose cloak and blanket. These are plaid or striped and favor bright colors: usually red or orange, with purple, pink, blue, or yellow. A bit closer reveals their beautiful ornaments, skillfully incorporating beadwork, metal, shells, bone, seeds, fibers, skins, and feathers, all in a vast array of colors and designs and set off against their dark skin. Large vibrant collars woven from thousands of beads; layers of rattling beaded hoop necklaces; long spiral brass armbands; complex headdresses that adorn the forehead with the morning star; intricate earring patterns that loop to other jewelry pieces. (All Samburu, male and female, have their ears pierced at the top and in the earlobe when young. The earlobe piercing is commonly gradually stretched long, to accommodate a vast assortment of decoration techniques.)

Though most of the beadwork and clothes are made by women, men too become highly skilled in adornment. While the women and especially girl children are occupied in nearly endless physical labor, with little time to doll themselves up, the young men's daily work of shepherding provides them abundant time to relax, while "working." Traditional hairstyles show this: all the village girls and women Monique knew kept their hair shaved. A clean-shorn head was considered the height of femininity. But boys from young grew their hair out, twisting it delicately, so by the time they were warriors it cascaded far down their backs in hundreds of fine ropes. The warriors spend hours maintaining and dressing their own and each other's hair. They plaster the long twists with ochre—the red pigment all Samburu learn to prepare from the local earth, mixed with animal fat or ghee—and form it, with all sorts of ornaments, into showy designs. (Some designs are practical: one popular style forms the top front section of stiff ochred twists into a sun-visor, like the bill of a cap, shielding the eyes from the sun's glare.) They also decorate their faces with natural paints, and adorn their favorite cows with paint or garlands and cow-earrings. And they gift heaps of bright beaded hoop necklaces to their young girlfriends, who wear these accumulated into huge piles, jangling in shifting collars around their necks.

All this adornment and specificity of dress is not only for beauty and fashion, however. These embellishments together with what type of cloths or skins are wrapped around the body and how the hair is worn traditionally have strict, definite meanings. They are marks of honor, shame, life station, and major happenings. Much fashion is only permitted at certain times, and forbidden at others. Blackened goat skins worn tied to the back at these specific events, tawny lion-skin garters secured below the knees only at another; coiled copper earrings normally worn only by married women but at designated occasions proudly worn by men; long strands of certain beads tied off with beetle shells, worn cascading from the ears down over the back at only one time by young warrior initiates. And

7

too many more examples to list. To properly describe the role of fashion in Samburu life would take an entire book.

Thus if you know how to read them, as Monique was learning, a mere glance tells you if this Samburu is young or a warrior or an elder, male or female, circumcised or not, married or unmarried; can inform you about transgressions or bad luck in the family, and how many warriors a mother has given the tribe. There is even one time you can see from what a mother is wearing how good a hunter her young initiate son is. You can see everything from the dress.

Now if you looked at how young Monique presented and knew how to read it, it would declare: "Here is a scamp. She is tough and all about action and does not care for tradition or frilleries. Watch out."

She had several beautiful beadwork pieces made by relatives or friends and given to her, and she admired the artistry in the craft, but she didn't favor wearing traditional dress or ornamentation. Neither did she love wearing the fancy western dresses you could find in the cities. Nearly always she went about in shorts, a t-shirt, and close-cropped hair, through all the adventures of her out-of-school life. When the situation required she wore what was necessary, but the minute it was possible she chucked it off and reverted to her native dress of scampery.

She did not intend to disparage traditions and cultural norms and roles. She knew others found them delightful and mean-ingful and wore them like a favorite soft goatskin shawl. She simply was not comfortable in them herself for more than a short while, and could not wait to throw them off.

Her rascal attire was also perhaps not natural to her, but born of specific events and circumstances.

When Maama covertly downed innumerable pints of Smirnoff and Grand Marnier to snuff out the life of Papa's child in her belly, fetal Monique stubbornly lived. When she was born weak, with raw, angry skin and dark spots here and there on her body, and internal pain that made her cry inconsolably, she still lived. After Maama was caught dropping her and she was instead raised by Papa and aunts and uncles, who left her crying and blanket-wrapped on a thin mat on the floor so that her skin would not rub off from handling, and bottle fed her there, she lived. Grandfather, *Akuyia*, visited often: shuffling into the house when his son could not see, he gently rubbed herbal oils on her skin to strengthen it and whispered blessings and prayers.

welcome, little one
grow strong
welcome
heal
welcome
live

She lived. She became used to being raised by aunts and uncles and Papa, and knew that Maama was something to be avoided. Her skin toughened up, though the leopard spots remained, and Papa took to joyfully prattling at her and tossing her in the air. Until the time her stomach landed just right into the press of his hand and diarrhea spurted all down his chin and chest. The uncles rolled in laughter and Papa too laughed until he cried.

"I'm never tossing another baby again."

He didn't. But the closeness grew with his daughter. As she outgrew babyhood and its fecal risks, he resumed tossing her in the air. She shrieked in delight.

One day when Monique was two or three, Maama viciously braided her hair, so tight that it pulled horrifically on her scalp and face. She could not stop crying from the pain. The cruel braids were too tight to even be undone. Papa and kind Aunt Napese took a razor blade and chopped them out the best they could, relieving her but leaving her head ragged.

"Come, let's go on an adventure," Papa said. He dragged her to the barbershop in town.

"But we don't shave girls' hair," the barber protested.

"You do this one's," Papa replied.

From then on Monique always had a shaved haircut just like her Papa, growing out perhaps a quarter inch and then shaved again by the barber.

Similarly, from her mother's malice and Papa's embrace, she stepped into her scamp attire. Papa openly mourned that the child he was so close with was not born a boy, with all the privileges and freedoms Samburu culture bestows: and she, fresh to the world, felt no allegiance to the usual ways and restrictions of women. Who would? So as far as the family and culture would allow she went around in simple western tomboy clothes—which were very comfortable and practical—and stuck with her father and uncles. She became referred to as her father's shadow or purse, so much did she accompany him.

As she grew, it became clear she was not only stubborn, but bright and inquisitive. She spoke early, and as soon as her mouth and brain could manage it, began asking interminable questions about why life around her was the way it was.

"You'll have to be patient with my daughter," Papa warned guests. "The first word that comes out of her mouth is 'why.'"

They'd laugh.

"I'm grateful she's curious and has a hunger for under-standing. But just bear with her."

After a few questions, the laughter was usually gone. Eyes narrowed and hands twitched.

Samburu adults, Akuyia and a few others excepted, really didn't like questions. Or being in the presence of children generally. Granny Ears reached for her belt just seeing Monique, even before her lips could purse up to form a *w*.

"Poor Monique," Papa sighed. "Born with the word 'why' in your mouth. You're destined for a beating in this culture."

It is not possible to adequately describe the role of fashion in Samburu life: it is also not possible to fully illustrate the depth of their relationship with their cattle, and to a lesser degree, other livestock. Their origin stories include God, Nkai, gifting them cows, specifically to *them*. They consider themselves *the* cattle herders, the only true ones, and when in the past they raided cattle from their neighbors they saw it as a triumphant liberation of the cows from those yonder idiots, to the people they should more properly be with and who would take better care of them.

Milk features in every day of Samburu life, practically and ritually. A village's milk supply is rationed out among the families by the matriarch, and as the main source of nutrition the ration means life or death. Fresh milk is poured out daily on the north side of the house for prayer offerings; a slim gourd of milk and a small wooden jar of ghee, made from milkfat, are included in a bride's traditional attire; the ghee is used in many rituals; a man's wealth is measured in his cows; and brides are bought with cows and livestock, among other offerings. The cows are nearly worshiped: although not actually, as it then would be awkward to butcher them, and this is done very joyfully when the time is right. Samburu relish meat, and use absolutely everything from their animals.

Papa too adored his cattle. Although he ended up taking many government jobs and flying and living all over the world, his heart remained a herdsman's. He was at his happiest camping out in his Land Rover, in the bush among his cattle under the starlight. He constantly thought about his livestock, and how to improve them and grow their numbers.

Traditionally Samburu men will split up their massive herds into smaller ones to be kept and watched over at their multiple wives' villages, their *manyattas*. The milk, blood, and meat provide for the wives, children, and other relatives. As Papa had been raised too effectively Catholic by the priests at school to have more than one wife at once, he put a large herd at his mother's manyatta, a smaller herd at his city house, and then shared out cattle generously with male relatives in exchange for them watching more herds. Papa was compassionate as well as generous, and applied these characteristics to his herd-keeping. He spoke a few minority languages and regularly visited conflict zones to buy cattle. At such times he often adopted back refugee individuals or whole families who wanted a safe place to live, and set them up with homes and their own cattle in exchange for tending more of his.

"Papa, who are these people?" little Monique asked when he returned with many new cows along with a family from deep within Turkana lands.

"Oh, don't worry. These are nice people. They're going to be part of our family."

"But Papa, why don't they talk? They don't speak."

"They only speak Turkana right now, but they will quickly learn our languages."

So it went, with family after family. They often arrived with absolutely nothing and speaking only their tribal language: neither Maa nor either of Kenya's national languages of Swahili and English. But the herds they were tasked with thrived, as did they. Papa put them at his varying family members' manyattas or at the Maralal house and placed their children in school. They all learned their additional languages and became woven into the family and community, either to stay permanently, return to their ancestral home once things had calmed, or forge a new future elsewhere.

3

The Manyatta

The little oval hut that was sometimes home to Monique was a place that all of her ancestors—thousands of years of little boys and little girls, who grew up into mothers and fathers and then grew up more into grandmothers and grandfathers, again and again for untold generations—it was a place they all would recognize as home.

It was made of many strong, straight branches and young tree trunks stood up on end side by side in a flattish ring, like many slim warriors standing tall and close around a fire. Ropes of strappy grasses tied these together, and also fastened long arching cross-branches on top to form the low, domed ceiling. Mud mixed with cow dung was pushed and patted in the walls and smoothed, to hold it all together, and branches were left exposed in handy places, to fasten or hang things from. The roof was thatched with sheaves of flattened grass, and animal hides or sheeting sometimes lashed down on top. A little sheltered opening was left here or there to let out cookfire smoke. This was all done by women's hands, as these huts must be made only by women.

The interior was one large roundish low room, perhaps high enough to stand comfortably or perhaps not, but always very comfortable for sitting and lying, with a dirt floor swept neat and tidy every morning. The entryway was an inviting domed hole: children walked straight in, and adults leaned down and stepped through. Inside nearby stood a large sheet of metal or wood which could be moved into place behind the hole and propped up with a few big sticks, to keep animals out at night.

A large, low cozy bed took up nearly half the room. In the center of the remaining floor a small wood fire burned quietly in its place, nestled among three good cooking-fire rocks.

The bed was built of wonderful, springy branches and twigs that had been gathered from the surrounding scrubland and forest, all carefully tangled and stacked together. A thick padding of leaves atop served as a mattress, and then several soft, beautiful skins from the tribe's cows long passed were spread on top, and tucked neatly into a huge log that ran along the side of the bed. This formed a smooth, sturdy edge that even toddler Monique could easily clamber up and slide down. The bed was wide: wide enough to fit a grandmother and great-grandmother and several grandchildren, sleeping alternately head-to-foot side by side in the space-saving way that Samburu share beds.

Back outside, just a very short walk in all directions were many nearly identical huts. A small child sitting in the entryway of one hut could easily throw a stone and hit another.

Overhead the rural night lit the land with soft, calm light from the moon and millions of stars that Nkai had flung bright and winking across the ink-black sky, spelling portents for those who read the language of the heavens. A few wakeful elders occasionally strolled between the huts in the starlight, quietly sharing greetings and laughter and news and stories.

As the strong sun rose each morning, the huts spilled out dozens and dozens of grandmothers, grandfathers, uncles and aunts, second and third wives and more wives, cousins and all kinds of cousins-once-removed and second cousins and babies and old folk and everything in between. There were a few small simple livestock pens, and much open space.

These all together made a small, clustered village: the manyatta. Here and there Monique could see a plastic jug, or t-shirt, or sheet of metal; something to indicate the modern age. Otherwise it was a Samburu manyatta exactly as Samburu man-yattas have always been.

A tall bush-fence ran all around the manyatta in a big, big circle. The fence was made from brown, dried bushes and thorny acacia branches all pulled and stuck together. It was as high as a grandmother, though tall children might see over it if they jumped, and Monique could peer through chinks in the interwoven branches. It was full of vicious white thorns the length of a thumb, each of which could slice an arm to the bone. No animal or man wanted to try to climb over or go through that fence.

And that was good, for Monique knew that outside the manyatta roamed lions, hyenas, and leopards, who would all love to tear a little girl or any other Samburu or their dogs or goats or cattle to shreds with their claws and teeth and gobble them up: and also elephants, who could easily crush them by accident or in a fit of rage. And also sometimes bad men, who would raid a village and do unspeakable things to the men and women and children inside.

The thorn fence was made with a few wide sections that could be pushed out and pulled back as simple gates. Manyattas have different numbers of gates depending on how large they are: Monique's grandmother's manyatta was large and had three gates. Each morning the gates were pushed out and left open, as folks and their animals came and went on their business.

As night began to fall, all of the manyatta's hundreds of cows and goats were gathered from the outside grazing lands, ushered into the large open area between the huts, and the thorn fence was pulled shut all around. The youngest calves and baby goats were secured in the simple little pens so they didn't get into any foolishness, or carried indoors if they were especially young or ill and needed extra warmth, or if the weather was cold and rainy. Once inside the baby goats settled curled neatly near the fire, calmly chewing their cud or sleeping silently, charming and adorable.

All the children trotted into the cozy huts and the adults stooped and followed, pushing the doors into place behind them. And they all, Monique and her relatives and their animals, slept peacefully, safe from the lions and leopards and hyenas that prowled outside, hungry and hunting in the silvery star-lit dark.

4

Granny Ears

The hut belonged to Papa's mother. The manyatta with its many huts was the home for not only Monique's grandmother, but all of grandfather Akuyia's wives in that area, and there were several. It also housed his four younger brothers' wives. Further it held all their combined relations, and that was dozens to hundreds more, depending who was home or away.

Monique's grandmother was Akuyia's First Wife. A few times a year he visited the manyatta and its wives and family, walking south four days from the town of Baragoi, where he spent most of his time with the wives and relatives there. After visiting a few weeks he would say goodbye and then again walk north four days back.

Akuyia was a deeply respected elder and patriarch, humble and kind and a famous healer, master of local herbs and materials to treat a wide range of sufferings. He loved children and their questions and ways, and Monique gave him her heart. Akuyia's decisions and wisdom had woven the huge family into existence, kept its far-flung web mostly integral, and brought much prosperity. It had been his decision to send Papa to school.

After Akuyia, Papa was the "big man" of the huge family: the eldest son of the first wife of the eldest son of the first wife, all the way back to the losing of all track of who was what. Papa was also by a great stretch the most well-educated and prosperous man in the clan.

This made Monique's grandmother, the wife and mother of the Big Men, the very proud matriarch leader of the manyatta. She was The Boss of everything inside: who must do what and who could not do what else; who should be punished for what; who would receive how much milk rations; who could stay in the village and who must be kicked out. Alas for Monique and all the children, Grandmother was known as *Nkiyaa*, "Granny Ears." No matter how far away you were, she always heard or learned of anything remotely naughty you did.

Granny Ears relished her role. She was bossy. She was mean. Uncalled-for mean. Her meanness was innate and unchangeable, just as her glinting eyes or darkest-chocolate skin. She was so mean that even her own grandchildren generally weren't welcome to sleep in her hut on her lovely, capacious bed. Instead they sheltered a couple huts down with Akuyia's much-warmer second wife, who Monique called Second Granny. (Second Granny also had a wonderfully comfortable and large bed, nearly identical except that its occupying grandmother was far more pleasant.)

Nkiyaa's notable meanness might lead one to wonder how she attained the privilege of becoming gentle and wise Akuyia's first wife. Well, Akuyia was just a man after all, and Granny Ears was the daughter of the most beautiful woman in many days' travel in the area: perhaps in all Samburu lands.

In her youth, Granny Ears's mother, who Monique called simply *Nkooko*, Grandmother (though she was of course her great-grandmother), had been a truly great beauty. Her skin was flawless and the color of ebony; her face was as perfect as any sculpted queen's; her body was the Samburu ideal, tall and with generous hips and a long graceful neck. She bore herself like royalty. Yet she also was exceptionally kind, gentle, and loving. In addition to her mother's charm, Granny Ears's father was also highly esteemed and just as remarkably kind as his wife. Akuyia likely believed their daughter would be an angel.

As in most Samburu marriages, Akuyia and Granny Ears were married having not known each other at all, with negotiations and exchanges of tea and sugar, beads and cows and other riches, made between Akuyia's representative male family members and Nkiyaa's father and male relatives. He would have had no idea what he was walking into, other than relations with the daughter of the most beautiful woman for a great many miles, and the child of well-esteemed parents with wonderful characters.

It must have been quite a shock to Akuyia after marrying her to see her throw her head back, slit her eyes, and start shooting out from her mouth streams of mean, vile disrespect and insults. Her abuse was heaped regularly and nearly universally upon all persons around, including heavily on her gentle parents and husband. It was issued in generous dispensation, like the noonday sun or monsoon torrents, without any need for a provocation. She had not inherited her mother's beauty: neither was her character like either of her parents. And it was as immutable as stone, despite all efforts to soften her. The toll her vitriol took on her kind and lovely mother was perhaps the most tragic: but that story is for a later telling.

Samburu and other Maasai men wear beautiful leather belts, richly beaded in bright colors and patterns. These are used to secure their waistcloths and also to carry their weapons, especially any knives and the *rungu*, a forearm-length bent or knobbed thick stick that is very handy for throwing, whapping people and animals, and waving around and threatening and gesturing with. Women generally don't wear belts, or carry weapons.

Granny Ears was again remarkable in this: after marriage, she wore a belt. Not even a common belt: a famous, vicious belt. It was cut in one long, wide strip from thick, iron-strong rhinoceros hide, and it was both a belt and weapon all on its own, known for having whooped the entire village through three generations. She could remove it in one second and be already whooping some poor soul on the next. As she strongly disliked Monique, the young girl knew far too well the metal-hard cuts of both that belt and Nkiyaa's words. Though the belt would leave bruises or even blood, Monique found the words the most flaying.

Nkiyaa, though highly formidable, was not a total monster. She was quite capable of showing love, tenderness, and loyalty when she wished. One day a sick baby appeared in the manyatta. Others had given up on it, but Nkiyaa took it in and lovingly sang to and tended and cradled it. She also sang to her favorite cows. Her love for her eldest son, Papa, was the sun and moon and the actual earth her feet strode upon. But to nearly everyone else she was mean. Viciously, universally mean. Monique was either simply no exception in receiving Granny Ears's generously-gifted meanness, or she reminded her too much of that unworthy woman Papa had married: Maama.

5

Little Girl in the Big Manyatta

Granny Ears could hear fun happening from any side of the huge village. She even seemed to be able to hear quiet leisure, and would come from afar bearing down like a lashing thunderclap on the hapless resting youth. Her fingertips lived at her belt buckle, so often were they actively removing the belt to whoop someone, or simply stationed in readiness. Monique and all the girl children tried to remain assiduously busy. Manyatta life requires endless work, so this was easy.

Every morning after the doors were pulled aside and folks stepped out into the bright sunrise, chewing on their *mswaki* toothbrushing sticks[2]:

- the livestock had to be separated, goats from cows, and all be milked, including the baby animals suckling their share

  Monique and other children helped separate and bring and return the animals and their babies. Only those few aunties that Granny Ears felt were up to snuff were allowed to actually milk. They milked into hand-pots that were beautifully carved from fat chunks of mahogany branch, often decorated with cowrie shells. Each pot had a leather strap attached, which the aunt wrapped

---

[2] Mswaki, miswak in Arabic, are twigs from the regional "toothbrush tree," *Salvadora persica*, which have been used for millennia across Africa and the Middle East to keep the teeth and gums clean and healthy. Use is just by chewing on them thoroughly. They generally work quite well.

tight around her hand. Then even if the cow or goat kicked, the pot was held steady and the precious milk kept safe.

• the milk was processed and stored

Much was used immediately for prayers, drinking, and tea. Monique watched her aunts turn more into butter-milk and butter and ghee. Any they wanted to keep fresh, they boiled in pots over a cooking fire or a *jiko*[3] and then poured into storage gourds or cans. It would stay good even without refrigeration for two to three days.

• the livestock must be taken out and watched over

Shepherding was usually the job of boys and young men, who used this time out in the bush also as free hours. They ranged over several miles, watching the animals, managing water and grazing, and practicing warrior-craft. They played, teased each other, showed off, shared happenings and gossip and lore, and twisted their hair and dolled themselves up, returning only for the late afternoon milking.

• the endless manure piles deposited by the livestock all around the village were tidied away, to where they were kept for construction and other use

This task was assigned specifically to the young children, who moved it all by hand, exactly as you would imagine. Children being similar worldwide, it was occasionally thrown. To clean up afterwards, they wiped their hands in the dirt and rinsed with a small amount of water.

---

[3] The jiko is a wonderful Kenyan improvement upon the small traditional metal field cookstove. A ceramic bucket, which serves as a heat sink, sits in the top of a small, easy-to-move metal cookstove, with three pot supports on top. It is so simple to make that the most rudimentary potters and blacksmiths can easily turn them out. Jikos can burn any fuel, but are commonly fed by charcoal, which they are very efficient in using.

- each hut's dirt floor was swept smooth, and the paths swept tidy and free of thorns

    Each family had a hand-broom made from a small thorn bush, which had been uprooted and twisted and coaxed into a "broomy" shape as it dried in the sun and dropped its leaves. Once properly formed and dried, this broom was truly excellent. It lasted nearly forever: generally until someone got sick of it and threw it into the fire.

- tea, strong, milky, and sweet, and breakfast were made and served, sharing with any visitors

    Samburu hospitality is absolute, and anyone seeking shelter at a manyatta overnight will be taken in, and fed the next morning. Just don't expect this at Granny Ears's hut.

- dishes were rinsed with a drizzle of water from each hut's water container and hung on branch racks near the fires

    The racks were made from sticks that were naturally resistant to mildew and bacteria, and helped keep anything hung on them fresh and nice.

... and that was just the necessary to get through breakfast.

After the morning chores, any girl or young woman not further occupied drew Granny's ire. Monique noticed she never beat boys into working. They mysteriously seemed to be allowed leisure when not shepherding, and drew their share of beatings solely for actual misbehavior or mouthing off. Only Papa would regularly chase them into working, if he was there.

There was always laundry to be done—washed and pounded by hand, at the river if it was running—ill or very young livestock to be specially tended to; water, firewood, and other locally-obtainable needs to be fetched; clothes and beaded adornments and ceremonial or household items to be mended and made; repairs needed on the fence or huts; and for the boys, various errands to be run.

Many girls preferred to go fetch the manyatta's water. Water-fetching was essential and always appreciated, and it could take a whole day. It was a job for women and children— strong men only fetched water for their livestock and themselves while out watching them—and often gangs of girls all under nine were the primary fetchers. The long walk to the river or waterhole and back, and the tedious time of collecting the water, gave hours for chit chat, and was so far that it was past even Nkiyaa's ears. It was one of the rare occasions girls were allowed to leave the manyatta, and see what else the world was composed of.

Samburu manyattas, and the villages of other Kenyan tribes, are generally located fairly far from natural water. Locals must travel thousands of hours a year to bring the village's water back, and once obtained it is precious and used sparingly. When the British arrived they exclaimed at this foolishness, and set up camp near the rivers and waterholes. They then quickly sickened and died from malaria and other diseases borne by water-based insects. These insects are primarily active at night, so Samburus avoid the pain and death they bring by setting up home outside the critters' reach, and trekking to fetch water by daylight while the pests are inactive.

In the old days water was transported in large gourds and carefully-stitched skin jugs. But plastic jerry cans, large 2-5 gallon containers with handles, had become ubiquitous before Monique was born.

Every water fetching day, about three times a week, the water-fetchers went around to all the manyatta's huts, collected the empty containers, and using long leather straps, roped them up into big jostling bundles on their backs. They picked up an axe or two, for firewood which they would gather along the way and for defense, and a couple big metal cups with handles to scoop the water. Then they paraded off neatly from the village, arrayed in their melange of bright Samburu and western dress, beaded and unbeaded, somber and quiet, without provisions or even usually shoes. (The thorns and rocks of the land quickly destroyed any shoes they got, and so in countryside life they generally went barefoot, and grew soles as tough as rhino hide.)

Once their dignified, quiet steps had carried them past the reach of Nkiyaa's ears, the girls looked at each other, grinned, and exploded into life. The rest of the long way they bounced and jostled and danced. They breathed in the expansive richness of the world and its sights and sounds and smells past the thorn fence, and relished their limited freedom. They were engaged in essential and exhausting service to the village, yet outside the fence it seemed they lived larger and freer. They trotted along full of energy and laughter and gossip and play along the way, the empty containers on their backs bumping along a syncopated accompaniment.

But alas for Monique, at this time she was too young to accompany them. Because this manyatta was not short of children, water fetching started only around the age of five, once children developed some strength and endurance. Very young ones could carry too little and held everyone up too much, and hence they were unwelcome. So, frustrated at missing the escape and the adventure, three-year-old Monique was left back in the manyatta with the other very little kids. She had to find other ways to stay out of Nkiyaa's reach and wrath.

She helped fetch and transport things around the manyatta, did a lot of sweeping, and inescapably had to be on manure duty. Once these were done, she went around trying to find someone she could pester with questions or ask for stories (this was not easy as Samburu culture is highly age-stratified and young children are generally shooed away). Or she would duck into a welcoming granny's hut, look for small animals or other kids to play with, or sneak to some far corner of the manyatta and fabricate dolls from twigs and wisps of grass or doodle in the dust, and hope Granny Ears would not find her.

Much of her time was spent, even young, dealing with the livestock and milk. When the cows and goats were milked twice daily by the "approved hands," every family provided gourds that were filled up. These were all lined up outside Nkiyaa's hut, and she dispensed them back out depending on each family's needs. Though the animals were originally from Papa's and Akuyia's stock and as the First Wife Nkiyaa was in charge of the milk, everyone held rights to it. No family could be unjustly slighted in their ration. It was an ancient form of milk cooperative. Monique and the other young children did much of the gourd-running, collecting gourds and sending milk to the various families. This was a wonderful time to pop into huts and get a cup of tea or a quick bite of whatever *ugali*[4], porridge, or other goodies they had on hand, and visit babies and see if anyone was up to anything interesting.

---

[4] Ugali is a corn meal porridge that is laboriously pounded and cooked down, typically until it becomes soft, doughy and formable. It is generally picked up with the fingers in bite-sized morsels.

Monique most loved visiting the kindest family members in the manyatta, who would not shoo her away. These were mainly Papa's younger blind brother everyone called Baba Senenkon, Second Granny, and her great-grandmother beautiful Nkooko, Granny Ears's mother.

Baba Senenkon was also Granny Ears's son; yet Monique never saw her treat him with a fraction of the adoration she did Papa. She hardly seemed to even acknowledge him as her son. This greatly saddened Monique. Baba Senenkon was blind, but he was also kind, handsome, patient, funny, and very clever and observant. He knew Monique's character perhaps the best of everyone in the village. It was he who gave her the nickname of Nailukiaa, "ears on fire."

"Why do you call me that?" she asked, giggling.

"You hear everything, no matter how far across the village it is," he answered.

She laughed. This nickname delighted her, with its imagery of her going around with flaming ears. (Her ears were also small and pointed up a bit, somewhat like little flames.) She also liked the gentleness he welcomed her with, and that even without being able to see her with eyes, he understood her so well. She could not fathom how such an excellent man could be unloved by his mother.

Perhaps the universe decided to lavish his missing parental love on him in other ways, as in time he became blessed with a large, happy family. He accumulated three wives, all in the village, and they each adored him and also got along well with each other—a small miracle. He eventually had sixteen children, all beautiful and well-mannered. The exception was his eldest child, his daughter Senenkon, who was a bit younger than Monique.

If in Samburu society you meet a man called "Baba" whatever, they are nicknamed after their child, as "Baba" means "father of." This commonly happens when a man's child is especially well-known. Senenkon from young was a miniature, duplicate Granny Ears. As if one was not enough for a village. They had the same grumpy, frumpy looks, and the same bossy, critical, mean-as-a-snake attitude. They were nearly inseparable. She was the only grandchild Nkiyaa truly loved, and Senenkon fiercely took Nkiyaa as her mother, even though her actual mother—who she chose to ignore—was right there in the village.

Baba Senenkon, being blind, was never occupied much with traditional male work, and from a young age was able to enjoy the relaxed life that was usually the privilege of elder men. He was a talented musician and carved flutes from discarded plastic pipes. He often sat outside his wives' huts and played beautifully for hours, sending endless melodies off on the manyatta winds. Monique loved to sit with him and listen to his music. It seemed to her he breathed into his flute all of his experience and reflections and complex emotions, and they came out as song and beauty.

Baba Senenkon was also an expert player of *ntotoi*, a traditional game similar to mancala, of moving stones in two rows of many cups in a wooden board. He felt the stones to count them, and held all their shifting numbers in his mind. He commonly beat his sighted opponents, playing daily for lively hours with other uncles or elder men, laughing and bragging and swatting each others' hands. Monique itched to come close and enjoy the raucous competition, but she could only watch sneakily from afar, as Samburu men have long strictly forbidden women and girls from playing or merely approaching the game.

Even kind Baba Senenkon could not break this barrier for her to cross.

Often Monique accompanied Second Granny, Akuyia's second wife, who was more a grandmother to her than Nkiyaa was. Second Granny was the mother of Papa's younger half-sister Aunt Antonella, who was a dozen or so years older than Monique and often stayed with their family. Second Granny had somehow lost an eye earlier in life, which Monique thought gave her a charming roguish, conspiratorial winking look. She was playful, warm and loving, and laughed loud, like thunder.

"She is so annoying," Granny Ears scowled on hearing her brash, joyful laugh. "Why does she have to laugh so loud. Like a hyena. It's so obnoxious."

Monique thought that she found endless criticism and whooping everyone more obnoxious, but had the brains not to say so out loud.

By far though, Monique's most beloved occupant of the village was her gentle, regal great-grandmother, Nkooko. Nkooko shared Nkiyaa's hut; yet she always seemed miserable inside it, hunched painfully like a trapped animal. She preferred to rest quietly outside under a beautiful big tree, leaning back and chewing on her mswaki or simply praying and communing. Nkiyaa's constant acidity and rancor wore Nkooko down terribly, and her sorrow was evident even to her tiny great-granddaughter. Little Monique loved to sit with her, and Nkooko would spoil her with quiet love and hugs. The pair often sat just silently holding hands. Monique was too awestruck by her great-grandmother's beauty and elegance to ever get bored sitting with her: although she would still ask questions.

Admiring Nkooko's flawless near-ebony skin: "Can I be dark like you?"

"Oh no, honey. You have to be born like this." (Monique was more caramelly-chocolate, and this was clearly not going to change to such a degree.)

Admiring her long, arching neck, and her height (Nkooko was easily six feet tall): "What about tall? Can I be tall like you?"

"We shall see, honey." (Also, nope.)

"Can I be like you when I grow up? Can I just *be* you when I grow up?"

Chuckling, gently: "I don't think so, sweetie."

Reflecting on Granny Ears yelling at someone a few huts down: "Why are you so pretty and your daughter is not?"

Nkooko, stifling laughter: "Shhh. Don't say that out loud."

Or: "Is she really your daughter? She's really mean."

Nkooko, sadly: "I know, I know."

When quiet Nkooko spoke to Monique, her words bore simple, earnest grandmother wisdom and love, in few words, often accompanied by a pat of the hand.

I wish for you all the goodness in life.

Be a good girl.

Follow your heart.

Be careful; be safe. The world is different now for your generation.

And, especially, often after a look at Nkiyaa,

Don't forget to be kind.

6

The Maralal House

When Monique was growing up, a reasonably-successful man would have at least four wives, each with their own huts and children, and perhaps a hundred cattle and goats. A highly-successful man would have a dozen or more wives and many hundreds of livestock. Akuyia had sixteen wives and thousands of livestock, spread over several manyattas. Ask the wives about this arrangement, and many may laugh and tell you this is a convenient way to get the men out of their homes and into another woman's, so they become someone else's problem. The multiple-wives arrangement is ancient and complicated: in many cases it resulted in harmony, prosperity, and simply survival; but in many others it brought drama, misery, poisonings, and ruin.

Papa stitched roughly this same ancient pattern for his life and his children's lives, but he stitched it across both old and new landscapes—and never had more than one wife at a time. He grew a small herd into thousands of cattle and yet more sheep and goats, all distributed out for care and breeding at varying manyattas. But as an accountant and then economist, brilliant and without tolerance for corruption, he was in high demand in government jobs, and additionally developed a few side businesses. This meant life near the cities.

So home for little Monique was often his mother's manyatta, yes, but also when she was young, most commonly home was the Maralal house.

The Maralal house was a large, airy single-story colonial house. Built by the British as an outpost home, it had housed small regiments of soldiers as they oversaw matters around what is now Samburu County. They had managed that region of the Northern Frontier District while it was walled off from the rest of Kenya, and were involved in the response to the Mau Mau uprising, the Maralal house arrest of Jomo Kenyatta—later to become Kenya's first president—and finally the necessities related to Kenya's independence and British departure.

The house sat up on a hill, and commanded a wide view from its shaded cement verandas, including in the distance the city police station and jail, and attached fruit orchards where inmates often worked, singing Christian hymns. The property's forty-acre allotment included a large pen for many cattle, and a vast garden that grew squashes and corn, collards and spinach, and tomatoes and potatoes. A thick, high hedgerow fence ran all around the property: a quintessentially British counterpart to the thorn fences encircling manyattas. The wooden gate at the road swung wide, easily accommodating a large automobile or herd of cattle passing through, and it connected a shaded vehicle parking area to the road outside. It was a short walk for the cows to large pasturelands downhill, and a short drive for Papa to his office, relatives, and places of interest.

Inside the house all had been built not for elegance, but for the basic dignified comfort and expedience of many people living and working together, and built wisely for the climate and for security, without electricity. (Monique would not live in a home with electricity until much later.)

Kenya is equatorial: a land without winter, and where the sun rises and sets at roughly the same times every day. Maralal sits nearly on the Equator, just one degree north, the same latitude as sweltering, tropical Singapore. One would expect it to be quite hot. However, the highlands' great altitude mitigates the heat, and places Maralal, at a mile plus a thousand feet above sea level, squarely in one of Earth's magical climate zones: the tropical highlands.

These lands reap the Equator's blessing of year-round sunshine for twelve hours a day; yet the temperatures generally only rise to the pleasant mid-seventies Fahrenheit, and drop at nights to the forties and fifties. Monique and her family shivered from the air's bite at the coldest depth of night—if they threw aside their cowskins and blankets and stepped out then—but they never experienced frost, ice, or snow. Neither would they truly scorch in summer. The climate is nearly perpetually moderate, and with abundant, consistent sunshine far beyond what temperate zones receive. When European colonists arrived they exclaimed over the incredible conditions. They declared the area the "White Highlands," ideal for European settlers. But that is another story; and one that did not go the way they intended.

These tropical highlands, like others scattered across the Americas, Africa, and Asia, are truly an agriculturist's paradise —in areas where there is plentiful water. But in much of the highlands there isn't. The climate experiences wet and dry seasons, and the streams and even rivers regularly dry up. Drought kills crops and herds, and wild animals and people. Finding water was a skill that Monique's people's very blood was a testament to: even so, they could not always find enough for all that they cared for and wished to keep alive.

The soldiers did not have these water-finding skills. But they had others. At the Maralal house they had built a large outdoor water store, an elevated metal tank, that held hundreds of gallons of water. It was fed by the city water system which had come into existence recently, but also was a standalone water source during drought or disruption. They installed a hand water pump near the house, which drew up water from deep underground. They also built a second outdoor water tank, with a clever place underneath to build a fire. It piped hot water straight to the bathtub in the house. Bathtubs are extremely uncommon in Samburu homes, but the British had wanted one, and a giant one at that, large enough to actually soak a cow. Papa also relished a mandatory piping-hot bath every morning. For toilet, a pit latrine outhouse sufficed, across a soft-grass yard on the back of the property. Monique tried everything to avoid going there at night, as she feared hidden snakes.

To ward off the evening chill and provide homely welcome, a cozy fireplace was built into one corner in the front living room. Around its crackling flames hundreds of Brits and their guests had smoked cigars, had tea, made negotiations, and told stories and shared news from the region and back home. Now it experienced much the same, but with Papa's family and guests exchanging the tea and stories. Down the hall, the spacious, warm dining area featured a dramatic, huge stone fireplace along one wall. In front of it lay a long, sturdy mahogany table, with expandable leaves and intricately carved wooden chairs. It had previously hosted decades of soldiers taking mess and mapping out strategy sessions upon it—reckoning with calamities dealt by nature, politics, illness, and local tribes—and it was now the daily meal-gathering place for Papa's entire family.

In the kitchen, the large back corner room, one wall was dominated by an absolute beast of a stove. Nearly impossible to find today, it was a massive specimen of the colonial enamel wood-burning type. It devoured firewood by the armsful; eight pots could bubble and steam at once upon its vast top. When it was running, the heat carried through the whole house and women fanned themselves and dripped sweat, despite the large stovepipe that diverted out the smoke and much of the heat. Another wall had two simple latched glass-pane windows that swung open for the cool breeze. The windows stood over a work table and a colossal, deep enamel sink with running taps, for washing up voluminous quantities of dishes. Stools were everywhere, and a storage area sat off to the side, filled with charcoal and firewood and pantry items.

It was good that the house had been built for a regiment, because rarely less than twenty people were there at any time. Daily the house filled with multiple generations of grand-mothers, uncles, aunts, cousins, people Papa had adopted into the family, and visitors. The house was always just buzzing with people, laughter, conversation, and work.

Mornings in the house began every day at 3:30.

When the first cocks crowed, little Monique opened her eyes. The night was still pitch-black unless there were no clouds, and then it was faintly lit by the crystal-white moon and stars. It was also its most piercingly cold, these few hours before dawn. Even if the cocks had been silent, suddenly carried to death by eagles or old age, Monique could still feel it was 3:30. Her body had learned the time, from the dark, the cold, and habit. It simply knew when to get up and start the day. She and any other children flopped out of bed and made their way to their assigned morning chores.

Over the next three hours, all the family—except Maama—scrambled into action. Everyone who stayed in the house and who regularly came by, the whole lot of nearly two dozen, had work to do. If extra light was desired, adults pumped and lit kerosene pressure lanterns. These, with their brightly-glowing mantles and glass globes, fascinated Monique. The little piston pump and loud hiss while operating reminded her of a tiny, fierce engine: one that threw out stubborn, intense light far beyond what was expected from something so small.

The first early-morning task was to light the fire under the outside water tank and start heating its water for Papa's bath. While he meticulously scrubbed the tub and waited for the water to heat and the enormous bath to fill, he turned his little brick-shaped battery-powered radio to BBC and chomped like mad on his mswaki stick.

CHOMP! CHOMP! banged out even over the radio and outside the bathroom. *My goodness,* Monique thought. *How is Papa still having all his teeth?*

At 4 a.m. on the dot he cranked up the volume, blasted BBC news loud enough for the entire compound to hear (they did not want to), and began his mandatory hour-long soak in the giant steaming-hot tub. He drained the entire hot water tank into it.

Papa's hot bath aside, the most central concern was, as always in Samburu life, the livestock. Even though this was the city home, Papa kept a herd of twenty cows plus a few goats and sheep on the property. By 6:30, when he would drive off to work, not only must the animals be sent out down the hill to graze the dew-grass, and then brought back up to be milked and the calves overseen in suckling their share, and all the milk processed and stored, but also: fires must be built in the jiko and the belly of the huge stove; tea and breakfast for all must be made and put out on the big table; and everything must be tidied afterwards, including the dishes cleaned and cow areas freshened up.

Of these morning activities, milking took the longest. A whole contingent of family, including the children and the most adept aunties, headed outside for this while everyone else attended to breakfast or other chores.

Monique loved prepping the cows for milking. First everyone carried out several heavy, dark, molasses-based vitamin blocks and plunked them down spaced apart on the long, low brick wall Papa had built in the milking area opposite the feed trough. Cows were brought, and lined up to lick the blocks or munch the feed. Everyone took their own milking cup, again beautifully carved from a fat chunk of mahogany and with a leather tie strap attached, and pulled up a stool to a cow, setting up tucked in alongside the belly so they couldn't be kicked.

At first the cows' teats would be tough and swollen, too hard to milk, and often nasty with filth. And so everyone must first apply a lovely, cleansing beeswax-based ointment. It softened and melted under the warmth of their hands as they rubbed it on the teats. Then with a sponge dipped in hot water they rubbed the teats down, wiping them carefully all over, again and again, until they were soft and clean and sweet-smelling. Once this was done, the teats could be worked easily even by young children's hands, and the beautiful, pure milk shot out easily, *tshewk, tshewk, tshewk.*

The aunties sang gentle, loving songs to the cows while they worked. Their tender praises rose as melodic incantations, lulling and charming the cows.

When the sun rises you wake with a full heart
full of desire to give us the milk

Your milk goes a long way
> *It raises our children, it raises our warriors*
> *who are mighty conquerors*
You are beautiful, you are wonderful
> *You fill us with pride*

The work settled into a trance of soft singing and shooting milk, punctuated occasionally with calls for Monique or another child to fetch this or move that, to send one cow or calf back to the enclosure and bring another. When things were going well, and the cows were relatively settled and not kicking, even little Monique could feel the ancient, powerful symbiosis. The family nurtured and cared for the cows, and the cows in return provided the glistening white milk that was the entire backbone of their life and culture.

Unfortunately the *tshewk, tshewk* and the aunties softly singing weren't the only sounds during milking. There was also the regular, loud *PWOW ... PWOW ... PWOW PWOW* of large, heavy, soft things hitting the dust. This was the herald of the last task. After the cows were all milked, they were sent out for the day's grazing, the vitamin blocks went back inside, and the aunties whisked the precious milk away for use and processing. The young children must freshen the milking area and move the manure, just as at the manyatta.

Monique repeatedly tried to get out of this. She yearned for the freedom to spend the day in the grazing lands with the cows and goats. Seeing whichever boy cousin or young uncle was getting ready to take the livestock down for the day, she pestered, "I want to go take them down. Can I today? I am much bigger, you see!"

"No, child. You are still too young. It is not safe for you. And you'll lose the livestock. Now get busy."

"Humpf."

But that was that. She and the other children had to clear the manure. Further delay would not get her out of the task: it would only add a whooping to it. But fortunately at the Maralal house there were large dustpans used for this. Moving the dozens of fresh cow patties to the manure pile was much faster and much, much nicer than at the manyatta. Poop was almost never thrown. Once it was all stored away, the children spread a layer of fresh, fragrant grass cuttings and clean sawdust all over the milking area. Now it was ready for the afternoon milking round.

As soon as the milking area was clean and fresh, the children dashed in for breakfast. Breakfasts at the Maralal house were amazing, nearly all made from scratch that morning. There was strong sweet chai, and ugali served with buttermilk, and sorghum porridge with wild honey and rich beautiful butter, and often fresh-baked sliced bread from the nearby baker, and various sides of vegetables and freshly-slaughtered and cooked meat, and anything else that had been picked up here or there. If they were lucky, there might be chapatis or mandazis, or Monique's favorite, the *mkonye* bread Papa sometimes brought back from the baker. The mkonye was formed in two clusters of small long loaves along a central spine, somewhat resembling a flat ribcage. Each small loaf pulled off easily and was a fresh, delicious soft bread. The aroma of fresh mkonye summoned all the children from far across the house, squealing in delight.

Chai

Kenya's tea is called chai, just as in India: *chai* is also the word for tea in Swahili. The British introduced tea plants as a cash crop in Kenya, especially in the highlands, in the early

1900s. It has grown there beautifully ever since, and is enjoyed by nearly every family no matter how simple, as well as exported on a massive scale. Tea, brewed strong, milky and sweet, was the first and most successful commodity (after beads) that the British could persuade the extremely conservative, spartan Samburu culture to adopt and trade for. It rapidly became so ingrained in the local culture as to be present in every house and hut, served every morning, and bags of tea and sugar are included *de rigueur* in wedding negotiation gifts.

Monique's family brewed delicious chai by first bringing a mixture of fresh milk and water to a boil in a huge pot; then handfuls of black tea were thrown in. A few cups of brown sugar were added, as well as any herbs and spices desired, such as the local wild mint, or cinnamon bark. However, Papa liked his chai plain, so plain it was usually made. Once the color, taste, and sweetness were right, it was ladled steaming-hot over a sieve into big cups or gourds. (Small teacups are not favored by Samburu, as they find them stingy.)

The family also had a proper British tea-service, on a tray with a teapot, large cups, saucers, sugar store, and milk creamer: tea made that style was served for guests, as well as placed on the dining table every morning for Papa and the menfolk to enjoy as they got ready for their days. The huge pot of chai was ladled out as desired from the kitchen, and was mainly for everyone doing the manual work.

Ugali and sorghum porridge

Starches were not a large part of the ancient Samburu diet, but they have been thoroughly incorporated for many generations now. Ugali is a corn meal porridge that while being heated in a pot is laboriously stirred, pounded, and flipped, using a wooden paddle called a *mwiko*. It is cooked and stirred typically until it becomes doughy and formable, but it can be made to varying textures as desired. (Papa, always extreme, over-cooked his ugali until it became delectable dry flakes.) A pillowy-soft neat mound of ugali is scooped out and served to accompany buttermilk, meat, or vegetables. It can be eaten with a spoon or picked up in small portions with the fingers and mixed with side dishes. It is standard breakfast and all-day fare, and second only to milk as a modern dietary mainstay for Samburu.

Sorghum porridge (*uji*), another ancient-heritage starch food, is made from a mix of sorghum and corn flours cooked in water, with or without milk, into a simple smooth porridge. Monique's family enjoyed it with butter and sweetened with sugar or honey.

Honey

The honey the family used was harvested by uncles and grandfathers, in the ancient way from wild beehives. They went honey-gathering regularly and kept the family in abundant supply. It was not processed at all other than rough filtering. Honey and brown sugar were the only sweeteners used at her home, other than rock sugar and a small amount of white sugar in the British tea service. Kenya has now mainly switched to modernized beekeeping using their own local styles of manmade hives to obtain honey: only a few people still harvest from wild bee nests.

Butter and milk and buttermilk

Milk is the main staple in the Samburu diet, and this was true for Monique and her family, even in the city farmhouse. Most of the milk was from the cattle, but they also milked their goats. The milk was turned into buttermilk and butter, and the butter was further reduced to ghee (*samli* in Swahili), which was used like oil and for cosmetic and ritual purposes, and for preserving dried meats.

Various sides of meat or vegetables

Because her family had many livestock, meat was plentiful. Goat was used with the frequency that Americans use chicken: goats thrived and reproduced prolifically, so the meat was abundant and cheap. Other meats in the household included beef, mutton, and a few hunted game animals. Samburu have rigorous cultural guidelines on which animals may and may not be eaten: they do not eat all types of wild animals. The main ones Monique's family hunted were various antelopes, along with bushpig and warthog.

They generally either roasted the meat (in addition to outdoor roasting, the main body of the huge stove could be opened, to fit a whole leg of goat inside) or cooked it into a stew or soup, with herbs or vegetables.

As with starches, the ancient Samburu diet is not rich in vegetables, but again this was expanded in Monique's family. The most famous vegetable dish was the regionally-popular *sukuma wiki*, chopped and braised collard greens, often mixed with a bit of meat. Sukuma wiki means "push the week" in Swahili: the highly-nutritious greens are used to "stretch" the meat rations. Other vegetables included tomatoes, cabbage, carrots, onions, and zucchini and eggplants (called by their British names, courgettes and aubergines). Monique detested okra (ladyfingers) and *terere*, a wild amaranth leaf that cooked up very slimy, but these were prized by the elders and appeared regularly on plates.

The vegetables and meats were not prepared fresh for breakfast: they were cooked for supper. Leftovers were usually still good the next morning due to the low nighttime temperatures, and were finished up with ugali or chapatis, or fed to the dogs.

Chapatis and mandazi

Chapatis were introduced in Kenya generations ago due to the long, robust history of Indians residing there. Chapatis got the most thoroughly adopted of all the Indian foods: the flatbreads are simple to make and work well with traditional side dishes. Made from wheat flour, water, salt, and ghee or oil, in Kenya you can find both simple single-layer chapatis and a popular flaky, layered one, similar to *parathas*. For special occasions or when they randomly felt like it or could be persuaded, Monique's aunts made delicious, buttery, layered chapatis, with homemade ghee and white flour, usually stone-ground by nearby Turkanas from excellent local wheat.

Mandazi are little, fried, slightly-sweet breads that taste somewhat like plain doughnuts or Native American frybread. Monique adored mandazi, but as with chapatis not everyone could be bothered to make them: they took a good bit of extra work. Her aunts mixed a fairly stiff dough from water, sugar, flour, and milk, formed it into triangles, and deep-fried them. Mandazis were served piping hot at breakfast, and then leftovers finished up at dinner.

It was Monique's aunts, the younger generation of cooks, who made chapatis or mandazis until she could make them herself. Her grannies never made either of these newer breads, instead cooking ugali and porridge in the ancient and simple way.

7

Papa, Maama

Papa only got his education as a punishment.

The British-influenced government had decided that all Kenyans—meaning at that time all the boys only, of course—needed an education. Very good! But when the ministers turned this principle to the many rural tribes who were still busily living independent, fierce lives in their ancient patterns: hunting with arrows and spears and knives, tending cattle, having bloody rites and trading many cows for a beaded and red-robed wife ... The same tribes who had only recently calmed their warring (especially the most-troublesome Turkana, Samburu, and Maasai) for some semblance of peace and national unity, and who would die of thirst itself, or go back to war, rather than give up their proud, customary ways, or give up their sons ...

The ministers stroked their chins. "Hm. Perhaps the best we can do is get each village to send one child for an education."

And so they tried this. Nervously.

They sent representatives to the villages and explained the policy. It was difficult to convince tribal elders and fathers that sons could be as valuable "getting an education" as herding and working in traditional ways. A few parents grasped the opportunity this could lend their families and chose favored sons to send. Far more were baffled or angry at men coming from distant cities to tell them to send their sons away. For people whose identities had always lain with their tribes, even the concept that they were part of a nation and subject to its policies and laws was novel, and often unwelcome.

The ministers must have worried their plan could not be carried out. But then a miracle occurred.

Somehow, everyone realized this policy meant they could get rid of the manyatta's naughtiest, most disobedient children by sending them off to school, which was usually a boarding school in a nearby city. It is a fact, even among the Samburu, Turkana, and Maasai, that every village has at least one problem child.

Voila! The policy was embraced and implemented quite widely, and all the naughtiest boys—and a few good ones—were sent away to be educated.

Papa was not one of the good boys. He was very naughty as a child. And so he was sent away from the manyatta for an education, to become Patrick as well as Kitamonge (PK to his friends and family), and to speak for his people in the greater Kenyan society and think of them.

Monique never heard how her parents' marriage had been decided. She never heard if her mother too had received an education, or what dreams she might have held for her own future. What she did hear, constantly, was the terrific sound of incredible, epic clashes between her mother and father. Chairs were thrown. Windows were broken: repeatedly. Yelling was the very least of it.

It is quite normal in Samburu culture, especially among men, to resolve conflict or grudges physically with full-on fights. Most often the relationship is undamaged the next day. This is a whole way of settling matters, well-understood, respected, and with its own known rules. Within this framework Papa had developed a fearsome reputation as a dangerous fighter when provoked. Even so, the one dishing out most of the action at home was Maama.

"Wow," little Monique said, as she saw her mother grab her father and throw him across the room. Papa mainly only countered in defense; yet even this was amazing to watch. When he threw things, Maama didn't even blink. She coldly took the hit or dodged, and adjusted her attack.

"Man," Monique told her little friends. "Someone should set them up for one of those paid fights. I'll ref."

Maama spent most of her rage on Papa; however, she also terrified and terrorized little Monique. It was clear from her earliest memories—her mother's face in a cold fury and usually an object or hand coming in for a hit—that Maama burned with hatred for both of them. She was the Queen of Violence, and unpredictable. Things might seem reasonably fine for a while, but then Maama would flip in an instant into rage.

If Monique accidentally dropped something, Maama pronounced horrific insults with vile innuendos about her tiny daughter's hands and smacked her. Once Monique overslept and failed to roll out of the bed at 3:30 to light the jiko and stove for breakfast: her mother again insulted her horribly and beat her soundly. Monique's many questions about life, already seen as irritating or impertinent by most family members, drove Maama into a fury. So did Papa's closeness with his child.

Once Monique asked, "Why do you hate me so much when I am so little? I have never done anything to you."

This too was answered with fury and beating.

In all the hustle and bustle and constant effort to keep life going, Maama herself never did any work. She relaxed and expected to be served, or complained and insulted people, including her husband, or "managed" others. She often spent the days out visiting friends, or on a stool on the veranda, drinking Papa's liquor he kept for guests and crocheting, yelling, and bossing people around. When she had other housewives over or went out with them, the time was spent flaunting their status and wealth, getting served, and complaining how horrible their lives and husbands were. Meanwhile everyone else, down to the small children, was engaged in endless labor to run the household.

Monique was not oblivious. If she had seen that her mother contributed to the family but struggled with her temper; or that she was kind but useless, she would have respected her, and possibly loved her. But with Maama bringing only abuse, in copious amounts, Monique felt very little tie of loyalty, regardless what her culture insisted she "must" feel. She simply knew her mother was vicious, like a snake, and to stay close to the door because that was the way out.

After a bad fight, Monique asked, "Papa. Why do we put up with that woman?"

"She is your mother. We must respect that."

"Why? She's horrible to you. She's horrible to me. She doesn't do anything around here. We don't need her."

"Monique! Respect your mother."

"I'm sick of all the fighting! And her yelling all the time! And beating me! I'll go find a *mzungu*[5] family and get them to take me away!"

This drew Papa up straight and he gave her a hard, silver-eyed stare. His daughter was only three years old, but he knew

---

[5] Literally meaning "wanderer," mzungu refers generally to foreigners, especially white folk. Most of the mzungus Monique saw hailed from various European countries, working with the church or visiting on safari.

she meant it: and she could possibly do it. She was precocious and determined. Maama was heavily pregnant with a second child, but that hadn't reduced her rancor or assaults. She would not dare seriously attack Monique when he was around or when he would shortly hear of it, but he couldn't be there all the time. And visiting mzungu families indeed came around regularly going to the Safari Lodge down the road, or were at church.

So shortly after this, Papa used his influence and friendship with the kind Turkana headmistress at the local girls' school, and persuaded them to accept Monique for kindergarten, two years early. Weekday mornings she was with the nuns at St. Mary's Primary School in town, and Papa picked her up after lunch.

The baby was soon born: a beautiful, chubby, happy baby girl. She reminded Monique of a dark-chocolate-skinned cherub, with deliciously slurpable cheeks and laughing light amber eyes. They named her Esther.

Esther was born somehow without Maama's hate. She still was not a good mother, but at least she was not abusive towards the baby. But while Esther was safe, it was just as bad as ever, or worse, for Monique and her father. Papa requested aunts and uncles to keep special eye on Monique and the baby. Maama showed no interest in raising either of them, and so Esther was cared for by Papa and Monique and various aunts and grandmothers, who were charmed and delighted by the cherubic infant.

In the afternoons Papa began bringing his daughters along to his office. In addition to his usual work for the county, he was preparing to depart the next year for government-sponsored study in Germany, and he had extra paperwork and studies to complete.

Monique loved the time in his office with just him and her baby sister. She played with Esther and peppered Papa with questions.

"What are you doing with all those numbers?"

"What is that funny language?"

"Why do mzungus have blue eyes?"

"Why are they so pale?"

"Why can't I have blue eyes?"

"Why are there people in the world who are different from us?"

"Why can't Esther talk?"

"What is this thing on Esther, anyway?" (On the baby's fat thigh a wide, bright-yellow crater had appeared, with weird floppy protuberances. It didn't seem to bother her at all, and was a mystery to the doctors, who suggested keeping it aired out and applying GV solution[6]. If anyone bandaged it Monique shrieked and removed the bandage, lecturing about its need for open air. Papa suspected she might become a nurse.)

"Why can other families be happy but not ours?"

"Why do you have to get a beating for asking questions?"

"Why do people have children they don't want?"

"Why do you have to fight somebody you sleep with?"

Wow, these questions, Papa thought. *Man. And how am I going to get anything done?*

"Here." He passed her a pen and paper. "Copy these words. All the way down the page."

"Write the numbers from one to one hundred."

"OK, now fill in the missing ones."

Monique loved learning and reading and writing, and happily complied.

---

[6] GV, gentian violet solution, was the panacea ointment of choice in Kenya at this time. Made from a chemical compound, the intensely purple thin solution is a medicinal dye. It is known for its antibiotic, antifungal, and anthelmintic properties, and was a very important topical antiseptic. After several months of its use, Esther's mysterious wound shrank and disappeared.

"Go play with Esther and take care of her. She is missing you. Talk with her so she can learn."

Monique also loved caring for her sister. Esther was generally an easy, happy baby. With others she was quiet and watchful, but with Monique she babbled and played. She loved lying on her back and waving her hand across her face and laughing at it. Since she was born, Monique studied how the aunts took care of her, and became an enthusiastic mini-mom. At the office, nearly all Esther's needs fell to Monique, including feeding her bottle and changing her diaper.

Monique was tall and strong for her age, and diaper-changing was well within her grasp. But Esther had grown so well under all the women's care and become so chubby and heavy that Monique could not pick her up to carry her to the discreet changing area in the corner. So Papa regularly had the scene over his shoulder of Esther shrieking in delight as her sister rolled her across the office to change her diaper, and then rolled her back afterwards.

"Yeah, you think this is just for fun," Monique muttered. "It's 'cause you fat, girl!"

Papa relished many aspects of Samburu and Kenyan life, especially those related to animals and nature. He especially enjoyed hunting with his brothers and cousins. Some of Monique's earliest memories were of standing on the Land Rover front seat, jumping up and down and shrieking at her father to drive faster, while they chased prey across the wilderness.

They were a bizarre new predator: boxy and wheeled with a roaring engine; fast and unrelenting. They cut a target animal—usually some sort of antelope—from its herd and drove it toward a trench her uncles had dug and covered with long grasses. When the antelope fell in, the uncles sprang down from their hiding spot in the bushes, and hogtied it with belts. They hefted it out and with a knife quickly made the ancient exchange of taking a life to feed more lives. Everyone enjoyed, right there, a bonfire and open-air feast of meat, especially the liver, sliced and fresh-roasted on hot rocks or over the fire. The rest of the animal came back in the capacious rear of the vehicle, to share out at the manyatta. Every part of the animal was appreciated and used. (But liver rarely made it back.)

Papa, being modernized and fastidiously proper, always acquired the necessary paperwork for meat hunting as well as any permitted collection items: skins, skulls, antlers, and ostrich eggs. He detested poachers and all types of corruption and illegality, speeding and cursing excepted. All his permits sat neatly in a drawer, and he displayed a beautiful trophy collection in the study lounge at the house, to enjoy and share with visitors.

Around this time, when he was bringing his two little daughters to the office in the afternoons, he went out one night for a drink. By chance he met at the bar some other county workers, from the wildlife and hunting office.

"Hey PK," they warned. "They're coming tomorrow to check your house."

"What? You know I do everything legally. What would they be looking for?"

"Some lady called in a tip that you have all these items poached, with no papers."

Papa thanked the men and rushed home. Anyone caught having poached the items in his collection would face a huge fine and likely jail time. The papers were crucial to prove their legality. He briskly trotted to the lounge and pulled open the drawer.

No papers.

He woke his daughter. "Monique. My hunting papers are all gone. From my study. Have you seen anything?"

She thought a bit. Then, groggily, "Oh, yes Papa. A few days ago Maama was burning many papers in the fireplace and smiling. I don't know what they were."

He groaned and woke up every person in the house but Maama and baby Esther. With light from the hissing pump lanterns, they had a very quiet, very busy 2-a.m. work party disposing of all of Papa's beautiful collection. The ostrich eggs were smashed and buried in the compost pile. The more durable items were driven off the property and buried deep in the bush.

When the enforcement agents arrived the next day while Papa was at work, Maama cheerfully welcomed them in. But not a single bone, antler, skin, or egg could be found: only a very tidy and empty study lounge.

All day Maama threw dagger glares at everyone. They all played unaware. And this became one of her many attacks Papa forgave or simply decided to overlook and forget.

8

From the Brewers to the Trough

E very day of his life, Papa contemplated how to improve his cows and their milk. The livestock benefited from traditional Samburu wisdom, built over millennia, that helped their animals thrive where others' would not. Papa also applied the most modern vaccines, dietary supplements, and veterinary care. Further, in his creative musings around this time he discovered a wonderful, economical secret to keeping his cows happy and producing well. It came from the brewers and bars.

Traditional societies nearly always have an alcoholic homebrew, or two or three. Incan regions developed *chicha* from maize and quinoa; palm wine is brewed from a myriad palm trees by people across the equatorial world; wide swaths of Asia have various homebrew rice wines, such as *tuak* in Borneo. Nearly wherever human society could flourish, someone found a way to brew alcohol, and it became woven into local culture, for better and for worse.

The Samburu, however, were for millennia among those few societies who didn't brew or drink much. Their traditional herdsman diet was very low in grains, consisting ideally only of milk, blood, meat, honey, herbs, some tubers, and some berries. The only alcohol they brewed themselves was sparingly-used honey wine, mainly for ceremonial purposes. However, this general abstention was absolutely not the case for other nearby tribes, whose cultures centered more around agriculture and who had developed traditional beers and spirits. By the time Papa was thinking of how to improve his cows' yield, the custom of brewing *busaa*, a gentle maize and millet beer, had come in from the Kalenjin tribe, and *chang'aa*, a powerful sugar-based spirit, soon followed from Sudan.

Chang'aa, usually 35-40% alcohol, is known for creating wild, blackout, violent drunkenness. Monique's uncles once, after a night of drinking it, got lost stumbling back to the manyatta with alcohol-blinded eyes.

"Eh, are these our huts?" one asked, blinking at vague shapes that loomed in the faintly silver-lit night, with roughly door-shaped spaces.

"Think so," another slurred.

"*Hodi, hodi*,"[7] they called out, and drunkenly hunched down to enter through the doorways. They promptly passed out.

"Jesus!" one exclaimed when he woke as dawn was beginning to lighten. He slowly, delicately extricated himself and went to carefully wake his buddies.

The "huts" were elephants. They had mistaken the space under the stomachs as doors, and slept underneath the bemused behemoths.

This is a funny story after drinking chang'aa: most stories are not funny. Most close elephant encounters also aren't funny. The uncles were exceedingly lucky they lived to bring their tale back to Papa and Monique.

Papa did not touch anything from chang'aa. However, the much gentler busaa held use for him.

The basic ingredients for busaa are dried corn and millet. The corn is ground, fermented with water and then roasted; the

---

[7] Called out on entering a home, to seek permission to cross the threshold. Roughly "Hello, may I come in?" Also used in crossing rivers.

millet is sprouted, then dried in the sun and ground into malt. These are mixed together with water and left to ferment. When fermentation is complete, more water is added to dilute the busaa as desired, and the sizable quantities of residue from the grains, called *machicha*, is filtered off for disposal.

It was these grain remnants, the machicha, that Papa bought for his cows. Every early morning after his bath, as the rest of the house was still hustling the day into action, he drove around to the local brewers and loaded the back of his Land Rover with huge woven sacks of wet machicha, oozing busaa. Long after the bags had gone and the vehicle had been left open in the hot sun, the aroma remained.

"Whew, Papa. It reeks of alcohol in here," Monique said. Baby Esther's eyes fairly popped out of her head from the fumes.

"Yes, that is my secret to how our cows give so much milk, so happily. The machicha! These grains are only half-spent, with much good nutrition in them still, along with a *wee* little bit of alcohol. It's so good for the cattle and they love it. And I only spend a few shillings for it! The brewers are simply glad to be rid of it, honestly!" Papa's silver eyes danced in delight at the arrangement. It was a cow-farming economist's dream.

The cows did love it. Papa and the uncles dumped the sacks into the vast wooden feeding troughs near the gate and the cattle, back up from the morning dew-grass, fed happily to their hearts' content and peacefully let themselves be milked. They were at their most mellow while eating the machicha. Evening milkings without it were much more troublesome.

One cow had a particularly strong bond with Papa, his Land Rover, and the machicha: Namada.

9

Namada

Papa named all animals after their characteristics, and Namada means "foolish." Namada was indeed foolish, and she was Monique's favorite cow. She was clearly extraordinary: very tall for a cow, with a strangely large belly and extra-long tail, and she was an unusual rich golden color, with a beautifully-formed head. Her huge, dark eyes were the size of teacups, elegantly rimmed with dark brown like eyeliner, and she had thick, long eyelashes. Her dainty light pink muzzle was dotted with brown freckles, and a pretty stripe of espresso fur ran up from her nose to the crest of head. Two tiny, nubby horns sprouted out like short ponytails next to her small ears.

"Namada, you are cuuute," Monique said, standing next to Papa and stroking her soft muzzle as Namada nosed around for munchables. "You are like a little thing in heels." Namada nipped at her. "You know, I am not edible. So stay away from me."

Namada whacked her with her long tail. *WHOOOK!* "Oh, you're violent too, huh? You don't like somebody you just whoop them." She laughed. "Papa, why did you name her Namada?"

"Is it not obvious?" he answered. Monique laughed again. "This cow is so foolish. She never follows any directions. You know, you direct cows a certain way. You raise them a certain way. You feed them certain things. Namada? Goes the opposite. She wants everything human beings are eating. She does not realize she is a cow. She is just foolish."

"She may be foolish, but Namada is just the best."

Papa looked down sideways at little Monique. "You like everything weird. Including people."

Monique could not defend her beloved Namada. She was definitely a weird cow. It seemed that in every herd nearly all the cows would be normal cows, doing normal cow things, and having a normal cow affect. Which for Kenyan cows is "Come near me and I'll kick you." But then there would be one weirdo, who was friendly and inquisitive and did strange things and was completely uninterested in being normal. There was always one. In her natal herd, it had been Namada. Papa had randomly acquired her on one of his livestock-purchasing expeditions before Monique had been born, and she quickly became not only Monique's, but everyone's favorite cow.

Namada's weirdness included being friendly to humans and thus easy to milk, but strongly disliking the many beautiful calves she bore. Whenever she had borne another pretty calf, maroon, or gold, or dark, and it was brought for nursing, she would kick at the poor little thing—*Pwoff!*—and it would have to be fostered out to another cow or hand-raised with a bottle. It seemed to Monique she was saying, "*You* guys can milk me, sure. Take all the milk you want. But those annoying little things? Nuh uh. No way. I'm not dealing with any of *those.*"

So Namada was a terrible mother. Beyond this, her weird behavior was mainly centered around food. She was a large cow, and gave huge quantities of milk. It took three people to milk her out. If she wasn't milked promptly, her udder became so huge and heavy she could barely walk. She would moo piteously and laboriously wander looking for someone to milk her, a trail of milk streaming *vrrrrrrr* out to the sides and behind. The resident cats and yapping dogs followed behind excitedly lapping it up, and Namada mooed aggrievedly and kicked and lashed her tail at them. If you wanted to find Namada, you could often just look for and follow a wide, parallel milk trail in the dirt.

Not only was the quantity of her milk remarkable, but it somehow had a preferred quality. Papa treasured it. All the other cows' milk could be sent out to friends and neighbors, but every drop of Namada's he reserved for the family. Whether it became chai, buttermilk, butter and ghee, prayer offerings, or was simply drunk fresh, it all had to remain for the Leparleens and their closest kin. And there was always plenty, even for twenty-plus folk.

But perhaps in need to make all this milk, or perhaps because of something else, Namada had a bizarre and prodigious appetite. She would eat nearly anything and everything, and drink voluminous quantities of water. Papa went to a nearby village of Turkanas who grew a lot of maize, and begged, "Please. Give me the husk, give me everything about the corn, give me everything that is left over from the farm. Please. Always keep that for me. I have a cow that eats everything."

It was true. Namada would nose at clothes on your body or the clothesline to see if they were edible, and eat all the grass and corn and leftovers she could get. If she found a patch of particularly nice grass, she could not be moved until she had eaten the last blade. She would finish her special bucket of extra food, and then toss it up in the air with her head inside, chucking it around so she could examine every inch and lick out any minuscule remnants from the bottom seam. Once the bucket was empty, she returned it to the ground, and drove it around with her nose first to one family member, then another, looking at them and mooing plaintively.

Moooooo. Look, it's empty. Where's more food. Add more food, please. Moooooo.

Namada was so brazen in her foraging that she regularly ambled across the veranda to the house's front door, and stepped *in* as far as she could (until her giant belly blocked her), looking around for any set-aside plate or cup or other tasty thing within reach. Her favorite daily gambit was to wander around to the two kitchen windows. Never mind only gaining access if they had been left open: she quickly learned to nudge them with her head so the latch fell and the windows swung out. She then stuck her huge cow head in, on her long neck, and nosed around.

Her inquiries began at the window above the work table. Were there perhaps any set-aside leftovers, or food or drinks in process? Anything within reach was munched and slurped up. Then she withdrew her head, moseyed alongside the house a few steps, and stuck her head through the second window over the huge sink and began explorations there. If she wasn't caught and stopped, all the dirty dishes and pots were thoroughly licked "clean" by her long tongue, *lllll-uhhh*. Ugali, mandazi, sorghum porridge, tea leaves, veggies, rice, stews: she would eat them all. Once Monique saw her delicately raise the yellow-enameled tea kettle with her pink mouth and slurp the last of the tea.

"Ggahh! Blech, Namada! You're nasty!" All day she kept gagging, recalling the cow lips and tongue slurping from the teapot.

Papa saw this many times.

"This cow is very unique," was all he had to say.

One time, he conducted a small experiment. He offered her an apple. She ate it. Next, orange peelings. She ate them. Ugali. She ate. Eggplant. She ate. A piece of scrap paper. She ate. A plastic bag. She tried to eat; he yanked it away. A dozen family members had gathered by this point, laughing and offering any bits of weird things they had.

"Look at this cow," Papa said. "Please, everyone. Don't ever feed her meat, because she will be eating people the next thing we know."

As wide as Namada's voracious palate was—and it was extraordinarily wide, wider than anyone fully realized—her definite favorite of all Things To Be Eaten was machicha. Once Papa began bringing it back from the brewers every morning and dumping the sacks into the cow troughs, a whole new life began for Namada.

At first, she peacefully went along with the normal cow morning routine: pre-dawn, go down for the dew-grass, graze a bit, and then come back up and settle together in the cow enclosure until milking time. Come out in turns, enjoy the machicha, and be milked.

That lasted about two days. After that, once her little twitching ears caught the echoing sound of the Land Rover's powerful engine as Papa sped up the hill on fourth gear, she would immediately raise her head and very loudly *MOOOOO* and go crazy, trying to get out of the enclosure and raising a storm and disturbing all the other cows. She wanted her machicha.

Papa drove in to this dysfunctional situation and said, "*Please*, anybody, when you bring the cows back up to the enclosure, *just let her out.* Let her come out, and stand right in front of the gate."

And so that's what Namada's mornings became. After the dew-grass, she snubbed the other cows in the enclosure and waited at the gate, or strayed around the property, nosing at the door and kitchen. As soon as she heard the *voom, voom-voooom* of Papa's engine straining up the hill, she yelled out *Mooooooo!* and came running to the gate and waited there, drooling long ropes of saliva, for Papa to drive in and unload the machicha.

He had her be served and settled for milking first, and then allowed the other cows over.

Monique watched her aunts surround Namada with their stools and lean against her giant tummy and milk her fat sausage teats into their milking pots while Namada happily plowed her way through all the machicha she could eat.

"Papa, she is so spoiled. She's manipulating all of us to get the machicha first. And to get the most of it."

"She thinks she is the Queen," Papa said. "She knows how to play her game *right.*" His eyes danced. Although everyone regularly cursed her a blue streak, and other colors too, they all loved Namada.

Even mean Granny Ears was bewitched.

Papa or one of the uncles brought Nkiyaa from the manyatta nearly daily in the afternoons. She would glare at everyone, then issue decrees at all the family about who was doing their jobs wrong, what different things should be fed to the cows, and so on. Then she ranted to Papa about who was misbehaving in the manyatta, who should come into the family, who should have their milk rations increased or decreased and why, who should be kicked out of the village ... (This was usually a young moran who was getting uppity.) But when the cows returned from their day of grazing for the evening milking, she suddenly ceased her pronouncements, grabbed her milking pot, strode off to wherever Namada was, and began petting her and singing sweetly to her.

Oh, you are the most beautiful one
    You've given us so many babies
    You give us so much milk
    We appreciate you very much
    Thank you very much

Namada happily mooed back: *Moooohmmm. Muuuuhmmm.*

We feel like you're the mother of all these cows in here
> *You're always so good*
> *You will get anything you want*
> *Oh, God must have known*
> *that we needed you as a blessing*

Muuuuhhh. Mohhhh.

You make the rains come down
> *You bring sunshine*

This made Monique want to gag just as much as Namada drinking from the teapot. Seeing her grandmother's cow-shaped soft spot could have tickled her. Instead it rankled. Nkiyaa never showed sweetness or sang to her, or to her son Baba Senenkon or even her own mother wonderful Nkooko. But she would cover Namada, and even other dumb cows, in praise and love. Monique only got covered in commands, insults, and belt-strokes.

10

Rose

One weekend morning Monique, free from chores, sat near the stove playing with little sticks she had imagined into a tiny wooden family. "This is a mzungu family," she announced. "They look funny, but see how nicely they get along. This is the papa, and the mama, and these are two kids. They do things happily together. They travel to different places and say 'How are you?' and 'What beautiful animals!' and smile a lot. We never hear them yelling."

(Her stellar impression of mzungus at this age was formed by the particular families that had come through the area, from different places in Europe or the Americas, often invited by her father to enjoy the charms of Samburu County. It had been a string of remarkably harmonious families and nice folk, likely due to her father only inviting that sort. She was convinced that mzungus were an entire race of pale, kind, happy-family people.)

Papa interrupted her. "Na'Monic, how long are you going to let this ancient creature go around dragging her belly on the ground?"

Papa had used the only endearing term he had for her: "my Monique." Regardless, she dashed the surprised family down on the floor and sprang up in anger. Papa was referring to her treasured old cat that had slowly limped in with him. She was a sweet cinnamon-cream tabby with beautiful light green eyes, and had over the years given birth to countless kittens that roamed outside. Monique had given her the dignified name of Bubbles.

"Bubbles is fine, Papa! Look, she is still happy and doing well."

Bubbles rubbed up against the little girl's legs and she picked her up, stomach and legs dangling down. Stretched out, the stinky old cat was nearly her length.

"Monique, Aunt Leticia can give her just one nice shot, and she can pass in peace. She will not need to suffer. She really will not feel anything." Aunt Leticia, one of Papa's cousins, was a veterinarian, and always kind to Monique and the animals. Papa had several times brought up the idea of putting Bubbles to sleep. She was truly ancient, and could honestly hardly walk. Yet the cat did still seem content despite her decrepitude. She even seemed happy.

"Papa, no. Look. She doesn't poop everywhere. She goes outside and nicely buries it. She's fine!"

Monique's health and fitness standard of pooping-nicely-in-the-correct-place was keen observation of old animal behavior, but it also was influenced by clearly-inept Baby Esther pooping whenever, wherever, all day long.

Papa sighed. But there was no time for him to persuade his daughter of the kindness of euthanasia, or for her to argue for Bubbles's dignity in natural death and a full burial: his cousin Uncle Le'e popped his head in the kitchen door.

"PK, some of your friends are here. In the front room. And they have some very *interesting* news." Le'e nodded significantly.

Papa sighed again and strode out. Shortly Monique heard him greeting men and offering tea. Her ears itched. Her twig family abandoned on the floor, she carry-dragged Bubbles out into the hall and plunked down where she could listen in.

"You know, your kid is always eating trash," one of the unfamiliar voices said.

"What? ... What kid?" Papa replied.

The men laughed. "You have a daughter."

"What? Of course I have a daughter! Monique?" They laughed. "The baby?"

"No, no, no. Another one!"

"WHAT?! There's another one?!"

Monique's hand froze mid-pet in stroking the purring Bubbles.

"Yes, man! She's always on the streets down by your scary mother-in-law's, eating out of the trash from all the restaurants and whatnot there."

"Out on the streets even in the cold," a voice added.

There was shocked silence. "How old did she look to be?" Papa finally asked.

"Oh, maybe seven, eight. Hard to tell! She's very skinny and dirty. She's in pretty bad shape, too: always coughing."

"And that big belly," another man interjected. "She's getting that big belly. The one from ... what?" "Malnutrition," one offered. "That's right, malnutrition."

"Oh my goodness," Papa said. Deep shock was evident in his voice. "My goodness ... Seven, eight years ... Yes ... Yes, I guess it could be ... Oh my goodness, that heartless woman."

He was quiet a few moments. Monique could feel his anger from outside the room. Then he turned the conversation to other matters: how their sons were doing, if they needed help with school fees, how their cows were, and so on.

Once he had finished discussing and passed them envelopes of money and seen them out, Monique chucked down Bubbles and accosted him. "Why do I have a sister and I don't know where she is? And eating out of the TRASH?! And dirty?! And

SICK?!" Tears sprang to her eyes and she balled up her hands into tiny fists.

"I just heard it too," he said. "Come on, let's go find her."

The Land Rover reached the neighborhood where Maama had grown up. Maama's father had owned several houses and store-fronts there before he passed, and Maama's mother lived there still. Maama's mother was definitely scary. As well as mean. Monique didn't like her at all. Rumors were that she practiced witchcraft, of the very worst sort; and that was why though her house was built in the modern style she had insisted on a dirt floor, and she always ran a small fire on the ground not far inside. *To cover all the smells and sights*, Monique heard an aunt say. *And she breeds snakes in there!* She shivered recalling this. Her sister had been living around this woman? With *snakes*?

Papa parked the Land Rover in front of the house. "Wait here," he sternly commanded.

She waited. The many minutes of muffled argument seemed like an eternity. Worse, she couldn't see or hear anything clearly. She felt through her pockets and found some nice rocks, a scrap of paper ... Then started searching around the car for anything interesting. Finally Papa came back out, holding the hand of a girl. She was very skinny except for a round belly, and quite dirty with long tangled hair, but definitely a few years older than Monique.

Papa opened the front passenger door.

"Monique, this is your older sister. Scoot over and let her sit with you." He gently added to the girl, "Get in, child. You will be OK."

Monique excitedly moved over and patted the seat next to her. The girl sat and looked down. She wouldn't look at Monique.

Papa started driving home. "Honestly, how could that woman be so heartless," he said through clenched teeth.

"I'm Monique. What's your name?" she asked.

The girl just shook her head.

Her hair was not tight-wiry-curly and short like Papa's and Monique's, but long and thick and loosely wavy. It was matted, and she was hiding her face behind it. Monique reached up and gently smoothed a chunk of the hair back, so she could see her face. The girl kept looking down, and Monique couldn't see her eyes: just long, thick eyelashes (*like brooms*, she thought, in awe), blinking down occasional tears. Even with the dirt and smudges, she was clearly pretty. She looked like some of the aunts in Maama's family.

"What's your name?" she asked again.

The girl just shook her head, burst fully into loud, messy crying and coughing, and hid her face in her hands.

"Her name is Rose," Papa said.

Once they got Rose home she was whisked away by a few clucking, exclaiming aunts who gave her a long, hot soak and started worked on cleaning her up and taking care of her. Monique watched them work, while also listening to her dad, back in the living room, explain to her uncles. His voice was ragged, and he sounded like he had aged ten years since that morning.

He said he and Maama had "dated" a while before they married, and apparently this was how Rose came to be. Maama told no one of her existence and hid this even from Papa. When they married and Maama moved into the Maralal house, she just left Rose behind in the "care" of her mother. This grandmother proceeded to nearly completely neglect Rose, not even feeding her properly and certainly not placing her in school. She had lived half-feral and often on the streets looking for scraps to eat, sometimes even sleeping outside, for all those years until Papa's friends found out and came to alert him.

Monique wiped tears of fury and grief from her eyes as she watched her elder sister get loving care, likely for the first time in her life. How could her mother have done this? She knew she was bad, but *this*?

One aunt brought some hot broth and helped the crying and coughing girl drink it. "Ohhh, baaad cough," she said. "Out in the cold too much. Poor child!"

Others gently worked at scraping the filth off of her—"Look at this caramel skin! And these eyelashes! Like a giraffe's!"—and untangling her hair the best they could. Some bits had to be cut off but they were able to save and smooth most of it.

"Ehhh, look at this hair!" one exclaimed admiringly.

"Arab," another replied. "Like that witch. And some of the other girls on that side."

They toweled her off and put her in fresh clothes. "Ohhhh, look! This poor little child is just beautiful!"

It was true. Rose was far too skinny and rather short for a Samburu—"Not enough food, for years," an aunt lamented—and she had a few small scars here and there, and the cough and belly, but she was clearly a beautiful girl. She was also shy and highly emotional, bursting into tears at any sign of tenderness. And no matter how they coaxed her, she would not speak.

Monique could no longer contain herself, and grabbed her hand. "Come on Rose. Let me show you everything."

She dragged her around the house and property, prattling to her new sister. "Here's Baby Esther. Just a few months old. She's your baby sister too! Esther, meet your big sister Rose. OK, come on Rose. You need to meet Bubbles, and Namada."

By dinnertime Rose had been introduced to anything remotely of interest at least twice. Monique was giddy. She had just gotten a baby sister a few months ago, and now here was this surprise beautiful big sister.

At dinner Papa was discussing placing Rose in St. Mary's (Monique squealed and squeezed her hand), when Maama walked in to take her place at the table. She glanced at Rose, said nothing, and sat down and began eating.

And that was how the three sisters came to be together.

It was astonishing that Maama could abandon her daughter in the first place. Again it was astonishing that she could, without reaction, see "Oh, here she is now," and feel no need to say anything, explain anything, apologize, welcome the child: nothing.

But for Monique this was a fulfilled dream she didn't even know she had. An unexpected phenomenal gift.

For Rose, it was the realization of truly desperate hopes. Over years of living cold, hungry, ill, unwashed, and unwanted, she often could not bear to even momentarily hold these hopes in her mind. So many other times focusing on the hopes was all that had kept her alive. Now they were fulfilled. A real home, plenty of food, love, sisters, a father who cared for her, and an education. For her it was rebirth. It was salvation.

11

The Last Broken Window

Papa brought Rose to the doctor the next day. Her cough was serious, as were her malnourishment and belly. But the doctors had experience and good medicine for all of these. With treatment, her missed vaccines, and a special diet to rehabilitate her, over the next few months Rose healed well physically. But she still was incredibly quiet, self-conscious of speaking, highly emotional, and shy. Instead of conversing she preferred to sit and with her large, dark eyes watch her new family and home in silence. Monique took to tickling her so she could hear her sister's voice, in laughter at least.

The night Papa brought Rose home he and Maama had an especially bad fight. By the end of dinner the sisters ended up hiding under the table while World War Three broke out over the thick mahogany top, dishes and chairs flying. Or rather, Rose and Esther were hiding: Monique was "watching the action from a safe observation point."

From that night on Maama's relationship with everyone deteriorated even further. That she had hidden Rose's existence from everyone, including him, and basically left the innocent child to slowly die of neglect: this was finally a sin so great that even Papa could no longer forgive, overlook, or forget. Maama became even more short-tempered and disrespectful with everyone around the house.

When school resumed Rose joined Monique at St. Mary's. Though she didn't know how to read or write, to keep her morale up she was placed in higher grades with kids near her in age and height, and the kind home economics teacher tutored her extra to help her catch up. Placing her with the older students also kept her away from the younger children, who were well known for viciously taunting any weakness or ignorance they saw in older kids.

As Rose settled into a routine and began catching up with the other students, she began speaking more, and finding her own interests. Classes above kindergarten were structured as boarding school, so Rose did not get picked up by Papa in the afternoons, and was only home on Sundays and school breaks. Monique saw her in brief moments here and there at school. She loved chatting with and encouraging her big sister, and delighted in her successes. Back at the house Baby Esther was still watched over by various aunts and grandmothers, since Maama was not up to—or trusted with—the job.

One day again during school holidays, Maama's mother came to visit, bringing Maama's younger sister Aunt Napese. Other than Papa's younger half-sister Aunt Antonella, the rest of his family had cleared out. They found the barely-tolerable-unpleasantness of having Maama around curdled fully into intolerable when her mother came over. The repeated whispered warnings of Grandmother's malicious witchcraft— and the truth of how Rose had been treated—certainly didn't help.

In contrast to Maama and her mother being so unpleasant, Aunt Napese was kind, gentle, and empathetic. She was like a lovely water lily that had bloomed out from a rank pond. Everyone loved her, and she was Aunt Antonella's best friend. Both teenagers, they were finishing secondary education at a boarding school in the far-away town of Wamba. During these visits at the house they spent hours holed up in one of the rooms, chatting and laughing about young woman matters. So were they doing again on this day, in the lull before dinner.

Fat, jolly little nine-month-old Esther was asleep in another bedroom, where beautiful, reticent Rose was also relaxing and sucking her thumb: a self-soothing habit picked up in her years of neglect. Four-year-old Monique was briefly free from chores. Twenty minutes ago she had come in the kitchen, yawned, and slumped down on the floor next to one of the kitchen stools. She crossed her arms over it, put her head down, and pretended to fall asleep. Fake-sleeping while actually listening to everything was one of Monique's favorite tricks. It was also a good way to avoid Maama. Bubbles too snored away, curled up and basking in the heat near the stove. The day was cool, and the warmth was welcome. Maama and Grandmother were cooking and talking.

Monique could of course have avoided Maama much better by not coming into the room where she was. Just go nap on a sofa somewhere. But in the adversarial, dangerous environment she had grown up in, her fierce love for her father—and her own survival instinct—drove her to keep an eye on what was happening around the house. She became, of her own initiative, a tiny spy. She could do very little: but she could indeed observe things in an effort to protect them both. She did not trust Maama. Ever. Especially not recently and especially not with Grandmother around. All day she had found ways to keep them in earshot.

"Look, here it is. It's ready," she heard Grandmother say. "One drop of this in their food, and they'll be finished."

Her eyes flew open, and she saw Grandmother hand Maama a small glass bottle, with a nearly-black liquid inside.

"Yes, just a drop. You put that in their food, first bite they're gone. And for sure."

Papa and Monique shared their dinner plate. Every night they ate from their special plate together, sharing everything. They always had, ever since she was a baby.

"Stir it in, quickly. He'll be home soon. Yes, just like that. Good. It will be the end."

Terror seized Monique, an icy squeeze deep in her gut, and she quickly closed her eyes. Her heart pounded.

They had not seen her eyes open.

Shortly there was the *voom, voom-voooom* of Papa gunning it up the hill.

Monique sprang up and bolted to the door. Maama and Grandmother startled, and their eyes followed her. As she ran, she heard snatches of muttering: *thought she was asleep ... who knows what she knows ... don't think she knows this ...*

Papa came to the door. Monique swung it open and jumped up and down. "Papa! Papa! I have to tell you something! It's important!"

"Heyyy, kiddo," he said distractedly. He patted her head and headed past her to the dining room. She sprang after him, pulling at his shirt.

"Papa! You had better listen to me this time! And I want you to pay attention *extra*."

"Hoh, wait, child. Let's have dinner." He sat down.

Maama immediately appeared with Papa and Monique's special plate. Monique gasped and froze. Maama spoke, her voice honey. "Whatever the silly girl has to say can wait. Eat first. Don't let her nonsense keep you from dinner." She gracefully handed him the food and utensils.

"The food! That's what I want to tell you about! Papa! It's a matter of life and death!"

"Death?!" Papa laughed. "What do you know about death, child?"

Chuckling, he set their plate on the table in front of him and picked up the utensils. He patted the seat next to him. "Come, let's eat."

"Yes, get on and eat," Maama said sweetly from behind Papa. She snapped her head and glared fiercely at Monique.

Monique felt herself sinking into deadly danger. Terror's icy grip had risen from the pit of her stomach to her heart, and now it squeezed her throat. Soon it would clamp over her mouth. Even if they would kill her later, she had to warn him. Before he took one bite.

"Papa!" she squeaked.

Papa finally perceived the tension in the room. He set down the utensils. Calmly he said, "Everyone, stay where you are. Speak, child."

Monique took a breath and focused on a spot of table and its woodgrain. She pushed the ice back down her throat.

"First Papa, send *her* out. I don't want *her* here." Maama was still in the doorway, her eyes shooting daggers. "Send her back to the kitchen with Grandmother. And make them close the door."

"PK!" Maama burst out. "This is ridiculous! Just have your dinner. Don't let her ruin it for you. It's nice and hot now."

"Yes," Papa replied, "We *will* eat. After I've heard from *her*." He nodded at Monique. "So it looks like it's best you step out for a bit."

Maama stood shocked, her mouth open. "But ... But you know her! That horrible child is a liar! She's full of all kinds of idiocy! I don't know how you can listen to that little bitch and not me, your wife! Why would you need to send me out?!"

Papa got up and escorted Maama, who was now screaming, back to the kitchen with Grandmother. He closed the door.

"You can get Aunt Antonella," Monique suggested. "She should probably hear this."

"ASUNTA!" Papa yelled down the hall, using her Samburu name.

She trudged in, clearly displeased at having her pleasant chat interrupted to have to sit at the table with Papa, Monique, and their lone plate of food. "What is this nonsense?" she began.

"OK child, now," Papa said. "What is it?"

Monique again focused on the woodgrain, tracing it with her finger. She relayed what she had heard and seen. When she looked up, Papa's eyes were gray stone. Aunt Antonella looked extremely skeptical and displeased, eyes narrowed and lips pursed.

"Papa, do you want proof?" Monique asked. "We can bring Bubbles."

"Mmm." Unlike Antonella, Papa was already inclined to believe Monique. That she was offering up her beloved old cat made the case even more serious. And it was a good idea. This needed to be investigated and settled. "OK, then. Go fetch that old cat."

Monique sniffled a bit and went and picked up Bubbles, who had relocated outside the kitchen to avoid the yelling women. "I'm sorry, Bubbles," she whispered as she carried her back down the hall. "You're a very good cat. Thank you for helping us."

She handed Bubbles to Papa and wiped her eyes. He placed the ancient cat on the table and turned the meat and gravy section of their plate to her. She started licking it up.

"Honestly," Antonella complained, after a minute of the three of them watching a decrepit old cat slowly and happily eat. "Do you believe this? This is ridiculous." She glared at Monique.

But the cat stopped licking.

She started foaming at the mouth. She fell over in spasms.

Monique's eyes filled with tears and she looked down. She could not bear to look at her poor cat. She twisted her hands in her lap and cried quietly. "Yeah. That's you and me, Daddy," she said.

"BITCH!" Papa yelled, breaking the shocked silence. He stood up and launched the plate. It flew through the window, smashing the glass, and scattered food across the yard. A few doomed dogs scampered over excitedly and wolfed it down.

"Monique, Antonella," he said, "come with me."

They went to the bedroom and collected Rose and baby Esther, who woke and babbled happily, and Esther's milk bottle and a thin mattress. Then he led them back through the house to the door. On her way past the dining room Monique glanced at the table. The cat had stopped moving.

Papa spread the mattress in the back of the Land Rover. "You girls wait here," he said, and went back inside.

In the car Antonella sat and stewed. *That* night was ruined. They could all hear yelling punctuated by slamming and things being thrown.

"Ladies, we won't be eating the dinner you made, because it killed the cat."

"That cat was old! It was ancient!" [*CRASH!*]

"What about the dead dogs in the side yard then!? Were they also ancient?!" [*SLAM!*]

"What are you saying?! What are you accusing us of?! Why do you always believe that little bitch over me?!" [*BAM BAM BAM!*]

"You're the bitch! Both you and your witch mother! See these dogs for yourself!" [*CRASH!*]

Monique sighed, stopped listening, and focused on Esther. She and Rose bounced and tickled and kissed her. They admired her happy amber eyes and slurped her smooth chocolate cheeks and fed her her bottle. Esther giggled her way back into a peaceful sleep, despite the yelling still coming from the house.

In a while it quietened, and Papa came out with a bundle of clothes and blankets. He passed these back to the children. "We're going to the manyatta tonight," he said, and started the engine.

After several minutes silent driving, Papa spoke, clearly, for everyone to hear.

"That's the end of it. They'll be gone by morning. They're never to return. I'm arranging things to set her up *nicely*, with a home and some properties to rent out in Lodungokwe. No one will be able to say I treated her unfairly. As long as she stays over there and behaves, this is settled."

Monique considered this. When a Samburu man sent a woman away like this, it meant the marriage was over. It was final. And Lodungokwe must be pretty far. She'd never heard of it.

"Monique," he continued, as the thorn fence came into the headlights.

"Yes, Papa?"

"Two things. First, you were right. We don't need her."

She burst into fresh tears, waking Esther. Despite her tears and gasping breaths, Monique's mouth kept breaking into a huge smile. "Okay," she said quietly. "Okay." She cried and gasped and smiled a few moments. Wiping her eyes and nose, she asked, "What's the second thing, Papa?"

"You are all to never, *ever* see that woman again."

12
Akuyia

The house itself seemed to exhale after scary Maama and even-more-scary Grandmother left. Everyone slowly relaxed as days passed without her: without screaming and insults and physical attack, without broken windows and objects flying. As the household recovered, family members and friends began streaming in for visits.

Papa was deeply shaken and hurt that the woman he had married had tried to take his and their daughter's lives. Samburu men, especially of his stature, are expected to always have everything well-managed and under control. Nearly falling victim to your wife's murder plot did not exactly indicate "having things under control." It had been highly dangerous; and now that it was survived, it was supremely embarrassing.

This great shock, coming so soon after the shock of discovering Rose and her abandonment, rocked Papa's faith in all his judgments and in his entire family and network. He had always trusted Monique: now he nearly *only* trusted her. He became skittish and depressed. Yet the three girls were delightful, funny and happy together, and this cheered him. His work and businesses and livestock were thriving, and his family showed him extra patience and respect while he emotionally reeled.

Shortly after Maama left, still during the long school break, the sisters were goofing around in the living room. Little Esther had invented a way to get sound from Rose: she farted into her hand and then held it to Rose's face, making her shriek and holler. Amidst this mischief a cry of welcome rose up from outside. Monique looked out, and startled in delight.

"It's Akuyia! Your grandfather!" she announced to Rose and Esther: then she threw her hands up, screamed, and ran off to the stove.

Its fire inside had become small and lazy: she quickly added fresh kindling and banked it up. She filled a pot with water at the sink, and put it on the stovetop. "Oh gosh, oh gosh," she flustered, and buzzed over to the dining table to round up the tea tray.

Rose walked in, her dark almond eyes questioning.

"It's for Akuyia! He's just the BEST, Rose! He's Papa's daddy and he's been walking for four days to come see us, *four days*, and he can meet *you*, and you can meet *him*, and I'm sure he'll help take great care of you, and he just *loves* his tea and I'm going to get it all set up for him! Here, come help!"

Rose poured the boiling water over the tea leaves in the yellow-enameled metal teapot, and they placed the little lid back on top so it could steep. Monique poured some fresh milk (Namada's, of course) into the milk creamer, and she checked that the the sugar store was full and that the light-gold sugar stones, which looked like pretty crystals, were heaped up nicely in their little dish. They placed a matching large enameled cup, saucer, and a small spoon on the tray next to the teapot, and added a few tea-time mint meringues from a tin.

Monique squealed and clapped her hands. She slowly and proudly carried the laden tray towards the living room. Rose shyly followed.

There was a knot of people near the door. Monique tilted her head around to look for her grandfather. She saw a few uncles she recognized as his traveling partners from previous visits. As always, his youngest son Apiyio was there. Exceedingly handsome, gentle and well-mannered, he was Akuyia's main companion and helper, and his apprentice in herbalism and healing. She had never seen Akuyia travel without him. There were a couple other uncles she didn't know as well ... And there was Akuyia! She suppressed another excited scream.

He stepped inside, attired as always in minimalist but still colorful Samburu traditional dress. He was tall, about 6'5", slim and well-muscled, extremely dark, and with a gentle, loving face. He was handsome and poised, in a simply dignified and civil way. He always shaved his hair completely off and wore a dapper khaki bowler hat when outside. Traditional strands of vibrantly-colored small beads looped decoratively around his pierced and stretched earlobes, set off against a simple white oval earring in each ear. He had left his tire sandals[8] outside, and moved his cheerful red-and-blue plaid shuka aside, preparing to sit. His rungu, the throwing/whapping stick, hung from his beautifully-beaded belt, along with a knife. His walking stick leaned near the door, his hat suspended atop.

He saw the girls standing with the tea set, and as he sat down regally on the floor—Akuyia was humble and simple, and often was more comfortable sitting on the floor than on a chair —he smiled broadly and beckoned them over. Samburu society

---

[8] Akuyia was a talented leather-worker and cobbler in addition to his other gifts, and he often made exquisite, meticulously-constructed leather shoes for himself. However, in his long travels he favored the common, locally-constructed tire sandals. These were plentiful, economical, and got excellent "mileage" on the rough trails, long outlasting most other shoes. They were— and still are—made nearly entirely from discarded car tires. A foot-shaped slab is cut for the base, tread down, and then straps fashioned from strips of the tire inner tube, or leather or knotted rope. Simple short nails hold them together.

is conservative about children not mixing much with adults, especially men, but this was another norm Monique completely rejected, and Akuyia too was exceptionally warm with children. Monique placed down his tea tray and sat next to him, beaming. The adults settled on all the chairs. Second Granny scurried off to get more teacups: Monique had solely brought one for her beloved grandfather.

"Thank you, little one," he said, as she poured his tea cup, resting properly on its saucer, and handed it to him. He helped himself to the milk and sugar. "Ehh, so this is Rose!" he said, looking up at her. "So lovely! Sit, sweet Rose." He patted the floor next to him.

Rose was too shy to look at him, her long lashes cast down, but she quietly sat. He passed her a meringue. Baby Esther toddled over and plunked in his lap, nearly spilling his tea. She snatched her own meringue with her fat hand, making everyone laugh. Akuyia patted her curly head as she munched.

Akuyia had much to discuss with this branch of the family. It had been many months since his last visit, and there were five wives and their children and grandchildren here down south, along with his four younger brothers' wives, children, and grandchildren. While the adults talked, he passed around a large white gourd he had brought. It was one of the wide gourds which when dried were wonderfully capacious, strong and light. Leather ropes were strapped around it, for carrying and keeping it tied shut.

Inside was chock-full of one of his most famous, coveted herbalist concoctions: small pieces of honey-rich honeycomb that had steeped for months layered with fragrant and healthsome herbs and roots. The honeycomb and honey had become delicious medicinal chewy bits and syrup. Papa forbade his family to chew gum: Akuyia's honeycomb was a wonderful substitute. It also seemed to heal everyone up, from any small illnesses they were afflicted with.

The girls sat silently savoring their pieces and sucking honey from their fingertips while they listened to the discussion. Even Monique displayed decorum in listening quietly. Akuyia would be visiting at the house and manyatta for a couple weeks, and there would be plenty of time to pepper him with questions and pester him for stories.

Though Granny Ears made it clear she did not welcome him, Akuyia nonetheless maintained politeness in being sure to go to the manyatta and greet her first of the wives there, as she was, after all, the First Wife. Monique and her sisters went with him.

Nkiyaa was sitting in her usual perch near the main gate where she could easily see and hear all the goings-on. Seeing the girls her fingers went automatically to her rhino-hide belt. As Akuyia walked in she stood up, thrust out her enormous chest (*Man, she has the jugs for the world,* Monique thought), placed her hands on her hips, slit her eyes and cocked back her head.

"Oh. What brings *you* here today?" she asked, in challenge.

Akuyia was standing in the traditional Samburu pose with both arms extended and resting atop his tall walking stick: he ducked his head down between his arms and hid his face until he could regain his composure and answer her politely, without laughing.

"Oh. I'm just here to visit my grandkids."

"Humpf," Granny Ears replied.

Nkiyaa was again unique among women in that she chewed tobacco, pinched out from a stash she kept tied in a corner of her wrap. She raised her chin, turned her head aside, and launched a disdainful missile of tobacco spit. She was a champion spitter. Monique thought she must be able to spit a mile; and likely knock out anyone she hit. This particular brown volley of contempt flew straight *PWAM* into the thorn fence about twenty feet away.

She then turned and with great show and noise, exaggerating every body movement, scornfully lumbered off into her hut. *Wow. A whole cow could ride on that*, Monique thought, observing Granny's swaying behind as she traipsed proudly away. *And not fall off.*

Akuyia and the girls grinned at each other and trotted to greet lovely Nkooko, and then went to Second Granny's hut, where they burst into laughter and spent a pleasant day. They visited with Baba Senenkon and the other village residents, and Akuyia inquired how they and all their families and concerns were.

When it was time to leave, Akuyia again found Granny Ears, to address her politely as the first wife and head of the village.

"What is it!?"

"Just letting you know I'm leaving."

"Good! You can leave all you want. I don't care!" Again she pinged off a round of spit, this time at Second Granny's hut, and stomped off, her whole body jostling a loud harrumph.

"Akuyia, how do you walk for *four days*, and arrive here? Safely?"

It was a couple days later and Monique and Akuyia sat on the Maralal house veranda's big step, overlooking the lands down the hillside. He had his tea (which she had brought, this time with tinned shortbread cookies), no one was bothering him, and the child had plunked herself down to interrogate him and suck up stories, like an aardvark hoovering delicious ants.

"Ah, well, you know, it's the route we take. That matters. We know the land and the villages between Baragoi and here very well. The people are good to us and welcome us and share any warnings or news. If we hear that there are bandits, for example, we take another path."

Monique had heard hushed discussions about raiders from Sudan, who frequently attacked villages and stole cows and sometimes did even worse things. It hadn't happened in Maralal, but it was a known danger, as were leopards, lions, and angry elephants, and roaring rivers and fearsome rains.

Monique listened as her grandfather talked more about how they traveled: always a group of two to five men, with their shawls and belts, their walking sticks and rungus and knives, and a few things they might be carrying, like the honeycomb gourd. It amazed her that he could walk just like that, basically with nothing, and travel village to village, be received with gracious hospitality, and end up not-lost at his destination.

(Samburu hospitality for travelers is absolute anyway, but Akuyia more than repaid his hosts. As the area's most-respected healer and wise man, he generously treated illnesses, offered sage advice on various matters, and settled feuds and arguments. Each village was delighted to have him stop by, anytime. They constantly tried to marry off to him any of their daughters. This rejected, as Akuyia had more than enough wives, they usually asked he at least accept a cow to bring along on the journey. It would be a contribution to his herds, a gift for him to give as he wished wherever he was going, or simply takeout beef, easily slaughtered on the road.)

Monique sprawled comfortably in the afternoon sun and listened. Akuyia shared the protocol to respectfully seek shelter overnight at a village; the best times to approach water and cross rivers, when animals would be the least threat; what times of year were favorable for traveling; and how they walked safely when they must cross through an area with many dangerous animals, especially lions.

"We let our own fierceness reflect out, so that the animals can see it. And we wear the big red shuka, very large and clear, as a warning for them."

Akuyia was finished with his tea. He was now ready for a smoke.

Akuyia rarely drank alcohol, but he too enjoyed a bit of tobacco, both chewed and smoked. Out of nowhere he produced his beautiful carved cow-horn pipe. Monique could never see where he carried it: it just appeared, as though conjured from the wind. He always wore a long beaded necklace on which hung a small ivory jar with a lid. He carefully opened it, and tapped out a wee pinch of tobacco powder into his pipe.

This was good: Monique knew she could ask him more questions while he enjoyed his smoke. She loved the smell of his pipe. The smoke carried a rich fruity, leathery tobacco scent, with pings of mint, which Akuyia ground a bit of into his tobacco blend.

"Akuyia," she asked, while he contentedly puffed. "How do you really sustain yourself, as you walk that far, *days* of traveling?"

"Well, when it's too hot I seek shade. And I sip my herbal water from my gourd." Monique knew he made a special drink from herbal tea and the fresh juices of some roots, and packed it in a gourd for travel. "And I keep myself nourished with my meat rations. You know them, yes? The ones you always help me with."

She indeed knew these well. A large reason she loved Akuyia's visits was that there was always extra slaughtering happening and much meat prepared in many delicious ways, thanks in part to the takeout beef provided by a village on the way. One of Akuyia's lesser miracles in her eyes was his ability to turn a normal slice of meat into an incredibly long thin meat string, with one knife cut.

"Here," he'd say, and hand her one end of the meat slice to hold taut while he held the other. Then with his free hand he moved his small, sharp-on-both sides carving knife through the meat in long, precise curves and careful twists, almost like cutting with a jigsaw. He transformed the entire meat piece into a long thin string like a shoelace. From Monique's perspective it was as though the meat was unraveling before her eyes. If you've ever seen an expert apple-peeler carve off the entire apple peel in one long unbroken string, it was rather like that: but with meat.

"There," he'd say. "That is how meat should be cut."

"Dang," was all Monique had to say.

Akuyia then took the long strands (he always prepared many), hung them, and smoked and dried them. When they were done and preserved to last well, he neatly wound each in a tight coil, and tied it with string. Several of these went in a pouch as he traveled for his rations. Any extra coils he packed into a gourd and covered with ghee. Ghee preserved dried meat beautifully: the coils would easily remain delicious and safe to eat for a year.

Akuyia's knives also fascinated Monique. Other people seemed to use just one or two knives for nearly everything. But Akuyia had a small army of knives, all forged by the local traditional blacksmiths and each with special characteristics and purposes. One was the short, thin, double-sharp knife he used for the dried meat coils and any other precise, fine carving work. Another was a longer, strong, thin, sharp-on-one-side deboning knife. Also there was a compact, sturdy chopper, for chopping roots and other very tough things. He even had a small pen-like, needle-sharp knife that was a traditional version of a lancet: this he used for precise piercing in his healing work. These and a few others all lived in the barracks of a simple leather pouch he wore on a strap over his back. When he went hunting for his herbs and roots (for "hunting" was how it seemed to Monique) he'd sling his pouch over his back and head out, pulling out each knife as was best used to help harvest his spoils.

As Akuyia was finishing his smoke, Monique asked him the question she had most wanted to, ever since she saw him step through the threshold.

"Akuyia, you see my big sister doesn't really talk much. ... You know what happened to her. Do you think she's OK?" She looked down and tangled and untangled her fingers. "Will she be OK?"

He looked at her gently. "I've been watching her, and looking, and yes, I think she's going to be OK. I really think so." He slowly nodded his head and looked off into the distance. "For now, she is just a bit quiet. ... If some day she can come visit us and stay in Baragoi, we can also watch her carefully there and take good care of her."

"That would be very good, Akuyia. No one can take better care of anyone than you."

Akuyia had immediately upon arrival begun taking care of everyone, both in the house and at the manyatta. He inquired after everyone's health and looked at each a bit. Beyond the family, streams of neighbors and community members, once they heard he was in town, came through the house to visit, seeking his wisdom and treatment. From the surrounding area he collected many herbs and roots, and set to work. He made medicinal soups and teas for everyone's varying needs, stuffed freshly-slaughtered meat with herbs and grilled it, and so on.

Monique watched him step out, cut some roots off nearby bushes, and bring them back in and start scrubbing them at the sink, with his kind son and apprentice Apiyio at his side. Akuyia's herbalism, as with everything he did, intrigued her.

"What is that herb, Grandpa? What is it called?"

Akuyia replied with a complex name in Maa that was impossible for her to pronounce, let alone remember. Her perplexity must have shown clear on her little face, for young Apiyio smiled at her gently. He repeated the name, and while Akuyia scrubbed, shared a simplified description of its wonderful benefits. Akuyia grunted in agreement and approval. This information also immediately fell out of Monique's brain. All Akuyia's herbs were like that. They carried complex names and workings, so unfortunately her great interest did not result in the knowledge "sticking" in her young mind. Thank goodness Apiyio was there to catch the wisdom so it would not be lost!

What *did* stick, however, for everyone in the house and especially Monique and her sisters, was the very memorable *taste* of the herbal concoctions.

Two were delicious. One was the herbal honeycomb. This he also made into a drink from hot water and the honey portion, especially during flu season when cold winds barreled across the highlands. He often added wild mint or some other fresh herb for extra benefit. Monique did not ever fall ill with a cold or flu while she was young: perhaps due to this intervention. The other delicious specialty was dried meat pieces that had been likewise long-steeped in a gourd, layered in honey and herbs.

These two delicacies were coveted enough to be fought over. And then a few of his herbalized soups and meats had a "unique" taste but were decently palatable. No one would fight over them, but they'd be contentedly eaten.

Akuyia's chai too was different: he first simmered much ginger root and some cinnamon bark and cloves in water until the water had taken on the flavors and color of the spices. At that time he added the tea leaves. Once it came back to a boil he removed it from the heat, added milk that had been heated separately, and stirred in honey. After he strained it into cups, he often served it with fresh mint leaves floating atop for beauty and freshness. His chai was eagerly drunk by all: except Papa, who only liked plain chai.

The rest of Akuyia's recipes, however, were varying degrees and flavors of foul. Rose and baby Esther took to shrieking and running/toddling out the other door each time he appeared with another strong, bitter, weird-tasting concoction "for your health."

Monique wanted Akuyia to never feel he or his efforts were unappreciated. And so she often ended up suffering through the taste thrice, drinking their portions in addition to hers. Many, many times.

Akuyia was deeply spiritual. He set aside special times each sunrise and sunset, spent in prayer at the north side of the house. Much of the rest of the day also found him in prayer. Monique knew he wasn't Christian, as she and her parents were raised by the nuns and priests to be. She found his sincere devotion to an allegedly damned pagan faith fascinating and impressive.

"What do you pray for, Akuyia? The most. And what do you pray *to*?"

"Well, I'm not, you know, I'm not the modern religious man. I am my own traditional religious person. I know there is a God above. That's the one I pray to. And He listens to everybody. It doesn't matter whether you are educated, like your father, or not educated, like we in my time were. We didn't 'go to' a school, but we were schooled in our own ways. I was raised by my parents; this is how they prayed. And this is how I've always done. I know I'm praying to a God, because everything always works out OK."

A few days later Akuyia sat quietly in the living room discussing matters with Apiyio and telling stories. Akuyia was the best storyteller. The stories were often about travel and occurrences he had seen: besides visiting family, Akuyia traveled widely to meet with other healers and wise men and discuss their concerns and experiences. They had grappled with all types of matters, and he shared many stories of these. He really got going though when talking about herbs: which ones you might find where; what their wonderful properties were to help people and animals and how to harness these properties; what they needed to appear in a location and why other regions might not have them. Often he would wander so far in his stories that not just he but everyone had forgotten which initial plant had begun the journey.

It was the quiet period before dinner. The milking was done and cleaned up and the cows back in their enclosure. A large fire was going in the fireplace for cozy warmth. Aunts and uncles and grandmothers were scattered through the house in clusters, cooking, laughing, and talking. Monique and the few other story-hogs among the children sat listening to Akuyia. Her sisters and visiting young cousins buzzed noisily everywhere, spilling out into the yard, telling jokes, playing games, and running in a game of tag. Papa was away, traveling on business as he often was; especially, Monique had noticed, whenever Akuyia was around.

Suddenly *POWWWW* an ear-splitting thunderbolt boomed. A typhoon-level downpour started dumping, without any warning. Shrieking kids dashed back in, immediately drenched, and huddled up near the fire.

Samburu County experiences all kinds of rain, from the oft-lamented "where is it?" to light mists to regular monsoon types. But this storm was abnormal. This rain was vengeant. It slammed in a fury everywhere as if it very much intended to drown everybody and then scour the earth clean. Lightning zapped and thunder boomed, more and more and more, and then lightning strikes moved right onto the property in bright sizzling columns. The metal roof amplified the pounding of the rain. It was deafening. The children all clustered together in the corner furthest from the door and windows, covering their ears and clearly terrified.

Akuyia spoke over the rain: "Is this normal?"

"It's really weird and it's scaring all of us," Monique replied.

Adults started slowly coming in to the living room, also alarmed. The lightning now was so thick it seemed like all you could see was lightning, stabbing from the sky to the ground.

"I don't feel comfortable about this either," he said. "Do you mind if I can get some milk?"

Second Granny immediately piped up. "Absolutely!" She strode hurriedly to the kitchen, and returned with the remaining adults and a long gourd filled with fresh milk.

"OK," Akuyia said, taking the gourd. "Adults, let's go. Outside. We'll all hold hands. Kids, you stay inside. You must close the door."

No one dared disobey Akuyia, and so the grownups strode out into the lightning-filled downpour, and the children closed the door behind them. But Akuyia had not said that they couldn't watch. Monique and the other bravest and least terrified children pressed up against the window.

The group of adults walked slowly to a raw gash in the ground where lightning had struck a few minutes before. Rain still pounded and lightning flashed and thunder boomed. Akuyia bent and slowly poured all the milk from the gourd into the new wound in the earth. The adults stood holding hands in a circle around it for a minute or two, clearly praying.

And the storm stopped. Monique was so shocked she nearly fell over backwards. The lightning and thunder ceased, the rain let up to just a few stray drops: and then cleared entirely. The sky again became innocently blue and radiant, as if nothing had happened.

The relieved, soaked, muddy-legged adults came back in and made their way to the bathroom and kitchen to wash up. Monique accosted Akuyia. There was no way she could stop her questions, impertinent or not.

"You can STOP the STORM?! You can send the bad storm away?! You can stop the lightning?! What are you? Are you superhuman? What did you say?"

He laughed and wrung out his shuka. "I love your questions, because they're quite interesting. No, listen. If you do believe in God, He will work for you. He will work a lot of things in your favor. All I asked for Him was, to not destroy us, because you guys are still young. It would be a shame. If we all perish, this day. So I asked just, to give us another day. And just stop this bad storm, just send it away. That's all I said. And I made my sacrifice I need to make. I appeased my God, and that was it."

❖ — ❖

Akuyia might have been able to appease God and end storms, but there was no appeasing his first wife Granny Ears, or ending her vitriol. Although the rest of his wives delighted in seeing him and treated him with sincere respect and tenderness, Granny Ears remained staunchly unimpressed and antagonistic, as she was with everyone except her eldest son. If Akuyia said it was time to pray, Second Granny respectfully hushed everyone; but Nkiyaa immediately started loudly pounding dried corn, or banging on a wall, just to be disruptive.

Worse, Papa and Akuyia did not get along. The men shared many characteristics: in a luckier world they could have been very close. But they were instead like oil and water. Papa loathed Akuyia's traditional ways, and Akuyia saw little to love in his son's unquestioning embrace of modernity and rejection of so many positive aspects of traditional practice. Papa was also, like his mother, simply rude to Akuyia and constantly argued with him. When Akuyia reprimanded Papa's ill-mannered and disrespectful behavior, Nkiyaa rose up like a spitting cobra. "Don't talk to my son! He works hard, he takes care of his family. *You don't.*"

Eventually the rancor from his eldest son and first wife wore even patient Akuyia down, and he felt the time was propitious to leave. The northern part of the family needed him back, and the villages between awaited his return visits and follow-ups on how their sick were healing, and their bothersome matters resolving. So invariably, after at most a few weeks, Akuyia would say his goodbyes and gather his few belongings. He checked that his knife and rungu were tucked well into his belt, threw his knife pouch and bright shuka over his ebony shoulders, put on his bowler hat, picked up his walking stick, and he and kind Apiyio and their other traveling partners stepped into their tire sandals and began the long journey north.

Yet again this happened. It broke Monique's heart to watch him go. It always did.

It seemed that as he stepped away, the spell of peace and tranquility and happiness that the house had been under traveled away with him. Her questions would again be met with reprimands rather than delight and gentle explanations. There would be no more stories of long travel and plants and their properties. Even the goodies Akuyia had left for them—the herbal honeycomb, which Papa had transferred to a glass jar "to be sanitary" and the leftover dried meat coils—would soon be eaten up to the last drop, and there would be nothing left from Akuyia, not until his next visit.

But at least this time she had some wonderful new things which would remain: her sisters, and a life free from Maama. And vacation was nearly over anyway. In a few days she and Rose would go back to school.

13

St. Mary's Primary School for Girls

B efore the advent of schooling, there were only two life
paths for Samburu children. Neither involved choice.

If you were born a boy, your birth was celebrated. You enjoyed
a leisurely childhood with minimal work—shepherding and a few
errands once you were old enough—and much play and freedom.
You followed the older boys and young warriors all you could,
and practiced spear-throwing, ran around, slid down mudhills,
and so on. As you approached puberty, you waited for the elders
on Mount Ng'iro to call for a new age-set gathering, every
fourteen or so years. Once the call came, you got initiated
through a series of rituals, including a painful circumcision
without anesthetic. If you were successful you were proudly
anointed as a warrior, a moran, along with the others in your age-
set. (If you were unsuccessful, you were killed or outcast and your
entire family was subject to long humiliation.)

Until the next age-set call-up, you served as a moran: the
Maasai equivalent of a local army. You were in charge of the
livestock and defense, and that was basically it. Daily, help the
livestock—the people's most precious, essential resource—find
feed and water, even in times of scarcity; keep them safe and
don't let them drown crossing rivers or be riven by the claws of
lions and leopards. Or be stolen. During these days and years you
had much free time and few restrictions, other than not being

allowed to marry, or seduce the wives of the elders, to the extent that you were forbidden to hang out or eat with women. So you hung out with your agemates and twisted each other's hair, cared for your cattle and planned raids to steal more from nearby tribes, and possibly were sent off to war or had to defend your village. You let off sexual steam by procuring many beads and using these to buy sanctioned relations with young girls, to keep you away from the elders' wives.

If you survived these fourteen years, you were relieved of duty, became a junior elder, and were allowed to start accumulating wives. Your family sent representatives to ask after any available girls in other villages who had attained puberty, and attempted negotiations. For this you needed wealth, gained through your own or stolen herds: you had better hope the cattle were thriving and not dying of drought or rinderpest. Once you successfully obtained one or more wives, you awaited the birth of children. The cycle began again.

If you were born a girl, your birth was likely ignored. When young you engaged in some play, but as soon as possible you were made to work around the household. You quickly, along with younger women, found yourself doing the vast majority of the village's manual labor. Once you reached an age that morans might find you pretty—nine or a bit older—they started serenading you with soft songs and showing up at your hut and negotiating with your mother and brothers about a price to buy your "company." If one was successful, he bestowed many beads upon you which you wore in a jangling collar about your neck, and the village exclaimed over your obvious desirability and beauty. Your mother built a hut not far from hers and you had to "accompany" the moran there as he wished, often nightly. Your consent was never sought. If you became pregnant, this was forbidden and your fault. You were prepubescent, still a child, and not allowed to be pregnant or give birth. Moreover, marriages are only allowed between different villages, and these temporary beading relationships were often within the same village. Any babies from this were cursed, and the young girl was blamed. You were taken out to the forest and given a brutal, very dangerous, excruciatingly-painful abortion. If you survived, you proceeded to what awaits girls at puberty.

At puberty, representatives of elders from other villages began showing up at your family's hut. The elders were at least fourteen years older than you, often much older. The representatives negotiated with your father and male relatives for your marriage, offering cows, beads, tea, sugar, and other wealth. Neither you nor your mother had any say. If the negotiations were successful, the families and villages on both sides began preparations for the wedding. You were circumcised: a crude, horribly painful full clitoridectomy without anesthetic, with the stated intent to remove your pleasure in sex. This was usually done two days before the wedding, unless you and the other girls had been rounded up and "batch-circumcised" earlier at the village's decision.

After this—if you survived—the village praised you as a pure and good woman. In the marriage ceremony you were sent off, beaded and adorned and wearing goatskins that had been beautifully oiled and rubbed with ochre. The only gifts from your parents (other than the wedding finery you wore) were a slim gourd of milk and a small wooden jar of ghee you wore on your back. These actually weren't for you, but were ritualized gifts to your new village, signaling the prosperity and care you would bring them. Your dowry remained with your father, under his control. You painfully, slowly walked with your groom and his best man to his village, where you likely knew no one. For the first month you lived with your new husband's mother, until the wound between your legs finished scarring over and she and other women built you your own hut. Then you joined village life as the new wife. You cared for livestock, did endless village work, and awaited the birth of children. The cycle began again.

These were the life paths for Samburu children. There was some variation if they were born into families of skilled trades—such as the astrologers, healers, or blacksmiths—but this was mainly only variation in the type of work they did.

It was from this path that Akuyia had diverted his naughty firstborn when schools were built and the calls came for villages to send sons. Papa still complied with the rituals of life and served nominally as a moran, but he relished the schooling path. He saw it as a far better option. Once he attained wealth and privilege within his family, he proceeded to divert into school every single boy and girl he could from the extended family, paying the fees for each if necessary.

Monique knew the traditional path well. It was all around her and had produced everyone she loved, and loathed. She was determined to escape it. She wanted nothing of beads, being stuck slaving at home, being seduced by older boys or sold to much older men. She was hell-bent on following, as much as humanly possible, the schooling path and claiming all the freedom and power over her own life that she could. Nothing could persuade her otherwise.

But she also knew—from young—that as soon as they could, her relatives would push her straight back onto the traditional path.

She clung to her faith that Papa would save her.

Maralal had at this time two schools: for boys, St. Paul's, and for girls, St. Mary's. Both were public primaries that went up to grade seven, and were Catholic boarding schools set up in partnership with Italy, featuring local management and Italian priests, monks, and nuns as teachers. Papa was the product of such schooling, and an adamant supporter of the public school mission, and the Catholic version. He insisted on public schools, not private, for all the children that he helped pay the tuition for. This was dozens throughout the extended family, including the adopted refugees.

Papa had long been a benefactor of both schools, and once Monique enrolled at St. Mary's he immediately joined the PTA. He had been schoolmates and was long-term friends with the husband of the headmistress, a kind, sympathetic Turkana woman the students called Ms. Mary, and this had helped him get Monique accepted for kindergarten before age four, rather than at the usual five.

Kindergarten, with its half-day schedule and relaxed curriculum of songs and play, was no problem for little Monique. However, she only managed to stay in kindergarten for a few months. Once the nuns realized that she was not only fluent in speaking English, the language of instruction, but also could already read it, they popped her up to first grade.

There she got in constant clashes with her first grade teacher, a short, stout, terrifying, easily-irritated nun. Monique couldn't fathom why other kids didn't know basic math or couldn't read. She found this distressing to the point of tears, and kept trying to "help" them during class. The teacher found this highly disruptive.

"There is only one teacher in this class!" the nun roared, and pulled her by the ear to stand at the back of the class. Or she shouted "Out, out, OUT!" and gestured forcefully with her short arm to go kneel in penance out on the veranda. The visual comedy cracked Monique up and got her in even more trouble.

This happened nearly daily.

After months of this, the nun announced, "That's it!" She stormed over to Monique and grabbed her roughly by the hand. "I can't take this anymore! And you're bored. Let's get you out of here!"

She dragged her out of the room and marched vigorously to the headmistress's office. Monique trotted to keep up, watching her teacher's veil swing side to side with each step like a fierce metronome.

"Sit here!" she commanded when they reached the office. She went in and shut the door, leaving the little girl on the bench outside, dangling her legs and wondering.

After a few minutes of muffled discussion, the door opened. The teacher glared at her and stomped off. Ms. Mary called her in. With a kind, laughing demeanor, she told her to sit down.

"Okay! ... What is your name again ... Ah, Monique! We are moving you to second grade. Is that okay with you?"

"Okay!"

"But listen. This school has teachers! Don't try to be the teacher! Okay?"

"Okay yes ma'am!"

The second grade nun was kind, and immediately welcomed her. But when she had Monique quietly read out loud for assessment, and the girl read fluently, she said, "Oh my dear ... I'm sorry but you're too advanced for what we're learning. I'm going to send you up to third grade. Follow me."

So she arrived at third grade, not yet five years old. The teacher was a pretty, tanned mzungu with amber eyes and toffee-colored hair that swung at her shoulders. Monique had seen her before, in a neighborhood not far from theirs. She had noticed she often carried two lovely large handbags: one seemed to be only for books. Papa and this mzungu teacher were the only people Monique had seen regularly carrying books around.

The teacher was wearing a calf-length dress with petticoat underneath and a scarf around her neck, but didn't wear a veil. When Monique was brought to the room, she looked at her with interest.

"Aren't you that girl who stays up the road from where I live?"

Monique was stunned by both the question and the teacher's accent. It was different from the nuns'. "Yeah?" she answered.

"Oh, I know!" the teacher said, to both Monique and her escort. "I know that family."

"Huh?" Monique said.

"Yeah, I know your dad. We went to Cambridge together. I'm Ms. Bridget. Welcome: please take a seat!" Ms. Bridget looked delighted to have this clearly-quite-young child of her friend get promoted early into her class.

Oh my goodness, this is great! Monique thought. *And that's why her accent is different! She's not Italian: she's British!*

Ms. Bridget was the sole non-ordained teacher at St. Mary's. She had moved to Maralal after meeting Monique's dad, and taught English and third grade. Her class was finally a fit for Monique, with a few students past her abilities in different areas, and she had to actually study a bit to catch up.

Thus at this time Rose was in upper primary grades, and Monique not far below. Baby Esther, now a large, strong, smart toddler, was still at home. She was extremely attached to Monique. When she had been gone only half-days for kinder-garten, as had been the plan, things ran smoothly. Esther managed mornings without her sister under the care of aunts and grannies quite well, and Monique joined her for the rest of the day, whether with Papa at his office or elsewhere. But once Monique got moved up into higher grades, school became all-day. Far worse, it was on a boarding basis. Monique moved in and took to the challenge well. But Esther was devastated.

Day after day her sister was completely gone, even at night. No matter which aunt or grandmother carried her or took her into bed—even Papa—the child screamed and cried inconsolably. She didn't sleep well. She didn't eat well. The usually easy, laughing, cherubic baby became a miserable creature who spread her misery into everyone around her. Monique's brief return when Papa picked her up on Sundays brought some reprieve: but when Esther was again separated from Monique she screamed and cried terribly.

This wretched situation continued for weeks, until Monique came back properly on school breaks. Then things were harmonious and happy. Esther once more began to thrive and returned to her usual happy, bouncing self. But when Monique went back to school, only out on Sundays, Esther again completely lost it.

By the time Monique completed third grade, the household was ragged. Grandmothers' faces bore new wrinkles. Gray hairs sprouted in Papa's tight curls. Even the younger aunts felt and looked haggard, far beyond their years. It is incredible how much one screaming baby can age an entire huge household.

"That's it," Papa said. He went back to his friend the headmistress.

When Monique returned to school in January for fourth grade, age five, two-year-old Esther proudly accompanied her. Though Esther was only admitted to kindergarten, she was permitted to board under Monique's care. Monique became known as "the little mother": other than during kindergarten hours, wherever she was, there also was Esther.

They shared the bed (fortunately Esther had already determinedly potty-trained herself), and got ready together. They had meals together, passing each other the best beans and grains and corn from their bowls. After Esther finished kindergarten each day she sat quietly squished in on Monique's chair in fourth grade. They napped together at the siesta hours, and Esther again sat with Monique during the late afternoon study hours, holding her sister's dress and alternating sucking her thumb from one hand to the other. She was well-behaved, and she delighted Monique's teachers, who saw the beautiful, happy, quiet toddler as a chubby little class mascot. Monique too was happy. The sisterly adoration was mutual.

They both still saw Rose occasionally in school, not just at home on Sundays. Rose had caught up academically with the other kids, and was now becoming bored and yearned for freedom. She hated being kept indoors. She took to strategically whispering in class so she could be kicked out and enjoy wandering and performing "penance" outside.

When Monique had gotten in trouble and was kicked out by the nuns, penance usually took one of three forms:

1) kneeling for long periods out on the veranda, which badly bruised her knees;

2) "walking" on her knees a long, hot sand strip the length of half a football field, which scraped up and burned her knees;

or

3) "cutting" the school lawns by ripping off the sharp, tough blades of grass with her bare hands, which terribly cut her fingers.

At these times Rose was often out there similarly employed, and they had time to chat and catch up.

The school was very strict. Moses had only ten Commandments, but St. Mary's had over a hundred rules. Forbidden: passing each other pencils, losing your soap, peeing the bed, not following the lesson, not finishing food, bringing in contraband, not ratting classmates out, making the bed improperly, forget-

ting to use your mswaki, skipping church, laughing inappro-
priately, falling asleep in class or study hour, and whispering,
including about course material. All of these and many other
infractions brought punishments that escalated from verbal
chastisement, to smacks, to actual beating or penance, to calling
the parents.

Papa was called many, many times.

Often he was called for Rose; but more often it was Monique.
In addition to the common infractions all the children were
subject to, Monique's mouth still got her in extra trouble. It was
not so much for helping other kids: they were better caught up
in the higher grades and the teachers also handled this more
smoothly, often even welcoming help. Instead again it was her
questions, about why things were the way they were.

"If Christ is all about love, why are you always punishing the
students?"

Out! Penance!

"Why do we get served this horrible food while you teachers
have ten-course meals? With wine?"

Out!

"When children make a mistake or ask a question you don't
like, why are they punished or beaten instead of instructed?"

Penance!

Additionally, by this time Monique's flaming ears had helped
her pick up a good amount of Italian from hearing the teachers
speaking it to each other, and she understood conversations she
was not meant to be privy to. This fed more interruptions and
questions: often about very inappropriate matters.

"What is *quell'infida puttanella*?"[9]

Out! Penance!

She also struggled with other aspects of school life.

---

[9] "that treacherous bitch"

The uniform was her nemesis. The white blouse that was worn underneath with its collar peeking out looked innocent, fresh, and perky; but it was incredibly, relentlessly scratchy. The long dress, worn over the blouse, was made of thin acrylic wool —the type that repels water, is impossible to wash, and is abrasive to touch—in bright Christmas green. The nuns distributed the clothing in sizes too big for the children so they could "grow into them": Monique's loathed green garb dragged the floor. It was an actual tripping hazard. Layered on top over the blouse and dress was a hot, heavy woolen sweater. This was screaming red: again with too-long sleeves and waist.

To adults, the look was crisp and tidy, if sized a bit large. The common colors of the Italian and Kenyan flags were obvious and appreciated.

To Monique, the look was Sad, Imprisoned, Uncomfortable Elf. And the imprisoned elf was hot and itchy as well as garish and tripping all the time.

The food was another formidable opposing force she had to contend with. She had been raised on copious beautiful fresh milk, buttermilk and butter and chai and wild honey; pillowy ugali and thick porridges; tons of just-slaughtered organic meats, freshly-baked bread, home-grown vegetables, and Akuyia's herbs and honeycomb ... But to begin with, the school, despite being in the capital of Samburu lands, served no milk. It is hard to convey how shocking this was. Every day of Samburu life—from birth to death—is centered around milk. But there was none to be found, day after day, for the students boarded at St. Mary's.

School breakfast instead was porridge so thin it resembled water, served in big, foul-smelling decrepit plastic cups with their insides peeling off in layers. And that was it.

Lunch was either corn, beans, or grains such as Job's tears and barley. These were boiled and served plain, without sweetener, butter, or seemingly salt. Sometimes for variety they were mixed, and then boiled and served plain. Boiled corn and beans, plain; boiled corn and grains, plain; boiled beans and grains, plain; occasionally boiled corn and beans and grains, plain.

Except that unfortunately these were not actually plain. They had somehow picked up notable populations of grain weevils, a global pest that travelers know well. Both the holes they left in the grains and their actual dead bodies, floating as well as embedded deep in the cooked kernels, were frequently apparent. To Monique they resembled disgusting tiny buffalo, black and with two little horns. The girls scooped them off the top the best they could, averted their eyes, and chucked them down onto the floor. The gruels were served with disreputable plastic spoons, which had been washed and reused so many times they were discolored, cracking, and crumbling at the edges. Monique used the spoon to remove the weevils, and then tried to secretly eat with her hands—again forbidden—rather than use the spoon.

Dinner was "ugali." This was not actually ugali, but simply a thicker porridge. On Sundays cabbage appeared. It was cut in huge hunks and boiled so long that it was rank and sulfurous, and when lifted on a plastic spoon, melted in pieces off it. Additionally most nights there would be broth with a piece or two of meat in it.

Monique *loved* meat. At home whenever kind uncle Baba Lkopina grilled freshly-butchered meat—his favorite activity, and he was excellent at it—he would come sneakily find her first. *It's ready*, he whispered. She stealthily made her way to where he was cooking, and he delightedly served her first, smiling and watching her expression. For she, of everyone in the huge household, enjoyed meat the most and most appreciated his cooking it. The love of meat, especially grilled, was something they shared in understanding.

So when she had first seen meat appear at dinner she had been delighted. But her joy rapidly fouled into disappointment, and then problem-solving. For nearly all the meats were strangely cooked, tough enough to seriously threaten teeth. The school bred beautiful soft, fluffy white rabbits on the property, which Monique was saddened to see killed. But somehow only their meat went into the kitchen and emerged as sustenance. The rest came out as rocks.

The worst offender was cape buffalo. These animals were plentiful and legal to hunt, and they are enormous. One buffalo could easily feed all 300 pupils at St. Mary's. One of the Italian priests, seeing this bountiful economy, loved to regularly hunt them: often Monique would round a corner to the sight of a giant buffalo in a cart, legs up in the air. But alas, buffalo is incredibly tough and requires long cooking or marinating—hours to *days*—to be able to be chewed. The cook either did not realize this or was not allowed such time. Neither was the meat cut small enough to be swallowed *without* being chewed. And so each night that the indestructible buffalo cubes appeared, the girls had to contend with how to get them down their throats without losing teeth. (The punishment for not finishing food was washing all the hundreds of bowls.)

As often as she could get away with it, when her turn came at the serving line and she recognized buffalo, Monique told the server, "My tooth is hurting and I cannot eat the meat. May I just drink the soup today?"

"Oh, since you told me and asked, OK." *Plunk* the server deposited the meat rocks back into the huge pot, leaving only the broth in her bowl.

When she had tried this too many times, her second strategy was to sit near a talkative classmate or two. When they were distracted—*zip!*—she ninja-speed transferred a chunk to one of their bowls. *Zap!* A second piece went to another bowl.

"Did God banish Satan to our kitchen?" Monique wondered. "Is he our cook? How can all this food be so terrible?"

She later discovered it was not the Prince of Darkness cooking their meals, but the overworked matrons, who also had to boil and bleach and hang dozens of bedsheets in addition to cooking and their other duties.

Monique ate and drank the daily gruels and broths the best she could. But over the weeks she invariably sallowed and thinned. When Akuyia visited while she was home on breaks he took a look at her, silently shook his head, and set to work on stews and restorative formulations.

As deeply as all these elements annoyed her, especially the harshness in several of the nuns and matrons, young Monique knew one thing for sure. School was her fortress. It was her path forward, and her deliverance. All of her goals depended on her education.

She also saw that the school made a huge difference in the lives of a great many girls. School, especially boarding school, was an excellent route to keep them from being beaded and impregnated by morans. They simply weren't around in the village to have their "company" negotiated for. It also staved off early marriage. Papa fiercely warned his brothers and cousins, "If I find that anyone has come asking the dowry price for any of these girls that I have personally paid the school fees for, they will face my wrath." He saved dozens of girls from untold pain, and likely saved many of their lives.

Beyond this, she saw that most girls came to St. Mary's without understanding English; forget reading or writing it. Many came without Swahili. Mathematics was a new concept to most. And several came, from the poorest areas, in such deep poverty that they arrived actually naked, without a stitch of clothing.

For children such as these, never used to the abundant food and comfortable clothes she had been, the scratchy uniforms and regular servings of simple porridge, weevils or no, were precious beyond measure.

These classmates were her first experience with deep poverty, other than the introductions to the refugee families her father adopted in. She took to the poorer and less-educated kids with a sense of protectiveness, and found that they were often more ready to be friends, and to talk freely about matters of real interest in life, such as animals, the stars and the sky. They were also less likely to engage in needless drama or complaints, about their hair or their parents not buying them this or that.

Beyond academic subjects, the school also made serious efforts to teach the children self-reliance and good habits and virtues, such as responsibility, orderliness, economy (bordering on stinginess), and cleanliness. Each dormitory had an overseeing matron, but the girls mainly had to take care of themselves. It was only the matron's job to provide what was necessary, instruct, and then check that the children had done things properly. Each girl had her own bed, which she was expected to keep tidy, her small tin handled and latched "box" at the base of her bed that held her few things, and her uniforms and a towel to maintain.

The strict expectations of responsibility, economy, and self-reliance were everywhere. For instance, at the beginning of each quarter the girls lined up at the matron's desk to receive their soap rations. It was all they would get until the next quarter, and with it they were expected to keep not only themselves but also their uniforms and towel clean. The matron emerged from her storeroom with a huge chopper and boxes and boxes of long four- by twelve-inch bars of hard brown soap. Each bar was marked into thirds every four inches. She cut these as each child indicated for easy handling, and sent them off with the blessing "Go put these in your box!"

When Monique stepped forward and the matron asked, "How do you want your bar cut?" she always answered, "In thirds, and then each third into square fourths." This provided twelve neat two-inch squares, one for each week. She requested the same for Esther.

Kids ran out of or lost their soap all the time. This forced a conundrum: be stinky, get beaten; bring contraband soap from outside, get beaten. Thus the school's strictness, meant to instill discipline and order, instead compelled many children towards theft. Stealing someone else's soap was the least painful solution. Monique avoided stealing or being stolen from by covertly making a small rip in her mattress cover and hiding her and Esther's soap in there.[10]

As spartan as the environment was, and as strict as the matrons and nuns were, the kids were still kids. They played and laughed and sang: they had rich friendships and petty fights. They were kept safe from serenading morans. They learned both national languages of English and Swahili, and mathematics, and geography, and history, and many other subjects. And they found ways to sneak freedom and other contraband delights. The most constant one for Monique and her sisters was Safari Lodge Sundays.

---

[10] Thus the strictness also fostered property damage.

14

Safari Lodge Sundays and the Magic Sleeves

Papa had endless flings with "normal" cars—Hondas, Nissans, Peugeot 504s—which he zipped around in to the office or bar when the *maram* roads[11] were easily passable. He'd keep one for a year or two, and when he tired of it, sell it and try another.

But regardless which secondary car had his momentary interest, his mainstay companion and true lifelong love was his Land Rover. It was his steadfast, reliable accomplice in endless rugged work and adventures. It easily handled the roads regardless of condition, and could traverse nearly any surface other than water. *Through* water at streams and low rivers was not a problem. Imagine the classic large, indestructible Land Rover from any safari film: make it bright red with silver bars in front and on top. That was it. Its back top interchanged between a hard top or canvas top—both with windows—or no top at all: Papa swapped these in a flash depending on the need.

Far beyond the daily boozy task of fetching the cows' morning machicha, the Land Rover fulfilled a huge variety of purposes. Transporting sick animals to the vet. Racing along in bush hunting, and bringing back the prize. Cross-country excursions to buy and drive livestock. Other excursions to help

---

[11] Samburu County roads at this time were commonly unfinished: just smoothed dirt, no asphalt or gravel atop. They called this maram. Road conditions ranged from "bad" generally to "impassible" in the rainy season.

his age-mates or cousins steal brides (a story for a later telling). Delivering donations to distant schools. Trading with remote tribespeople. Camping out in. And completely-illegally and very unsafely transporting twenty-odd thrilled, screaming children on Safari Lodge Sundays.

The school was intended for year-round boarding except for holidays and school breaks. But the headmistress allowed some leeway in pulling children out for family time, especially if this could be explained in the language of the School Values and Rules.

"Er. Can I pull the Leparleens on Sundays?" Papa asked.

"What for?" Ms. Mary asked.

"Well, they need to go to the barber and get their hair cut."

It was that simple. Cleanliness was next to Godliness, and regular haircuts were a great portion of cleanliness in the school's eyes.

And so every Sunday when he was in the country, after church Papa led the large flock of Leparleen girls—his and the extended and adopted families'—while they demurely filed out from the school grounds and into the Land Rover. As they drove away the girls' heads were turned back, eyes increasingly filling with life and delight. The feeling at seeing the school shrink smaller and smaller and get further and further behind was intoxicating. It was winning the lottery: it was jailbreak. This feeling was the first of the Sunday delights. The moment the school could no longer be seen the carload burst into a loud cheer, and normal conversation began.

Papa dropped some girls at the house to relax while the others went to the town barber shop. The barber now did thriving business in shaving girls' heads. When all was ready, they piled back into the Land Rover, packed in every available nook and cranny like laughing, goofy sardines, and Papa took the whole giant lot of them to the Maralal Safari Lodge down the road for fruitcakes and Fanta.

Papa was allergic to driving at a legal—or even reasonable—rate of speed. And the Safari Lodge, technically down the street from the house, was actually at the very end, miles away, long after the "street" had become a ridiculously uneven, boulder-strewn, climbing path that could no longer honestly be called a road. And so every Sunday Papa gunned it like a delighted silver-eyed madman up the rough hillside path with twenty packed, excited kids screaming maniacally and hanging on to each other for dear life. (Papa used the Land Rover's canvas top on these days, so the inevitable head-bashing-on-the-sides was inconsequential.)

As the vehicle skittered along uphill and dipped and rocked over boulders, like a drunken pirate's boat in a wicked storm, the mass of goggling, screaming girls surged and pressed this way and that. Squashed up against the window, Monique squinted out over the rocky hillside below. *Man, I hope it doesn't tip. What is this? You can forget about it!*

Once they pulled up at the Lodge, they all toddled out on their adrenaline-weakened legs, grinning in the joy of freedom and adventure and having simply survived. They piled in at dining tables on the spacious veranda.

The Safari Lodge, being up on a hillside plateau, was blessed with deliciously cool breezes which stirred the huge trees and flowering bushes all around. There was a wonderful view of wild areas in the lower distance where many of Kenya's most famous creatures freely roamed. The lodge had installed a water trough quite near the veranda, and here the more relaxed animals came to drink, comfortable with people nearby and watching them.

Papa ordered each child an orange Fanta and an English tea cake that was absolutely stuffed with dates, raisins, and all kinds of dried fruits. For children who had been sugar-starved through a week of St. Mary's porridges, this teatime was nectar and manna from heaven.

Papa and the children happily sat and chatted and drank and snacked and watched the animals and listened to the Lodge's music playing, for hours. In the far distance roamed buffaloes, warthogs, and rhinoceroses. Handsome zebras strutted on the grounds and drank at the water trough. So did a whole range of the beautiful varied antelopes that Samburu County is blessed with: shy, adorable bushbucks; elegant long-necked gerenuks; large, regal elands. Baboon families waddled and spied suspiciously on the girls. Cute, alert vervet monkeys, silver-tan with black faces, swung freely wherever they pleased. (The girls knew not to feed the animals, or bring anything with them, as the monkeys would snatch it.)

A tremendous variety of birds hopped and flew and perched and ran. Besides the innumerable chortling songbirds that flitted among branches, down on the ground the girls watched chunky, spotted guineafowls with their blue turkey heads strut and squawk. In the distance they could spot tall secretarybirds, which nest high in acacia trees and look like very fancy large white-and-black eagles comically perched up on cranes' legs. These run beautifully along above the tall grasses: and then dramatically stomp their lizard or rodent prey to death, tossing it up in the air to gulp down whole. Monique's favorite bird was the aptly-named superb starling. These are small but spectacular. Bright platinum eyes gleam from a black head, above a vibrant copper-orange chest. The rest of its plumage cloaks it in iridescent shifting shades of blue, purple, and teal, with white accents.

Groups of giraffes, both in the distance and near, majestically sauntered and browsed on high tree branches. Of all the creatures, the monkeys and giraffes approached the closest. One particular giraffe loved to amble up to the fence at the veranda and lean its head down on its long neck right over the tables, seeking pets and scratches. Monique marveled at its huge head and strong neck muscles, and admired the gentle dark eyes the size of teacups, with their amazingly-long, broom-like lashes. Once she reached out her hand to feel its velvety muzzle, and that was her mistake. The creature opened its mouth and stuck out its long, tough indigo tongue and licked her all the way from her elbow to her fingertips. It was incredibly slimy and covered the shrieking girl in thick giraffe saliva.

"Ohhhh, it's *nasty!*" she squealed. She shuddered, then leapt out of her chair. "Aaaagh, nasty, nasty, *nasty!*" Papa and the girls laughed and laughed while she ran around looking for some way to wipe it off. Having felt that surprisingly tough, harsh tongue, she thought, *Man, no wonder you have no trouble eating those thorny acacias!*

Eventually the children had their fill of animal-watching, the sugar high wore off, and they became hungry for Real Food. Papa herded them back into the Land Rover, and they hurtled along screaming down the hillside. They pulled up in front of The Buffalo bar in town. The Buffalo had a very effective sign of an actual enormous buffalo skull hung over the door. The huge skull was painted white and the long curling horns painted black. Monique found it quite impressive.

Among his other businesses, Papa owned a different bar in town, Lkishili. It was the town's first bar: Papa had given it the age-set name which he shared with all the warriors from his age set, similar to how the West names generations. Both Lkishili and The Buffalo had very popular meat butchering-and-grilling eateries attached to them. Papa owned these and knew the butchers/cooks, who did their work to his exact expectations.

Papa and the children crammed around a long table. The cook greeted them heartily and began charcoal-roasting vast quantities of fresh, local goat: often ones Papa had brought earlier. The smell was amazing. The children had to be mindful not to openly drool.

When the barbecued meat was ready the cook chopped it up and served it out: huge mounds of delectable, perfectly cooked fat-dripping cubes, sometimes with sides of ugali. He then began roasting more.

It was incredible. Forget receiving manna: the girls now were *in* heaven. Perhaps it was because the gruel-fed children were protein- and calorie-starved and on the verge of kwashiorkor and malnutrition: or perhaps it was just always that good.

Once they had eaten all they could, Papa made sure that each child had a small extra portion, perhaps a quarter pound, of roasted meat. This they wrapped carefully in plastic wrappers that the cook gave them.

Papa drove them all back to school, after their "haircuts," and the girls again docilely filed in and went to their dormitories. The nuns and matrons didn't suspect the contraband barbecued goat parcels neatly concealed in the folded red sweaters they carried. They usually arrived back at nap time. When the matron was gone they stealthily smuggled out the precious meat piece by piece to the remaining children, who huddled up under their thin blankets and secretly ate and licked their fingers in delight.

Monique, however, put these modest smuggling efforts to shame. The other kids took one small packet to smuggle in and share out. Monique went whole hog. She used the enormity of her uniform to advantage. She tied the huge sweater around her waist, with the two giant sleeves in front. These she stuffed with small package after package of takeaway meat, up to the limit of what would look suspicious, and then she wrapped the arms around her in a meaty hug and tied the cuffs again at the back. Her waist had easily two to three pounds of goat cube parcels in the lumpy sleeves tied around her. To hide the bumps and bulk, she pulled up her long dress several inches, and let it hang all around over the sweater arms. This was perfect. It just looked like she had hitched up her dress and tied it with her sweater: something the nuns encouraged when the students were coming or going or running around, so they didn't trip on their long garb.

"Wow, you can smuggle food *that much?*" Papa asked, impressed.

"I got a tribe to feed," she replied.

She walked in confidently and relaxed. She was not caught.

The sweater served further as the "serving dish" for the meat. She passed some to kids clandestinely, or switched sweaters with them and they wore it tied for a bit while they sneakily removed meat from the sleeves. At recess she gathered her group of kids who never had parents come take them out or bring them food. They sat in a circle, their sweaters on the ground, obviously playing an innocent game every time a matron or nun glanced over. The game actually was: switch spots around the circle and take turns discreetly pulling out a piece of meat from Monique's sweater on the ground here. And then eat it very sneakily, all compressed in your hand, so it looks like you're laughing or sucking your thumb or biting a hangnail. The empty wrappers Monique rolled into tiny tight parcels and tucked under the thatch of the grass, with a quick prayer: *Jesus please forgive me for polluting Your green earth.*

The first time she tried this it went smoothly and she was delighted. She was able to share out so much meat that she no longer felt guilty enjoying it herself first at The Buffalo or Lkishili. This became her regular scheme. She always saved the last package for little Esther, who loved the extra rations over the following days.

"So, who was eating last time, from that sleeve?" Papa asked, laughing, as she busily stuffed and tied her sleeves another Sunday. "I wish all the nuns were generous like that."

"Me too," she replied. "Then I wouldn't have to hustle this in the first place."

Papa replied, still laughing, "Just don't get in trouble. I don't want to hear any phone calls."

"Oh, don't worry. It's food. It's swallowed upon arrival."

"As long is everything is cool."

"It's gonna be cool."

After recess one day, when they lined up to go back in after the usual game of Move Around the Sweater and Eat the Meat, a terrifying huge matron sniffed the air.

"I smell something!" She whipped her head and flinty eyes around, sniffing. "Who has food?! If I find it, you'll be punished!"

The girls all played innocent. They were not caught. All the meat had been eaten by then anyway.

Monique did this every Sunday that Papa took them out. She did it for years. She was never caught. The matron didn't even sniff it a second time. God only knows how many kids benefitted how much because of the extra nutrition produced from that red sweater's magic sleeves.

15

The Bicycle

O ne day, out of nowhere, there was Sophia.

It was near the end of a school break and Monique saw a girl only a couple years older than her had moved in next door. Despite her proximity, she seemed like an exotic creature from galaxies away. She was pretty and carried herself with assurance and boldness, and played freely as she wished around the area. Monique, when not in her school garb, wore whatever random faded t-shirts and shorts were in the house. Sophia wore bright, lovely dresses, often in elegant shades of pink that contrasted beautifully with her dark skin. Almost every girl Monique knew had the close-shaved haircut that rendered them nearly indistinguishable from boys. Sophia had beautiful long hair, much like Rose's, and it was often braided and adorned with satin ribbons. If Monique had home shoes at the moment, they were either the local tire sandals or a pair of beat-up, dirt-covered secondhand shoes Papa had brought back from somewhere, which everyone at the house shared and which featured various holes displaying your toes.[12] Sophia's feet were

---

[12] Samburu life and the ground itself relentlessly ate shoes. Also for some reason they kept randomly disappearing from the house. Commonly children's shoes went missing but occasionally adult ones as well. The dogs were suspected, but no one actually saw any evidence, so it remained a mystery.

always in beautiful, clean sneakers. To Monique, everything about her spoke to class, grace, style, and freedom.

Papa knew Sophia's dad from government circles. He said the family were Maasai, which was why they spoke Maa with an accent, and that her father was a diplomat, so they probably wouldn't be here long. They were only staying in Maralal between assignments.

Sophia was a revelation for Monique. Kenyan girls too, even ones who spoke Maa, could be different, and stylish, and free. These things were not actually reserved for mzungu girls.

Yet the revelation was not to stop with how Sophia dressed and carried herself.

Monique soon discovered Sophia had a bicycle. A *girl*, with a *bike*. It was even shiny and beautiful and pink, with long ribbons on the handlebars. And *Sophia rode the bike*! Her braids and ribbons bounced and streamed behind her as she happily rode along the red maram roads in the sun, effortlessly traveling faster than Monique could run, her sneakered feet not touching even for a moment the mud and dirt.

This was a miracle. It was incomprehensible.

In Monique's experience boys and men commonly had bikes, and cars, but girls and women never did. Ever. They had to walk everywhere, or get a ride from a man. Sophia and her bike seemed to break all laws of existence. Monique could not understand how Sophia could be riding it.

When she lazily rode past the house gate one day, Monique flagged her down. "How can you ride a bike if you're a girl?"

Sophia blinked at the question. "I ride a bike because my mom allows me."

Monique goggled at her.

Sophia continued, "We had a bike at the home in Washington, and in Switzerland. My mother said of course I can also have one here." She looked at Monique, puzzled. "You don't have a bike?"

Monique was silent, trying to process this world-shaking information.

Sophia shrugged and rode on, the ribbons on her bike and in her hair trailing behind like wafts of perfume, like banners of freedom.

Oh wow. Monique thought. *Wow. I wish I could have a bike. Man. What a nice way to be free.*

All the next week at school she fantasized about having a bicycle. She imagined herself riding away from a furious Granny Ears, who could not keep up and was left behind yelling and waving the rhino-skin belt. She realized how quickly she could go see a friend: without having to walk so long each way, she could play all day and still be back before dinner. Other kids would gather around and ask *her* questions about the bike and how she could be riding it. And she could have adventures, and something to write about in the endless "what I did over school break" assignments. No one wanted to write about shoveling manure.

The next Sunday as they were all eating their grilled goat, Monique screwed up her courage.

"Oh, I *really* would like a bike, Papa."

"What?"

"I would really like a bicycle. Like Sophia has."

"Sophia ... Who is Sophia?"

"Papa! The girl next door! The Maasais, with the dad you know, and with the *bike!*"

"Oh. Sophia. Yes. A bike. ... You want a bike. ... OK. I'll get you one."

"OK! Yes! Great!" Lit up in pure joy, Monique ferociously bit into her meat. She chewed in a daydream of delight, imagining herself riding around. But then she suddenly stopped and considered: after the goat they were going back to school. She'd have to wait, not just a day for the bike, but through the whole *week* at St. Mary's.

Oh, man. Waiting was hard. ... But for a bike? Her very own, shiny beautiful bike? She could wait! Yes, absolutely! She could wait!

All week at school Monique was unusually agreeable and compliant. She was patient and worked hard. When tasks were boring or in the minutes before falling asleep she remembered the promise of the bike, and fantasized what it might look like and how she might look riding it. This immediately restored her, in delight and anticipation.

The next Sunday Papa brought them home as usual. The moment he switched off the engine, Monique leapt from the seat, leaving Esther sitting, surprised. She dashed around, looking everywhere. Papa never presented gifts properly, but left them somewhere to be found. Could it be in the yard? No. Ah, probably back where the car parked! She skipped there. Only the Land Rover and Papa's second car sat there, gleaming. *Oh, it's probably in our bedroom!* She stifled a squeal. She ran and flung open the door; but the bedroom held only visiting cousins, surprised and looking up at her. Shoot. She checked the other rooms. Nothing. She sprinted behind the house, and looked in every corner and in her special area under the water tank. Surely it would be there! But no. She couldn't find it anywhere.

She ran to Papa. "Papa, where's my bike?"

"Oh, I haven't gotten it yet. I'll get you one."

Haven't gotten it yet?! This cut deeply. No bike? *No bike?!* She had waited a whole *week!* How could this be? This was Papa. Her beloved, generous, honest, could-do-no-wrong perfect Papa. He adopted whole families; he sent everyone to school; he bought endless treats and gave out funds to help everyone. A bike was nothing by comparison!

OK, she thought, he had probably just been too busy. It was only one week. He did work hard. He would get the bike. He said so. She'd just have to wait again.

Again Monique cheerfully faced the week at St. Mary's. Her mind moved to obsessing over if the bike would have a bell or a horn. Which was better? How would it sound? How far away would people hear her? Again hope and glee sustained her through the days of school.

The next Sunday again Papa picked up the Leparleen clan. When they arrived at the house she dashed everywhere, looking. It wasn't in the yard. It wasn't in the parking area. Not in her bedroom, or the other rooms. Or behind the house, or under the water tank.

"Papa," she asked, "so where's my bike? I'm still waiting for it."

"Oh. I haven't gotten it yet. I'll get it for you."

What?! Still no bike?! This was truly surprising. But she knew Papa. She saw him endlessly doing amazing things to help others, and always keeping his word. He would definitely get her the bike, his Na'Monic, his purse, his shadow, the one who had saved his life. Work just must be very busy.

She waited again. Spring was turning warm, and her acrylic-wool school clothes were becoming hot. Wouldn't she feel so cool and comfortable with a breeze rushing over her as she rode her bike? Ah, how delightful! And she would only let nice kids ride it and fly in the wind. The mean ones would remain earth-bound, itchy and hot and tugging their uniforms and getting dirt on their feet, looking sadly after her. Ha ha!

When Papa brought them home this third weekend, and there was still no bike, no bike anywhere, and Papa only saying "I'll get it for you," Monique stormed off. This was becoming too much. How busy could Papa be?

And yet it would get worse. Week after week she waited, to each Sunday find no bike. Over the Easter holiday it was Monique still stuck earthbound, sadly watching Sophia ride her bike.

Returning to school away from Papa and Sophia became almost a respite. Irritation and cynicism colored over her fantasies about her bicycle. She became sullen and grumbly. She was often punished by the nuns.

In early May, hand-pulling grass in penance, she suddenly blurted to her friends who were being similarly punished, "You know what? I'm gonna make a song out of this, because I'm tired of begging."

"What are you on about, Monique?"

"That bike! I'm never seeing a bike. Ever. And he's not willing to do it. My father. He keeps saying, 'I'll buy it for you, I'll buy it for you.' It never happened." She rose up, throwing fistfuls of torn grass from her stained and cut small fingers. "I'm done begging! I'm going to *retaliate!*"

"How're you going to do that?"

"By creating a *song!*"

"What?!" The other girls laughed and threw their grass at her. "How can you retaliate with a song?"

"You watch. You'll see."

Later that very week kind Madam Headmistress addressed the class. "Children. Madaraka Day is coming up, June first.[13] The whole city will gather at the stadium, and the mayor, our patrons, and all the dignitaries will be watching. Your class will get a turn to perform along with the other classes and the boys from St. Paul's. We want to put on a good performance for this distinguished audience and important day. Would any of you like to compose a song for us to perform?"

[13] Independence from British rule came in a somewhat complicated manner, so Kenya celebrates on two separate days: Madaraka Day in June and Jamhuri Day in December. Both are festive holidays, with large public celebrations.

Monique's hand shot up.

"Yes, Monique. You can compose a song for us?"

"Yes, Ma'am. I already have one ready."

"Wonderful! What is it about?" The headmistress and nuns loved themes that reflected a simple, happy childhood.

"A bicycle," she innocently said.

"Splendid! Let's hear it!"

And so the ground was set for the coal of revenge smoldering in her tiny heart to burst into glorious flames, for all to see.

The weekend before Madaraka, Uncle John visited. One of Papa's younger half-brothers without children of his own yet, Uncle John took some kindly interest in Monique, and she in turn shared some of her shenanigans and thoughts with him. He and Papa took their tea out on the veranda. Monique played idly a ways off, her back to them, so she could employ her usual trick of listening in without suspicion. John cast his eyes towards her and gave a little laugh.

"Uh oh, PK. You are really going to be embarrassed about this."

"What?"

"Monique has formulated a song about the bike."

"WHAT?!" Papa looked over at his daughter, who clearly didn't hear a thing and was innocently teaching her stick doll a new dance. He sighed and lowered his voice. "I'm always afraid she'll do something contradictory. I have my position to watch for. So many people depend on me."

John laughed. "Nah, she's just being creative. It won't be too bad, I'm sure."

Monique looked up. Innocently she called over, "Hey Papa, where's my bike?"

"I don't have it yet, Na'Monic. I'll get it for you."

"Okay!" she said cheerfully. She turned back to her doll. An evil smile spread across her face.

Madaraka Day finally arrived. On the stadium grounds all the girls clustered with their watchful teachers in the seething, hot mass of six hundred kids from both schools. Sheltered stands at the front were indeed filled with all the region's Important People, who could relax and watch from the shade. Other spectators filled simple benches and all the grounds nearby. The students were tidily attired in their school uniforms. Aside from formality, this kept them neatly herded through the event. All from the same region—many from the same families—and generally with shaved heads, distinguishing even girls from boys could be a challenge. The uniforms immediately signaled which school each kid went with.

The St. Mary's children were in their full regalia: long, bright green acrylic wool dresses, scratchy white shirts with collars peeking out, and hot, thick, screaming-red sweaters on top. The overhead June sun radiated fiercely, broiling the children in their thick sweat that the synthetic fabrics wouldn't absorb.

Finally the time came for Monique's class to perform. The nun signaled, and they began their song and dance, in Swahili.

My bicycle will not fly
It has a trumpet bell
rumba rumba[14] *ha ha ha*
Let's go again, ha ha!

---

[14] The rumba is a dance movement similar to the twist in the West. The shoulders, hips, and feet all shimmy and boogie opposite each other.

My bicycle is wide open
And the trumpet shall sound
rumba rumba ha ha ha
Let's go again, ha ha!

My bicycle has bells and they sound like
ring ring ring ring
rumba rumba ha ha ha
Let's do it again ha ha!

Monique led the kids in singing a verse loudly and joyfully: then, cranking imaginary hand bicycles they comically buzzed around in circles clockwise. Stopping still, they again delightedly yell-sang a verse, then cranked their bicycles and buzzed around counterclockwise. Again and again and again the kids loudly sang and cranked bikes and tooled around in circles.

The spectacle was so humorous and delightful the entire audience and even the most dour nuns were cracking up. For them it was a simple, funny, cute performance about a bike. But when the laughing nuns signaled Monique and the kids to stop, she threw her eyes to where Papa sat with Uncle John, up in the stands with the other bigwigs.

Papa was leaning sideways, nearly falling off the bench. He was gasping, and laughing so hard he was wiping tears from not only his eyes, but his face and neck.

He had clearly gotten the message. His daughter knew he would not buy her a bicycle, and she had found a way to publicly stab at him: yet in a way that could not get her—or him —into trouble.

At that moment, she didn't care what any further outcome would be. She got her one wish: to sing, there on Madaraka Day with Papa and everyone watching, about the bicycle she never got. She didn't get the bike, but she got her small revenge.

Afterwards Papa stepped down and with the teachers' permission ushered all the St. Mary's students aside. He sat them down in a clearing to the side of the stadium grounds, and served out from a waiting truck bed hundreds of individual Fanta bottles, snacks, and various treats, restoring and delighting all the hungry, dehydrated kids. He had forseen something like this coming, and prepared a kind peace offering, for all the hundreds of children.

But his daughter was indeed never to receive her request, of just one simple bicycle.

16

Fetching Water

Papa left for his studies in Germany. The sisters remained at St. Mary's: on breaks uncles brought them to the Maralal house, or more commonly put them at Granny Ears's manyatta.

Nkiyaa ranted openly about the uselessness of the girls. This had begun with Monique's appearance in the world, and expanded to generously include each sister as they arrived.

"You are pests in my son's life! You suck everything from him!"

"You are just a leash, holding him back!"

"You take everything from him. You are nothing! Why should you be given his time or any kind of support? You are not worth it. You should be let go!"

But despite her vitriol, Papa trusted that she would keep them safe, knowing that *he* at least valued them. The one thing Nkiyaa feared in life was her son's displeasure.

Monique could never get over the hurt from her grandmother's words, or understand her disdain. She made many attempts to show extra respect and try to win a modicum of welcome.

One morning she led her sisters into Granny Ears's hut. Her grandmother was sitting near the fire, chomping on her mswaki. Seeing the girls, she looked up, and spat *PWAM* on the distant wall.

"What is it?!" she barked.

She took her mswaki in her fingers the way fancy ladies in advertisements held cigarettes on long sticks, and started thwapping its chewed end with amazing force on one of the cooking rocks. *BOM! BOM! BOM!*

Monique stood there, eyes growing wider and wider.

Her grandmother glared at her. *Well?! What the hell do you want in my house?*

"O-oh," Monique managed, "We just came to say hello." (Greeting your elders is essential in Samburu etiquette.)

"I don't need your greetings!" Nkiyaa snapped. "Get the hell out."

"Oh, OK."

Rose and Esther, behind, had already disappeared into thin air. Like retreating from a cobra, Monique demurely stepped backwards to exit. In case something was thrown.

Monique had been five for a while, and was tall and strong for her age. She had finally been allowed to join the manyatta's water fetching for several months. Rose and little Esther often partook in other tasks inside the village, especially beadwork or watching babies. But every chance Monique got she volunteered for any duty that got her out of the manyatta and that much further away from Granny Ears, especially fetching water.

"Monique!" one little friend exclaimed as they sauntered to the river. They walked barefoot on the rugged path, their metal water-scooping cups and empty containers bumping along strapped on their backs. "Your mean granny is always taking the first milk and shooing everyone away and disappearing with it behind her hut. For a long time! What is she doing back there? Is she drinking it? Rubbing it all over herself?"

"Why don't you look and see?" Monique smiled.

"Eeee-Ahhhh! NO! I'm still in pain from the last whooping she gave me!"

Monique laughed. "She's praying. You know the custom. Take good milk and pour it on the earth and then make prayers."

"But dang, she's gone so *long* with it! And what would your mean granny pray for anyway?"

"Oh, you know," Monique said, toeing at a beautiful bright blue lizard just off the dusty red path. "*I* don't even dare go listen. But definitely blessings for her cattle, and for her son."

"That wouldn't take so long."

"Yah, but then also probably revenge on everyone she hates. One by one."

"Oh."

The girls babbled through a rich repertoire on these sojourns. It was the only time adults could not overhear. They blabbed freely about food; recent whoopings who had received for what; what they were playing with and new dolls they had constructed; beadwork they or their sisters or mothers were working on; school, for those who were in school; and village news, especially new wives their fathers were taking, new babies, new calves and what the animals were up to.

Rarely someone might broach the news of circumcisions, beadings, a girl who had been taken into the forest for an abortion and whose screams had rung for a mile, or was married to a much older man and disappeared, crying and walking slowly away to a far-off village. But more often they did not talk about these, even with each other. These matters were taboo. And they were terrifying. The girls tried to relegate them to the dark of nightmares, or shove them into the abyss of things-that-would-surely-not-happen. Even though they somehow knew they could not all be escaped. In their speech and all the hours they could, the girls simply preferred to live in the sun.

Perennially-popular was dreams for their futures.

"I want a very handsome husband."

"I want my husband to give me a nice house to live in."

"I want ten kids."

"I want the most beautiful beadwork ever at my wedding. We will work on it for two years."

"I just want to have a happy family." (Many families were indeed happy.)

And then Monique would pipe up. Something like:

"Psshh. You fools take all the husbands you want. Have them all. All the beads too. I don't want any of that nonsense."

The girls would laugh. Monique was always weird. "What do you want then?"

She rattled off any of her long list of impossible, heretical desires:

"I want to tour the world; see the world."

"I want to learn ten international languages."

"I'm going to invent a car engine that runs only on air."

"I want to live with people I don't know and learn their culture."

"I want to drive the biggest car that exists anywhere in the world."

"I'll adopt fifty kids and educate them all."

"I want to drive the world's fastest car."

"I'm going to house all the homeless and refugees."

"I want to be a pilot."

"I'm gonna open a huge hospital for all the kids who are hurt or sick. We will treat them for free."

"I want to put all men in jail."

"I want to see women become more educated than the men."

These made the other girls goggle or choke with laughter. Monique's interests in philanthropy, other cultures, and feminism, and her obsession with speed and engines, were all utterly bizarre.

(When Papa heard such talk, he would reply, "Mmm. And how are you going to make that happen?" And then ignore her very detailed, exact explanation of how she was going to make it happen.)

Suddenly one of the tiniest girls came scurrying back. She had blasted ahead to check things out at the river. "Guys, guys! The river is dry! It's all dried and muddy and nasty!" She made dramatic choking noises, clutched at her neck, and fell over.

Ah, nuts. The water fetching gang trotted ahead to confirm, their containers bump-bump-bumpiting on their backs.

It was true. It wasn't dry exactly, but it was not going to be good.

Along the riverbank stood grand, stately trees with branches that arched over the water. When the river was running properly, its power could easily sweep grown men away. Those times, or even when it was just half full and lazily lying around, getting water was fairly straightforward, thanks to the trees. Monique and the other bravest and surest-of-foot kids would step out on the muddy bank, lean way over holding to a sturdy branch or strong root with one hand, and use the other to scoop water again and again, passing the cup back to the kids behind. This was quite fun. The trees were gorgeous and gave cooling shade, birds cackled and cooed up in the branches, and there was a great view down the river both directions and into the water, revealing many interesting things.

The river called all life in all its diversity to it. They commonly saw zebras, giraffes, wild cats, wildebeests, antelopes, monkeys swinging in the trees, buffaloes, and many hippos.

"When hippos are around," one of her uncles had told her, "you must walk very slowly and peacefully if you wish to leave the river with your life. Once irritated they are amazingly fast, and can bite you clean in half. Worse, they are actually vegetarian, so anyone smote in this fashion will not even be eaten. They just bite to rid the earth of you and will leave your dead body there in spite."

A myriad birds in endless variety of size, color, call, and behavior also congregated around the river. The kids had even seen the legendary vampire finch, known for drinking the blood of cattle, visiting to wash up. Sometimes leopards were in the trees, mellow and relaxed. Monique once watched one cutely lick its paws and wipe its face, again and again, just as the village cats did. Endless creatures partook of the bounty of the river.

But recently the river had been getting lower and lower. She had especially enjoyed these visits: the river gave out some of its rarest treasures as it dried up. The riverbank itself transformed. The boring muddy ground, once dried, revealed itself to actually be many exquisite colors of sand grains, like a rainbow, jumbled together and sparkling. Beautiful pebbles shone among the grains: she jammed her pockets full of them. Wild water chestnuts—small, sweet, juicy snack tubers that you could sometimes find in the earth—grew in their clusters along the bank, just waiting to be triumphantly discovered, pulled, and munched. There was also often interesting debris or large pieces of wood. Monique always wanted to drag these back to decorate and make art from, but they were too heavy and the distance too far, so instead the kids shoved them aside and sat in their shade.

As for gathering water from this day's river, it was clear that it finally was just no good. The river was reduced to a long, wide strip of mud with pitiful puddles here and there of very dirty water. The girls sighed. They would have to detour to one of the waterholes.

Waterholes were dug by strong warriors while caring for their cattle, at specific points where signs indicated there would be water underground. Most people would die of thirst before detecting such a place, but Samburu know exactly what to look for. Birds often gathered: hidden water supported nearly-hidden life that their sharp eyes spotted and they feasted upon. A big tree was another sign: it was sustained by water somewhere near or underneath. Darker earth and greener vegetation both indicated moisture. There also often tended, for some reason, to be a large rock. Upon digging, it would reveal itself to extend deep into the earth, with an underground stream or trickle alongside somewhere. And if a waterhole, natural or warrior-dug, existed nearby but you didn't know its location, you could watch the animals. They would show you the way to water.

The girls had all learned from older kids where the nearby waterholes were. The older girls had been taught when small by ones older than them, who were now wives. These had learned from ones older than them; and so on through an unbroken line of five- to twelve-year-olds stretching into the distant past. If a new waterhole was dug by a family member or tribesman, or one of the old ones dried up permanently or was fouled by an animal carcass, that knowledge was also passed through the families and the children.

"Shall we go to Big Rock Snake Hole?"

"Yeah, it's closest."

"Closest to death, if there are snakes!"

Big Rock Snake Hole, an hour walk along the river then cutting back through the bush, was dug at a rock formation that included a giant boulder and a flatter rock where snakes often sunned themselves. Monique loved fetching the water here, as long as it was clear of snakes.

Kenya has many deadly snakes. Venomous cobras in several species and colors, constricting pythons, the stout puff adder and sleek black mamba, and the beautiful shy, tree-dwelling boomslang, bringer of a spectacularly horrific death whereby you bleed from every orifice. Everyone knew of someone who had died horribly after being bitten (or squeezed) by some local snake. Snakes were nearly the only thing Monique feared.

Today though no snakes were sunning themselves or apparent nearby. They would not be in the waterhole itself as they avoided such cold places.

The cool, moist path curled around the boulder and behind it, and then went down a series of almost-steps and toeholds and handholds dug into the smooth earthen side of the deep, dark, cave-like waterhole. Many children were not brave—or foolish—enough to go in such a place. But from young, Monique always seemed to end up on this kind of assignment. She was tall and skinny for her age, and could reach farther and squeeze in tighter than other kids. More importantly, she was daring. She was not only unafraid to climb the tallest tree, slide the highest hill, or go in the deepest hole that could be found: she relished it. The adrenaline gave her a rush of courage. It made her feel brave enough to do anything.

So today again doing the scooping fell to her. She said a prayer and then crept down the toeholds and handholds to the ground below. It was pitch black. She felt for the water line, and began carefully scooping with the big, handled metal cup. She didn't want to get mud or pebbles in the cup, and sometimes that was nearer the surface than expected.

She crept back up the toeholds and handholds and passed the full cup to a child halfway up. That girl passed it again, and it traveled a railway of small hands until it reached the jerry can. The girl stationed there dumped in the water (usually it was light brown, but at this hole it was crystal clear, cold, and especially delicious), and sent the empty cup back.

Monique had already re-descended with the second cup, and it soon was filled and on its way. The two cups went back and forth again and again along the small-hand railway, coming in full and heading back out empty.

Kids not needed for the water line gathered firewood nearby, kept watch over the filled containers so no opportunist from another manyatta would come take them, or relaxed and kept an eye on the sun and the lateness of the day. And watched for snakes.

They were lucky the waterhole was so full still. Sometimes when the river was low or someone had just taken much water, the waterholes held only a tiny puddle or trickle. At those times they'd use their hands and the cup and dig deeper the best they could, and then set the cup sideways in the dribbling water and wait. Filling the manyatta's water containers could take many hours. If they ran out of time they brought back what they had managed to get, and it was carefully rationed. At such times the livestock too had trouble getting enough water. Everyone in the manyatta, old and young, wore worried faces, and the adults prayed for rain.

But usually there was enough water. This day too the cans all filled. The kids hollered to Monique, and she climbed fully back out, blinking in the bright sunlight.

The hard part now began. Using the leather straps, each girl roped as many full, heavy water containers on her back as she could manage. One wide piece of leather strap went across her forehead and tied back to the load, so her head and strong neck could help bear the weight. Bundles of firewood sticks got lashed on top of the water, right behind her neck. They assigned lighter cans to be hand-carried by every child who could pos sibly manage. Smaller kids just toddled along cradling a gallon or half-gallon of precious water. When all was distributed, they began the much slower trek home, the water and firewood looking from a distance like high hikers' backpacks: but much heavier.

A couple hours later they wearily passed through the open gate in the manyatta's thorn fence, and leaned over and slid their heavy burdens off. As usual, it was already near dinnertime. Clucking mothers, aunts, and grandmothers distributed out the water and firewood to their respective huts, and all the pooped girls had a short period of grace to rest. Even Granny Ears understood how exhausting fetching water was, and appreciated, in her own way, their efforts.

Monique spotted her beloved Nkooko sitting under her favorite tree. With the water fetched, she could go take some rest with her. It would be several minutes until Nkiyaa would start yelling about idle children.

As Monique approached she noticed her great-grandmother's shuka, draped like a cardigan over her shoulders, was dark-colored. So were the other fabrics she was wearing. She knew Nkooko chose these dark tones to wear when she was feeling especially down. She sat quietly next to her, and picked up the long, elegant ebony fingers in her small caramelly-chocolate ones. Looking up, she saw that tear trails streaked from her great-grandmother's beautiful eyes down her cheeks and even down her long neck. *Oh my goodness*, she thought. *That's a lot of crying.*

"What's wrong, Nkooko?"

Nkooko sighed and wiped her tears with her shuka. "Ah. I am just wondering. Why does God have to keep me here so long, just to be disrespected and abused by my own child?"

Anger flared within Monique. *Stupid mean-ass Granny Ears. What did she do this time?*

She thought a moment.

"Let's throw her to the wild animals to eat her," she suggested.

Nkooko burst into laughter. She laughed and laughed, and leaned her head back on the tree. New tears, of laughter, began streaming down. Monique too giggled and grinned alongside, and began full-out laughing.

After a minute or two of catharsis, Nkooko finally wiped the tears away. She looked at Monique and patted her hand. "You always know how to bring things around to be better. You always find the comedy in everything."

She pulled Monique in and hugged her tight. "I wish for you all the goodness in this world. Ah, child. Please. Never forget to be kind."

17

Jimmy the Afro-German Shepherd

Papa had been gone nearly a year to Germany. Monique had no idea where that was. She just knew it was another country, super far away; you had to take an airplane to get there; and Papa was away on important studies for his work and he was still not around and that was no good.

At school the teachers and matrons oversaw her and Rose and little Esther, and during breaks so did her extended family. Sometimes Akuyia walked from Baragoi to visit, and he pampered and fed them and filled out their bodies that had grown thin and sallow. But there was no Papa, not for a long time. Every three months or so he came back for a few days, but then again he left.

A few times over the year, the headmistress called Monique and her sisters to her office to read them a letter that Papa had sent to the school for them. The envelope bore interesting stamps and markings: Ms. Mary said it too came from Germany on an airplane. Papa told them funny things about life there, such as the existence of snow and how it behaves, and exotic food like sausages and warm cabbage sauerkraut. He asked how they were, and told them to study well and be good.

"Later in life I'd like to send you anywhere in the world to study," Ms. Mary read, and paused to look at the girls significantly, "and you can see these wonderful things too."

This prospect thrilled Monique.

She finished being five, and turned six.

A few weeks later, school vacation arrived and the girls came back to the Maralal house. The following Tuesday was quite hot. Monique hid from the sun in her favorite not-so secret playing spot under the water storage tank. The raised tank provided a large, cool, shaded area underneath, about six feet across. The space was plenty tall for a young girl and her friends to sit under and play, but low enough to exclude big kids and adults. Monique was tying grass stalks into little dolls and bossing them around, and with her finger drawing an imaginary house for them on the metal tank floor overhead. A nearby condensation drip off the tank created a handy little mud patch. Mud-drawing and writing on the tank bottom was her favorite pastime in her hours under there.

She debated whether to give her family one of those amazing flush toilets that the nuns had in their convent, or an ordinary pit latrine. Just as she had decided upon the easier-to-draw latrine, she glanced out and got a shock. A tall, handsome man dressed in a western-style suit had suddenly appeared out of nowhere, right next to her hiding spot. He reached under and pulled her out, and then threw her up in the air and caught her in a big hug. She squinted at him.

"Papa!" she squealed.

"Heyyyy, kiddo." Papa smiled, his silver-grey eyes dancing. "Look. This is for you."

He reached into a jacket pocket. He gently pulled out a small, mewling ball of black fur streaked with tan.

Monique squealed again and carefully took it in her hands. It was a tiny drop of a dog, a little perfect puppy with all its parts (she immediately checked), that fit curled up on her two gentle palms. Papa set her down and she cradled the puppy to her chest, swaying and cooing at it.

She heard happy laughter and looked up: a mzungu family, a mom and dad and two big kids, all with straight reddish-brown hair, were standing a bit behind Papa and watching her, obviously pleased. Papa was always bringing people back from his trips, to meet his family and visit Kenya and Samburuland.

"They were my host family in Germany," he said. "The dog is a gift from them. A proper German shepherd boy dog. Say hello and thank you."

Monique was amazed. How could a dog could come back on an airplane? Letters, yes, and people: but a puppy? It was unfathomable. An unfathomable delight.

"Hello! Thank you! This is my baby," she announced to the mzungus. They smiled and Papa laughed.

"They don't understand English very well, Monique."

"Does it have a name, Papa?"

Papa nodded and pronounced something incomprehensible. It was probably German. Monique stared at him. "No. That name is too hard." She thought and stroked the puppy's soft black and tan head. "I always wanted a brother named Jimmy. This will be my Jimmy brother. Little Jimmy dog."

Papa laughed. "OK. Take Jimmy and go play. I'm bringing our guests to the Safari Lodge. Don't forget to introduce him to your sisters."

Jimmy became the Best Gift Ever for Monique. Her sisters were also delighted with him, but he was indisputably *her* puppy. He drank copious bowls of Namada's milk that she brought, and shared her food from the plate she shared with Papa. He sat where she sat; slept where she slept. They went everywhere together, laughing and flopping around.

Alas, no vacation can last forever; not even if your Papa is back after a year away and you have a new puppy. Monique went back to school. She became very depressed at leaving Jimmy. The puppy too was distraught. He lay around listlessly for days awaiting her return. When she came back briefly on Sundays, or longer on school breaks, Jimmy was ecstatic. He licked her feet, stood up and hugged her with his forearms and licked her face, and did not let her out of his sight. But then she would leave, and again he would mope and pine.

Papa tolerated this dysfunction until Jimmy had grown into a clambering long-limbed half-grown dog-puppy. Then he decided it was time for him to start becoming useful and have his own proper dog training and life and business, not just moon around after Monique.

First, Papa placed a rubber band with medication on it near the base of Jimmy's tail. After a few days the tail fell off.

"Papa!" Monique shrieked. "Poor thing! Why did you have to do that to him?"

"Na'Monic, you know we dock our dogs' tails. So the neighbors know they're ours. And he's a special breed, you know. We need to keep him this way."

Monique cried quietly at Jimmy's lost tail. Jimmy didn't seem to mind at all that it was gone.

Papa said, "Jimmy is going to be a farm dog; he's going to be a guard dog; he's going to be everything. The best dog. He is special. And he's to keep you safe when you take the cows down, now that you're nearly old enough."

Hearing that she could soon finally quit Manure Duty and go out herding with the cows cheered her immensely and quenched her irritation.

Over the next few weeks back at school she contemplated Papa's serious intentions for Jimmy. If Jimmy is so special, she thought, maybe Papa wants him to be the father of other dogs for us. Little Jimmy dogs running around just everywhere. A whole herd of amazing dogs. Maybe many herds of amazing dogs! Like Papa's herds of amazing cattle.

But alas, the next indignity Jimmy suffered was the loss of his testicles, at Aunt Leticia's veterinary clinic.

"Papa!" Monique cried. "Why did you do that? Now we can't have any more Jimmys!"

He looked at her seriously. "Listen, I told you he's going to be a special dog. I don't want him to have to worry about puppies or any of that. I want Jimmy to just be Jimmy."

Again Jimmy didn't seem to mind. He now was a rangy, raw-boned very-big puppy, the kind that people might think was full-grown if they haven't seen a real full-grown German shepherd. He was finally kicked out of the house, and slept at night in the red earth and green grass underneath Monique's window at the front of the house.

"See? He is partial to me," she giggled. "So many windows at this house, but he will only come and sleep beneath mine."

"Yes, he is not a fair guard dog," her father replied. "He's such a firestorm. He's supposed to be going around and taking care of the *whole* family. He just takes care of one person."

Jimmy also by now had outgrown eating all the ugali and milk and whatever Monique fed him and developed a huge proper dog appetite and needed proper dog food. Papa insisted on only the best, most natural food for everyone, so every day the uncles slaughtered a goat for Jimmy. They pulled off a few pieces for the family, but basically half was his breakfast, and half his dinner.

Jimmy was trained to absolutely only eat offerings from the family's own hands: never anything from others, or even any small animals he caught. "Because," Papa explained, "such a fine dog like that, many people would want to drug him and steal him. Other bad people might put out poisoned meat. If they can kill our guard dog, then they can rob us or steal our cattle. It is too dangerous. Dangerous for us, and most dangerous for Jimmy. He *must* know to only eat what we give him."

And he did. It was a fresh, organically-raised goat a day, and Jimmy quickly became huge and sleek and radiated exuberant health. His coat and his eyes shone brightly; he was covered in strong, rippling muscles; he was quick as a whip, and as smart as many people. He delighted in running giant loops around the property and bossing around the other dogs and coming back to pant and smile in his beautiful clear brown eyes at Monique. He clearly communicated his feelings through his eyes and bark, when happy barking *Arrrooo! Ar-Ar-Ar!* When the uncles teased him, snatching the nice, fat leg bone he was gnawing and cleaning his teeth on, he complained bitterly: *Arr! Wrarwrarwrar!*

Watching this one day, Monique observed his simple studded leather collar, and her uncles' richly beaded beautiful leather belts. "Why don't you guys make a nice collar for him?" she asked. "You know, bead something up?"

Uncle Le'e snorted. "For a dog? Oh, please."

"That's really biased," the girl grumbled. "He's our dog, you know?"

"You treat him like he's a human being," Le'e said.

Which she did. Nights when he whined outside her low window, she sneakily cranked it open and ushered him into the room to sleep. Then in the early morning she quickly shooed him out, lest Papa find out.

At last Jimmy started his final training. For the Leparleen clan, this included a secret to making great guard dogs. "Once in a while, Monique," Uncle Baba Lkopina said, "they must eat the bees."

146

Kenya has many, many colonies of strong, wild honeybees. These were the source of the delicious honey Akuyia and the family and other locals used. The bees make huge, fat, round hives hanging high in certain trees, or dangling tantalizingly from a strong root on a cliff face. Samburu see the bees as another fierce though tiny tribe to battle and raid, to trick away from their stored treasure and then seize it: the prized, rich golden honey and honeycomb.

Baba Lkopina had already explained to Monique how the honey is obtained. When a hive is found, the uncles and grandfathers—only men were trained in honey hunting—plan their raid. At the designated time, they gather their materials, including some small bundles of dried lichen and a couple sticks of wood. They prefer to do this raiding, like most other types, at night: the bees are calmer then. At the tree, they burn the lichen. It makes a thick smoke that rises up all around the hive, and both drives away and stuns the bees. Whoever in the group that night is best at climbing strips naked

"Naked!?" Monique interjected. "Why naked?!"

"Because bees trapped in clothing will sting the most certainly, and the worst," Baba Lkopina replied, and then continued.

The uncle shimmies up, carrying a strong knife and a lit wood piece and a large skin bag. Taking care to disturb the bees as little as possible, he first checks the tree and nest for dangerous snakes. Any he finds, he dispatches with the knife. He carefully places the lit wood so it keeps emitting smoke, and so the glowing ember lights his work area. Sometimes the hive is just one big fat hanging circle: other times it is several all next to each other, or entwined. The honey-hunter carefully slices off into his bag as many large portions of glorious honey-filled honeycomb as he desires for collection and he deems prudent to attempt. If all has gone well, he descends, throws on his waistcloth and belt and shuka, and all the raiders rejoice and triumphantly return home with their stolen treasure.

That's how it's done. Both the honey and comb are prized. Monique's favorite was the honeycomb, especially prepared in Akuyia's special fashion, layered in a gourd with its honey and herbs and sometimes pieces of dried meat.

Normally during a honey-raid the men made off with much of the bees' goods but left the dazed bees alone, to recover and rebuild. But when a Leparleen wanted to train a guard dog, he would also quickly scoop up a handful or two of the bees while they were knocked out, and drop them in their own small, soft goatskin bag to bring back.

On the honey-raid early this morning, Baba Lkopina had done just this.

Monique was fascinated. She watched her uncle carefully open and tip his small bag. Out tumbled a palm-ful of dazed, slightly buzzing wild honeybees into the plate of goat meat he had hacked up for Jimmy. They stuck to the blood and viscerals and started to buzz less sleepily and more angrily. At this point Monique became skeptical of this whole business, and considered rapidly backing up. But Uncle motioned for Jimmy to eat, and he didn't hold back. He immediately wolfed down the whole plate of goat bits and nosed down the last wandering bees on the plate and gobbled them as well.

Monique was astonished.

Even more astonishing, within moments, Jimmy transformed. He became wild. His mouth began foaming; his ears sprang up; he suddenly looked around viciously, like a truly scary guard dog.

Monique had never seen her sweet companion this way. She was horrified.

"Jimmy! Jimmy! What's wrong with you? What's wrong?"

He bolted off to the house. Some uncles and cousins who hadn't been around in a while were visiting and talking with Papa in the shade of the veranda.

RAWF! RAWF! RAWF RAWF RAWF! Jimmy dodged and lunged at the interlopers, yowlping out ear-splitting huge barks and flashing his white teeth.

"Ehhh, good boy," Papa laughed. "It's OK. Down, down."

Papa calmed Jimmy and his terrified guests, who had leapt their skins in sudden despair for their lives.

Papa looked over at little horrified Monique and delighted Baba Lkopina at Jimmy's feeding place. The dog trotted back to them, happy and wagging his stumpy tail.

"Ho, Na'Monic," Papa called over. "Now he is ready. You will be safe when you go down with the cows. Enjoy your guard dog. Why don't you take him now? Go check on that foolish Namada and see how she and the others are going."

Thus Monique and Jimmy began some of the best hours any girl and dog could possibly dream of.

Long before dawn every morning when she was not in school, she woke at her usual 3:30. She went outside and got Jimmy. Now with Papa's blessing she left the pre-dawn duties of fetching firewood and lighting fires and helping cook. She finally got the job she had been so long coveting, of watching the livestock: both taking them down the hill before dawn so the animals could feast on the morning dew-grass, and then taking them down again after milking for the day-long grazing.

When the night sky was only beginning to faintly lighten in the east, Jimmy and the tall, slim six-year-old walked by starlight with the cows and goats and sheep out the gate, along the road, down the hill, and across the rich, wet, cool grass in the pastures of the quiet grazing lands. Each grass blade was adorned with dewdrops, and each dewdrop reflected the starlight. Walking the pre-dawn field was like treading a dark carpet woven with millions of sparkling crystals, mirrored overhead by innumerable stars flung in twinkling silver splendor across the purpling black sky. Each step she or a creature took made a small footprint of void blackness in the vast field of shining dewdrops.

The beauty often took Monique's breath away. Beyond beauty, the early morning grass was essential to the animals' health. It seemed to hold a special nutrition, and all those sparkling dewdrops, when eaten with the lush grass, carried enough moisture to quench the animals' thirst for most of the day. *It's like their breakfast and tea too, all at once,* she thought.

They passed further into the grazing-lands of grass and scrub and forest, the animals munching where they pleased. The sun slowly rose in splendor, filling the sky with vast, untameable changing colors. The landscape brightened and details came into focus. A multitude of birds began to warble and squawk and brag to greet the day. It seemed to Monique that the birds' morning exuberations expressed what she felt—what she thought Jimmy and all the animals also felt: an overflowing love and praise for life and its sustenance generously provided, and for being present in a glorious, new morning. The bird songs felt like psalms.

She and Jimmy hustled the animals back up the hill and into the enclosure, so they could be milked during the machicha-fueled milking time and receive any necessary care. She still helped milk them, but afterwards she no longer had to clear the manure. Instead she went straight to enjoy breakfast, and Jimmy had his. Then they took the animals back down again, this time for the day.

Once the sun was properly up and the animals were properly down in the grazing-lands, it was non-stop motion for Jimmy. Monique ran alongside or lay back on a hill and watched as he circled and rounded up strays and divided and gathered and drove the animals, barking and running, all day. As noon neared he moved the animals to the nearby water-catchment areas. Most of the year they held small, transient ponds of good, fresh water. He divided and drove the animals in folds: in towards the water to drink, and then out, and then drove the next fold in. First went the cows in folds, and then the goats, and then the sheep. After the water Jimmy drove the animals into shade: the day grew hot in the afternoons.

Monique was nominally "in charge," and she carefully watched over and gave extra care to any young animals who were out with them. But she found the shepherding job—long arrogated by the boys and young men to themselves—indeed gave incredible, delectable freedom. She was often just rolling around in the grass and playing, or enjoying the sun, or picking berries, or making grass dolls, or watching various creatures, or digging for water chestnuts, or simply watching Jimmy and the animals from afar. Jimmy did nearly all the work. She did not need to command him: even though he was still not fully grown, he had a sense of time and what the animals should be doing when. In fact, it was Jimmy who often reminded her when things needed doing or it was time to move.

Yap yap, yap-yap-yap!

"Oh, it's time to go and get the water, yeah. OK, let's go."

Around three in the afternoon the shepherding day ended, and they led the animals back and into the compound for their second milking.

After that, Jimmy's day of work was done, and he was free. If Monique was in her room he would go around to the front and lie under her window. If she was in the kitchen, he'd lie under those windows, until wandering Namada kicked at him. Wherever she was, often Monique would hear a low grunting whine outside, from a very big puppy who missed his best friend, but knew he was not allowed inside. *Mmmm. Mmmm. Mmmm.* She would laugh and go out and sit with him.

At dinnertime Jimmy received his standing order for his second half-goat or something else newly slaughtered if the previous half had been needed during the day. And every few months, he would indeed eat the bees.

18

Ms. Bridget

When Monique landed in Ms. Bridget's class for third grade, she didn't know her world was about to change.

Her whole brief life, people had treated her questioning mind as a curse. And truly, what good would such a mind be, in a girl destined for the traditional path? Papa tolerated her questions (generally), as did Nkooko, Baba Lkopina and a couple of the kindest nuns. Only Akuyia had truly welcomed and delighted in them.

"You know we have the Swahili saying, *Kuuliza si ujinga*,[15]" Monique asserted to Granny Ears once. "Why then am I always called stupid for asking, and getting a beating?"

"Stupid girl! No one has time for your questions!" Granny Ears replied, and whipped off her belt. Most of the uncles, nuns, and matrons had a not-very-different response.

So when she arrived in Ms. Bridget's class, she was wary. But over the days and weeks she discovered that Ms. Bridget, like Akuyia, truly welcomed and encouraged questions. She also encouraged the children to discuss matters—of any sort—in her class. Over the months Monique began to relax. She blossomed. Not only she, but every girl spoke freely in class. There was not any matter they felt they could not discuss. They also were encouraged to help each other.

---

[15] "Asking is not stupidity." An analog to "there are no stupid questions."

"How is it that you are better than me in this?" she asked a classmate about a mathematics procedure. "How do you do this thing?"

"I do it this way," the girl happily replied, "And then I do this, and this."

"Ohhh," Monique said, and smiled. And they became friends.

The classroom openness allowed Monique for the first time to develop strong social skills. She was no longer only the babysitter or whipping girl. She made friends with nearly every girl in the class, despite the age gap, and many remained friends decades later.

For the first time she could ask questions freely, discuss anything, help any students, and make friends. These were not only acceptable, but welcome! And this teacher knew her father; indeed had in a way followed him back from England. Further, Ms. Bridget was young, beautiful, extremely classy, well-educated, independent, gentle, and kind. Monique loved having her as a teacher, and saw her as almost a fairy godmother, or like Nkooko, someone worth *being* when she grew up.

When Monique began finding delight in class, first in English, Ms. Bridget noticed. She told the girl, "English is like this. It's fun. And it's not the only subject you can learn in school. There are a *ton* of subjects you can learn. So keep learning. Keep going. Go, go, go."

"But then how do you finish?"

"Education is never completed in one sitting," her teacher replied, smiling. "There is a *lot* that will come your way. And maybe you will find a niche, something you particularly fit and link with, and then you can do that."

This reminded Monique of Papa saying education was never completed; that you can learn even at seventy.

Oh man, Papa would love this woman! she thought.

"I don't know why you think this woman is everything," Papa said when she was again extolling Ms. Bridget's virtues and wisdom.

"She is," she replied. "She's my teacher. She's great. So I don't understand why you can't believe what she says."

Papa looked at her sideways but said no more.

When the wonderful year in third grade ended, Ms. Bridget told her, "Remember: you can always come and ask me anything you don't understand. And you know where I live."

It wasn't long until a break came in fourth grade and Monique screwed up her courage, grabbed a book and notebook, and trotted to Ms. Bridget's house.

"I-I didn't finish my English," she stammered when Ms. Bridget opened the door.

Her teacher laughed. "What didn't you finish? It's not like you to not finish anything in school. You are the kid who gets punished for staying up all night learning and not going to bed!"

It was true. Monique had begged Papa to smuggle her a flashlight and batteries. The school's electricity was switched off at 7:00 and not long later the girls were supposed to be asleep. She regularly pulled the flashlight and a school library book from under her mattress, and read underneath her blanket. She was unaware the blanket was so thin that the flashlight lit her up like a lantern. *Bing!* Many times the matron yanked the blanket back and disciplined her with a beating. The girl just read again a few days later, and got beaten again. Eventually she learned to hide the light better.

Ms. Bridget welcomed her in. Her house was also the colonial brick type, but smaller and built a bit later. It was incredibly cozy, warm and feminine, with a fireplace going and sofas in front of it, and lovely rugs spread on the floor. A huge bookcase held a great many books. She had electricity, and brought Monique a glass of orange juice from the refrigerator, and sat her down at the fireplace to review the "unfinished work."

At one point Ms. Bridget said, "I like your questions."

"Why do I usually get a beating when I ask questions?"

Ms. Bridget looked straight in her eyes. "Don't stop asking," she replied. Monique was surprised at the force in her gentle teacher's voice. "Your questions are a sign of courage," she continued. "They will take you far. You know, it is true that when you ask questions people can use it to isolate you from the group. But when you stop asking questions, you stop thinking. So *don't stop*."

Wow, Monique thought as she walked home. *My questions are a sign of courage.*

She was floating.

"Hey guys," she said to her sisters another day during the break. "Instead of us just wandering the neighborhood wasting our time and playing with the kids, let's find something constructive. Let's go learn from Ms. Bridget."

Rose looked at her skeptically.

"She has orange juice, Rose! And snacks. And her house is super-cozy."

"Oh, Monique always knows where to get the good stuff," Rose said approvingly.

From then on they often went together to visit the English teacher. She welcomed them and brought cold orange juice and snacks. Ms. Bridget's lovely dog, a golden retriever she had brought with her from England, calmly let itself be pet and

cooed over and then lay down at her feet. After a few minutes
Rose reached the limit of her focus, and excused herself to go
run races and play jacks-with-rocks and the forbidden ntotoi
with the neighborhood boys and listen to all their nonsense.

Esther and Monique remained. Ms. Bridget read them stories
from England, and histories, snuggled up on the couch together
in front of the fire, or in the back yard with Ms. Bridget in her
rocking chair under a beautiful big tree and the girls sitting
near, and the dog running around happily. If they weren't
reading, they asked her questions or received encouragement,
often while Ms. Bridget was carrying out her daily chores with
simple dignity.

As Ms. Bridget scrubbed her laundry and hung it up, she told
Monique, "Don't be afraid to pursue your dreams in life. And
when you're turned down, don't be afraid to try again. Find
something that works for you, that gets you nearer your goals.
There is never an end to what you can do."

Another day as Ms. Bridget was cooking, Monique asked her,
"How did you become independent? How come you're not like
other women that need a man to have a life?"

Ms. Bridget laughed. "No, I'm OK. I'm totally OK. You know
I've worked hard for everything I have. I got my education. I
don't need anybody." She smiled at Monique. "I can pay my
bills: I'm good! I moved here, remember? From so far away. All
my family and friends are in the UK, and I'm here." She looked
at her seriously. "Complete your education. It will open
opportunities for you that you never dreamed of."

Wow, this woman is amazing, Monique thought. *Surely Papa
would like her. Wouldn't it be wonderful if she could be our
stepmom? Oh my goodness!! And I've seen her light up when Papa
is near ...*

"Nope," Papa said when she prodded him.

"There's a lot of good things about this woman!" she said.

"What do you know about that? You're too young for that stuff. How do you know this?"

"I *see,*" the girl replied. "I mean, how can you not *see?*"

"I'm not looking to *see* anything," he snapped. "I don't have time. I have a career, a whole career, ahead of me. I have all the responsibility of the manyatta and the house ..."

It broke Monique's heart that Papa could not be persuaded to marry Ms. Bridget. She eventually gave up suggesting the match. But she kept Ms. Bridget as her friend and inspiration, and as often as she could went with her sisters to go bask in the educated, classy, independent femininity that they each in some way admired and loved. And to get orange juice and cookies, and snuggle her dog.

19

Ndurume and Lorekesho

Leparleen family life, like any typical Samburu family life, was mainly all about the cows. But that was definitely not *it*. Not even for the livestock. There were many goats, chickens, sheep, other dogs besides Jimmy (they were mainly useless), and also later some camels appeared.

Among the animals at the house that got shepherded daily, the next Big Boss of the field, after Jimmy and then the humans, was indisputably The Ram. *Ndurume*, The Ram, he was simply called. You would only be wondering *Which ram?* if you had not yet seen him. One time, and you knew.

Ndurume was not just big: he was vast. He was mean. He was strong and tough. He was stinky. All of those even by the standards of rams, who are all big and mean and strong and tough and stinky. Normal rams' horns curl once or perhaps twice and then point neatly downwards: Ndurume's twisted upon themselves a full three times and then pointed viciously and bizarrely straight *up*. His eyes were yellow and bulged out like an angry frog's. His nostrils constantly streamed enough mucus for all the livestock combined. He was so massive, several hundred pounds, much of it wobbling fat, that the ground literally shook as he walked. When he bellowed a challenge, it was like a thunderclap.

Ndurume was so intimidating that he had become nasty in all meanings of the word. The other livestock got loving attention from time to time from family members, who sang gently as they picked and worked over them, keeping them clean and sleek and pretty. The sheep were all neatly shorn as needed. But not Ndurume. Because no one would or even *could* touch him, his fleece was never cleaned or shorn or even a random branch plucked out. It grew thick and wild and matted and full of various bits of unpleasantness he had gotten into but not fully out of. He became nastier and nastier, and his tangled and brambled coat just added to his intimidating bulk. It may also have made him crankier from discomfort. Maybe he had rashes under there. Or maybe he just relished being The Mean Ram.

Regardless, one look, and everyone knew not to go near him. But even if people intended to have nothing to do with the stinky, huge, frog-eyed spawn of Satan ram, he definitely had his own designs upon them.

Ndurume was known not only for menacing folk, but indeed ramming them without any provocation or warning and sending them flying. Boys and men, that is. If he saw a boy or a man, he would dig powerfully at the ground with his sharp hooves, and snort challenges, lowering his massive head and wagging it side to side. If the poor chap didn't get out of the way quick, he'd get it. Dozens of Samburu menfolk—especially visitor menfolk, who were unaware and easy targets—had been jarred abruptly out of a conversation or pleasant musing, suddenly finding themselves splayed on the ground ten feet from where they had been, with sore buttocks and a face full of dusty earth.

When Ndurume encountered a girl or a woman, he'd again lower his head and snort and paw. But his bulgy frog-eyes looked up from under his lashes with disgusting ram lasciviousness.

"Ew, Ndurume, you're nasty," Monique said. "Looking at you makes me nauseous." He wagged his fat, crusted tail and lumbered away.

"How can you even move that thing?" she asked, referring to the tail. "It must weigh ten pounds all on its own."

One day after watching him send some unsuspecting young cousins flying, Monique turned to Papa.

"Was he really from a normal sheep family? Or did someone create him? Like in a lab?"

Papa laughed. "What a question is that?" Everyone wondered about Ndurume, but a six-year-old considering an experiment-gone-wrong origin was a surprise. "I don't know about his family, but he is The King. That is all we need to know."

"Where did you even find him?"

"I honestly don't remember. Somewhere on my travels. You know if I see something I like, I buy it. I just found him somewhere."

It was true: if Papa heard rumors of an interesting breed or single specimen of livestock, especially cattle, even hundreds of miles away, he'd go check it out and buy it if he liked it. He regularly went with Baba Lkopina and some of the other uncles as far as Tanzania or Ethiopia for animals to drive back overland to Samburu County. This was how he'd developed his extraordinary livestock lines. He'd probably seen a weird-looking young ram lamb during his travels, had his interest piqued, and brought it home to see what it would become.

What it became was Ndurume. After years of maliciously ramming dozens of boys and men, Ndurume had now become a living legend in his own right, not only in Papa's huge family, but in the region. Hundreds of people knew and laughed about The Ram.

Normally if a person has a livestock specimen that has become legendary, keeping that animal might become a challenge. Naturally many others will want to rustle it, for the acclaim, or for breeding its extraordinary qualities into their own animals— or just for the generous servings of meat. Neither Papa nor any other Leparleens feared for Ndurume though. In their view, he was an untouchable, invincible, grumpy, stinky sheep god that they were lucky to be hosting, and as long as they continued caring for him and not incurring his wrath, he would keep breeding his strength and size into their herds.

No one feared for him, that is, until the day Lorekesho came.

Lorekesho was even more legendary, and far more dangerous, than The Ram. He was a Samburu outlaw who lived in the wild, roaming a wide area around Maralal. Like all Maasai, Samburu men are commonly tall and strong. Six feet is a rather minimal adult male height. Lorekesho was preternaturally tall and strong, even for a Samburu. He was nearly seven feet tall and thickly muscled, like an American NFL player, and was burdened with no responsibilities, other than taking whatever he wanted, from anyone he wished, at any time he pleased. No one could stop him. He was easily stronger than two men combined, and the local police were armed only with billy clubs and not much courage or conviction, which are both very necessary if all you have is a billy club. He had been raiding the area around Maralal for years, from the time The Ram was only a mewling lamb.

"Lorekesho" is not a man's name in Maa. It means "The Rapist."

Besides taking all the goods and slaughtering all the animals he wished, Lorekesho viciously beat and raped women, of all ages from teens to grandmothers.

He had never been stopped. He was itinerant, so no one had any idea where he might be at any time, and no one could keep up their guard forever. He wandered as he pleased, and would observe everything around him from behind a random bush, up in a tree, or atop a hill. When he happened to spy a nice goat or sheep that appeared could be taken without too much trouble, he would walk up to it, chuck it up on his back like a schoolchild slinging up a light backpack, and carry it away into the bush. He often carried women too into the bush. Besides these, he was known to simply drop down out of a tree as travelers were passing and demand their goods, which they mutely handed over and hoped to escape otherwise unharmed. People did not dare stop him. He could kill them easily with his knife or just a shove into something hard.

Monique had been warned about bad men. She had been warned specifically about Lorekesho.

The view from the house looked down towards the city police station with its attached jail. Between lay several acres of open land, preferred grazing areas for the animals. It was a small realm of lovely countryside, with bush-lined trade paths and a forested area. For centuries people had crossed small streams there, singing and laughing and talking, traveling to their villages. Women without fear had regularly walked the paths in their bright clothes and with bundles on their backs or heads. It was a natural crossing area, shaded here and there by trees and bushes, with seasonal streams of good water and a history: of being a place where travelers—some knowing each other, others not—crossed paths and exchanged greetings and news as they went their ways.

However, nearly all that traffic had ceased for several years, due to Lorekesho's occasional prowling and hiding in those bushes and dropping out of those trees. Monique had never known the area in its vibrant natural state.

One day, she sat on the veranda with her uncles, looking out over the paths a few hundred yards below. Her dark, alert, almond eyes followed the top of a very tall man's head bobbing along behind and above tall bushes as he traversed the routes. She had seen that man before. Once, while fetching water, she had even seen him up close, as he had passed their little gang of water-fetching girls on the path. He always wore colorful clothes, and though he was tall and strong and had a bright, smiling face, she got a very bad feeling every time she saw him.

"Uncle Le'e, who is that man, really? Do we know who his family is?"

"Do we even know who *he* is? No. He's The Rapist. That's who he is. He is bad news."

Monique shivered. She had overheard some of that bad news, about him taking people's things and animals and beating people viciously and doing horrible things to women. She didn't understand why all the dozens of strong men around her and the police didn't stop him. After all, they all were or had been warriors, supposed to protect the animals and people.

"Why don't you stop him, Uncle? It's not right to let him keep going around terrorizing people."

"Who's going to stop him? Me? I'm half his height! You think he's going to listen? What am I going to do to him? He'll break my neck! The police? With their little sticks? No!" Uncle Le'e laughed and leaned back on his stool and took another sip from his cup. "No. That man, you just have to avoid him. Leave him *alone*."

The other uncles looked at her seriously and nodded their heads in agreement.

Monique was silent, but inwardly she raged. Here the grown men were, so many of them and with all their power, and they just made excuses and let that one bad man keep going around, doing terrible, evil things.

"Well, that's okay," she said, leaning forward and taking up her cup. "I'll have Jimmy with me. I'll just let Jimmy take care of him."

The men burst into laughter. Uncle Le'e snorted at this fantasy: a little girl and her dog "taking care of" Lorekesho. "Pfah. No, you just stay safe. Jimmy is good: have him with you. Or always other people. Just avoid that man. And don't come bringing him to *me*, whatever you do."

"I'll let Jimmy take care of him," Monique quietly reasserted, and watched The Rapist's head disappear into the forest shade.

When Lorekesho finally did come, it was a complete shock. It wasn't long after Monique's discussion with her uncles. She was still six, and enjoying her long school break and shepherding. Jimmy, still in his early herding days, about eight months old, had just driven the sheep and goats from the water to join the cows under some of the trees in the grazing lands. They all stood contentedly munching in the shade of the quiet, warm day.

Suddenly, *POOM!* The earth shook and huge Lorekesho dropped out of a tree and landed standing, grinning at Monique.

Before Monique could scream he strode to The Ram and bent down to seize his legs.

Jimmy flew into a frenzy. But he was still only a big puppy and had no idea what to do, other than leap wildly around Lorekesho, barking ferociously and snapping. Monique bolted about twenty feet away and stood screaming her loudest. Ndurume, with Lorekesho's arms gripping his legs, rolled his yellow bulgy eyes and bucked and screamed wildly. Lorekesho focused his strength despite the multi-species howling cacophony and slowly, awkwardly began to lift huge four-hundred-pound kicking and screaming Ndurume off the ground. Two inches, then six, then a foot, then, amazingly, up onto his back.

Lorekesho turned to walk off with the ram. He took one slow, staggering step, then another.

Tears of rage and impotent despair streamed down Monique's face. She continued to scream, watching her beloved nasty ram, who was utterly terrified, get hauled off by this horrible man. He would surely slit his throat and butcher him into pieces and barbecue him bit by bit over coals in the wild. Globs of Ndurume's melted fat would stream greasily down this disgusting man's chin, and he would say "Mmm-mmm, that's good" as he chewed Ndurume up and swallowed Ndurume, and despite everyone's absolute burning hatred he would steal nourishment from his slaughtered victim. Nourishment to continue raping and pillaging.

Jimmy still leapt and barked and nipped uselessly. Monique's fantasy of Jimmy taking care of Lorekesho suddenly stood out to her as stark nonsense, and tears choked in her throat. It was all so horrible and so wrong and yet it still was happening and there was nothing they could do.

Suddenly Lorekesho stumbled. The ram fell. Lorekesho stumbled a few feet further and bent over, breathing hard and resting his arms on his knees.

That was all it took. Ndurume and Jimmy and Monique and all the livestock immediately ran like a breaking tide, all the way out of the grazing lands, up the hill, along the road, and through the gate. When they arrived Monique and Ndurume were still screaming and Jimmy was still barking like a maniac, nipping at the heels of the slowest animals.

Monique ran straight inside. Her uncles were sitting around in the living room and looked up, surprised. They had been having tea. Of all the ways in which British colonialism stamped the countries it had been present in, teatime may well be the influence that stuck the firmest and widest. Even in the most simple Samburu homes—remembering that the Samburu hardly had anything to do with the British as they are a remote tribe and for decades were walled off from the rest of Kenya—even then, amazingly, there will be teatime, every day. The uncles were all comfortably seated in their melange of western and traditional dress, with cookies and snacks and the British tea service and cups of chai.

"What is it?" snapped Uncle Le'e.

"You're having TEA?!" she yelled. "Jimmy and the animals and I are running for our lives from that rapist monster and YOU'RE HAVING TEA?!"

"Of course we are having tea! It is teatime! Now, what nonsense is this? What happened with the animals?"

Monique quickly relayed the occurrence, and urged, "Go get him and stop him! You're all here! He's got to still be nearby!"

"Oh, no, that's impossible that that happened," Uncle Le'e said, and laughed. "You must be imagining things. These are PK's animals! Who would dare mess with them? And even more, *Ndurume*?!" The other uncles laughed with him. "No no no, it's impossible."

Monique's terror transformed in an instant into fury: white-hot fury.

"You don't believe me because I am a girl. And I am accusing a man. And so you are making excuses for him! But if a boy shepherd ran in here, you would believe him!"

Le'e clicked his tongue. "Ho, speak respectfully to your uncles. It's not this. It's just that we think you must be overreacting."

Monique could not believe her ears. "Never mind, I changed my mind. You are sexist, but you're really saying this because you're all cowards and now that he has actually attacked, you don't want to have to do anything!"

"Ho, child!" Le'e's hand went to his rungu.

"I'll tell my father you didn't chase him: you didn't even believe me. You just sat around taking your tea. You dummies need to take this seriously! He almost managed to carry Ndurume away! Do you really think he will give up so easily? He will try again!"

At the reminder of how Papa would feel, Le'e let go of his rungu. "Ah, yes. Well, the animals are safe, you said? It's settled for now then. I'll mention this myself to your father and we'll see what he says."

Monique was furious. She turned and stomped out. "Come on Jimmy, let's go."

She tramped to her hiding area under the water tank. She sat there crying and stroking Jimmy, who crawled in and snuggled up next to her. She was angry to be so disrespected and disbelieved, and angry at the utter uselessness of her uncles. Poor Ndurume! And he had been so terrified! Even worse, the police station was *right there! With* its jail! And yet all these men would do nothing. They were all useless.

In an hour or so Papa came and found her in her hiding spot. "Papa!" she squeaked. He tossed her up in the air and caught her in a hug. Her tears had dried, but now they sprang back.

"Ah, Na'Monic. Le'e and the others told me what happened."

"Do you believe me, Papa?"

"It is a crazy thing, but yes, I do believe you. You don't lie." Monique hid her face in his shoulder. He patted her back and continued, "It is fortunate that our stinky sheep king is so heavy! And it is very fortunate you had Jimmy with you."

"Yes, but Papa, I think he will return!"

"Ah, I don't think so. But you know, just in case, I think maybe we should send Jimmy for a little extra training."

"That's a good idea, Papa."

"OK. Come. Let's go share our dinner."

20

Akuyia

Around this time, Monique fell ill. Part of her stomach started swelling and an area under her ribs hurt. She began passing out regularly at school, so they sent her home.

Papa took her to all the modern doctors nearby. She was checked repeatedly for everything they could think of: but no one knew what was happening or how to treat it. Meanwhile week by week her swelling and pain increased. She began losing the ability to eat. Papa now took her to the best hospitals in all of Kenya, driving her—in pain—the many hours to Nairobi and back. Again no diagnosis and no treatment. All they could recommend was rest and care at home. Even the local nuns, who had considerable experience with illnesses of the high interior, didn't know what to do. Day by day she grew weaker, and was able to eat and do less and less.

For months she lay slowly wasting away on the living room sofa or her bed, only able to watch other children play or go off to school, and not join in herself.

Besides being in pain and exhausted, she became terribly lonely and depressed. Papa went to work every day, and Esther and Rose remained at St. Mary's, only coming back briefly on Sundays and school breaks. Visiting Ms. Bridget or anyone else was out of the question. She could even only see Jimmy the few moments she felt strong enough to hobble outside. One of the young boy cousins was now taking out the livestock with him. Her aunts and grandmothers at the house, who also didn't understand this disease or how to help her, cared for her the best they could. But in truth that was very little, and her illness continued to progress.

Soon she was unable to stand and became nearly completely bedbound, and in agony. She was barely able to even drink more than a tablespoon at a time. Her hair began falling out, her skin turned pasty, and her stomach swelled so much that she looked ready to give birth. Only her head and belly remained large: everything else shrank to skin and bones. She stopped spending most of the day on her bed or the sofa, and instead lay around inhabiting the floors, as she could not fall off them.

When she sensed she needed to use the restroom (which wasn't often, since she could hardly eat or drink), she very slowly and weakly scooted, dragged, and rolled herself through the house. She stopped at the kitchen for a sip of water, and then dragged herself out the back. She stopped and puked the water up, and then slowly rolled and dragged herself again along the soft grass in back to the latrine. After her meager business there was done, she repeated the procedure to get back inside. It took hours.

At this time Papa was called away on a three-week trip to London. Local doctors had mentioned that he could attempt bringing her to India, where they heard there was treatment for a disease that looked much like hers. *Otherwise*, they whispered (but Monique's still-sharp ears heard) *it is likely just the end for her.* Papa got things ready to travel to India after he returned from London, and he left, assigning Uncle Le'e to check on Monique regularly and report to him via Papa's office telephone.

Monique received the news of going to India with some encouragement: at least Papa was still trying to save her and would return. But she had lost hope in doctors and lost hope of being treated. She also did not think she could live the next three weeks; much less travel anywhere afterwards.

One morning soon after Papa had left, as she was lying on the living room floor in her terrible state, a miracle occurred.

"Ho!" she heard, as she was dozing, barely conscious. She slowly opened her eyes. Ebony feet were before her nose. Then a tall, dark man squatted down looking at her with great concern.

It was Akuyia! Incredible! A few scant tears sprang to her eyes: she did not even have the strength to be able to cry properly.

"Why are you lying down? On the floor? Why aren't you in school?"

Since her pitiful babyhood, when his prayers and herbal-oiled-hands had incanted healing and strength into her, Akuyia had never seen Monique ill. Or in any condition other than cheerful, buzzing energetically everywhere, climbing trees, and beating on her cousins.

It was hard for her to speak, but she quietly and slowly got the words out. "I am sick."

Akuyia gently caressed her sunken cheek. "Ahhh, child. No wonder." He sighed and shook his head. "No wonder. ... I was ... I could not sleep. For many days. I kept thinking about you. I kept dreaming about you. That something is not really right. I just had to come."

"Oh, Akuyia ... I don't know how much longer I am going to stay alive." She cried a few more insubstantial tears, and then they dried up. "I heard the doctors say, 'I think it's just the end. For her. We can't treat whatever she has. It's not known.'"

Akuyia hushed her and touched her swollen belly, right below her diaphragm. The child immediately screamed in pain.

"Oh, I know what the problem is. It's your spleen. It has to be bled. Doctors don't know this. But we do. We Maasais treat this the whole time."

"What are you gonna do, Grandpa?"

"Just lay there, I'm coming for you back. I have to journey somewhere quickly, because I need to fetch some things. I'm going to the neighbor for him to help me. Try to drink a little."

He spoke to a grandmother who was in the house: she appeared with a thin broth to slowly get a bit more fluid into her, and he left.

In a few hours Akuyia reappeared with the kind neighbor (he was also their local blacksmith) and a few relatives he had gathered to come help. Their faces were serious, and softened with worry and care.

"OK," he said, "I'm going to take you outside. It's going to be slightly painful. But it's going to be OK. You believe me?"

"You're the best doctor in the world. There's nobody like you. Everything with you is always good. So I believe you, Grandpa. Whatever you want to do, I know it's gonna work. And it's gonna make it better."

He carried her out to the car-parking area, and carefully laid her down on her back on some soft skins that had been spread there. The other adults knelt nearby, and did as Akuyia asked to help finish preparations.

They neatly spread out alongside her several bottles of oils and traditional medicines and piles of different freshly-cut and cleaned herbs, roots, and leaves. A nearby jiko had already heated water and was now cooking something herbal. Near her shoulder was a small wrapped parcel: inside, soaked in medicinal oils lay a leather-handled, black metal knife. Forged by the blacksmith, it was the size of a paring knife, and only used for the spleen-treating ceremonies. These were clearly surgeries, with their own precise supplies, procedures, and checklists. The knife was kept carefully buried at a designated location between ceremonies, after being cleaned and re-soaked and re-wrapped. Akuyia had walked to where it was buried at the blacksmith area and dug it up, in addition to preparing the other materials.

Monique was wearing a dress and underwear. Akuyia asked if he could roll up her dress. "I don't want the blood to be all over it. I need to work on your tummy." She nodded and he gently raised the dress and draped it like a shuka over her upper chest and shoulders, so she wouldn't get cold.

Akuyia looked down at her, his face full of sorrowful compassion. "We're now ready. It will hurt a bit, but you will get better. So don't cry, don't cry, don't cry."

This immediately made Monique cry.

Two of the adults held down her arms, and Akuyia made a first small cut on her stomach, near her spleen. There was no anesthetic. At that first cut, she passed out from the pain.

Akuyia worked carefully but quickly: he had done this ceremony several times before, and *he* at least knew this disease well, even if the doctors didn't yet. He made two rows of small, shallow vertical cuts in a circumference around her stomach near her waist, in her skin layer. Then he made similar but shallower small cuts at spots on the back of her neck and her shoulders, on each toe, and then each fingertip and knuckle.

Monique woke when he was working on her hands. She was surprised to see that the drops of blood coming out were not the bright red she was familiar with, but black like charcoal.

"Ah, little one," Akuyia said. "It's going very well. See this black blood? All this is bad blood. This has to go. I'm sorry, honey. I know it hurts. But it has to go."

She cried and passed out again.

When she woke, Akuyia was gone. Uncle Baba Lkopina was there, and smiled gently at her. She was not in pain, surprisingly: only rather sore. She felt herself all wrapped up and oiled and things different around her body.

Baba Lkopina showed her where Akuyia had meticulously rolled up certain small, soft leaves that were used like gauze, and placed them on each cut when it was time to stop the bleeding. Then a healing herbal oil had been spread all over the areas that were worked on. Last Akuyia had gently and securely wrapped her stomach, which had already shrunk and reduced in pain a great deal, all around with huge, long, strong, soft leaves, rather like a large, fresh green abdominal binder. Smaller cuts along her arms and legs too were covered in leaves. It seemed that everywhere she looked on her there was something green.

Akuyia returned and smiled. "All right, little one. Let's get you inside."

He carried her in and set her half-reclining on the living room sofa. A cozy fire had been lit for warmth. The atmosphere was wonderful. It seemed to not even be the same room that for months she had been suffering and preparing to die in.

Akuyia passed her a cup of light broth. "Can you drink this?"

Indeed she could. She finished it immediately. This was the first time in months she could drink so well. After that first cup she was ravenously hungry.

"OK honey," he said. "Now just drink this."

This second cup was extremely dark and bitter, with a massive, almost throat-cutting acidity. After the first sip and grimace, she drank it all without hesitation. Akuyia nodded and smiled. Taking the empty cup from her, he said, "That will clean your insides more. You will probably throw up; you will probably have a runny tummy. But I will be here until you can walk and run around again."

Over the next many days Akuyia personally tended to her all day long. He brought her endless restorative soups, delicious meats, and herbal teas. He sat and massaged her feet to help improve her circulation as she rebuilt her blood supply. In the first days when her cuts were still raw, he kept her clean and comfortable, carefully sponge-bathing her, and bathing her wounds with healing herbs. Once a day he brought her a small cup of traditionally-prepared fresh blood from the animal that had been slaughtered for meat that day. This is a common Samburu drink enjoyed frequently by warriors to increase their strength, or by anyone in recovery from serious illness or blood loss.[16] Likewise once a day a deeply nasty, bitter, pitch-black herbal tea appeared in the cup to be drunk: she pinched her nose and downed it without question.

In a week she was up and running around again. Her wounds healed quickly, without infection and with almost no pain or soreness. Her swollen tummy and its pain disappeared, and soon her hair began growing back and her skin regained a healthy luster. Her hearty appetite was matched by the endless food Akuyia prepared or directed family members to prepare, and she started putting weight on again.

"Look at me, Grandpa!" she exclaimed, jumping around and showing off. "I am all souped up! I am thick, I am growing fat!" He laughed. "I have, like, nice color on my skin now! See? And

---

[16] Samburu make their blood smoothies by an ancient method. Blood is harvested either in the slaughtering process or as a small "blood donation" from a living animal by carefully piercing the large neck vein with a special arrow-tip. The collected blood is beaten and twizzled with an herbal stick which is known for decoagulating and cleansing the blood. The stick is thrown out and some milk mixed in to take away the iron-heavy smell of the blood. This makes a highly-nutritious drink that can be made without hurting the animal, when done wisely.

look at my hair!"

Monique had been so ill that she hadn't asked Akuyia why he had come alone this trip. He usually traveled with several men. And she had never seen him arrive without his son, kind young uncle Apiyio, the apprentice he had for years been passing all his knowledge to.

Now that she was recovering, she saw Akuyia seemed to bear a deep sorrow and heavy weight about him. He also seemed suddenly far older. It was evident all the time, she realized: she had just been too desperately ill to pick up on it before.

She thought back. A couple months ago an uncle had very quietly passed some secret news to her father, who looked more and more ashen as he spoke. Papa had refused to answer when she asked what had happened. Her flaming ears had only picked up *terrible to happen so young ... brain hemorrhage ... very sudden ... nothing could be done*

She realized what it all must mean. A wall of horror and sorrow hollowed her stomach and slid against her backbone.

She made Akuyia his tea and brought it to him on the veranda. He was quietly watching a spectacular sunset unfurl its splendor across the horizon. As he sipped his cup, she somberly asked, "Akuyia, something happened, in our family. What has happened?"

She did not ask about Apiyio by name, as traditionally it is disrespectful for Samburu to mention the names of the dead, especially recent departures.

"Ah, child," Akuyia said, and looked down.

After a long moment he looked back up, not at her, but again into the sunset and its shifting colors. Tears were welled up at the bottom of his eyes.

"I lost the only son I had."

Akuyia continued making all his healthsome soups, grilling freshly-slaughtered herbal meat, and preparing medicinal recipes. Monique realized that healing her was not only mandatory to him because of his love for her and his calling as a healer. It was also a distraction from his grief and a way for him to keep busy and keep living day by day.

He spoiled her with much of her favorite hot herbal honey water and honeycomb "gum," and these in her mind offset the taste of several of the nastier preparations, which kept coming. Whenever she saw Akuyia standing with a plant or root at the sink, she just knew it was going to go down her throat somehow. The root that was the main ingredient in the daily bitter, nasty black tea was itself ugly, lumpy and horrid-looking. Watching Akuyia clean it, she asked, "What is this tea for, Grandpa?"

"Oh, this one? This one is good. It will build the resistance you need in your body. Your immunity system will be amazing. Even in the future, for years to come. You will not pick up anything from anybody easily. It will probably take a lot for any sickness in the world to really get to you. Because I'm gonna keep your body good, for hard times ahead or whatever."

Monique suddenly got a feeling of foreboding, that he was preparing for his days there with her to end.

"You may never live in this country long," he continued, "but you know, when you're good to live wherever you want to live in the world, you'll always be OK. As long as you take care of yourself."

Now she knew it was true. Soon he would leave. She felt tears welling up.

Akuyia may have sensed her despair: he looked at the chopper he was working with and grimaced. "Ah, look," he said, "It is time to take this knife and my others for a sharpening. Would you like to come along?"

"Oh yes!" Monique jumped in glee, her sorrow momentarily forgotten.

Akuyia took meticulous care of his knives, always using them for their correct functions, cleaning and drying them immediately, and wiping them with special oils to keep them shiny and bright. Yet even the best-kept knives wear and need sharpening or replacing, and at such times Akuyia headed to the local traditional blacksmith, who in this area was their neighbor a bit down the road. This same man had helped with the spleen-treating ceremony.

"Ah, welcome!" the blacksmith declared in delight as they arrived. "Ehh, look how well you've recovered!" he beamed at Monique. She grinned in response. "What brings you here, sir?" he warmly asked Akuyia.

While the men examined Akuyia's beloved knife regiment in his pouch, discussing which could be sharpened and returned for more service and which were best retired and a replacement brought in, Monique wandered and drank in the sights. The blacksmith had several apprentice helpers hard at work, and many wares they had made were on display.

It amazed her, no matter how many times she saw it, to watch the blacksmiths. With only the most rudimentary tools—fire, rocks, a hammer and tongs, and simple bellows made from animal skin and sticks—they worked and twisted and drew red-hot metal into all kinds of shapes.

This particular blacksmith focused on making traditional knives. Samburu culture has specialized knives for everything. Here you could see the proper types for all of the common uses, such as deboning and chopping and cutting; the spear tips and arrowheads used for hunting and for bloodletting; and very specialized knives, like the ones Akuyia used in his healing work, ones for the ear-piercing done to young children, and for the circumcision rituals of upcoming warriors and wives.

Monique's eyes lingered on the type used for the decorative tooth removal ceremony, and she stifled a laugh. Many Samburu ritually pop out, with this certain knife, their two lower front incisors. This is considered a sign of strength and beauty, and open to both genders to participate in if they wish. Her grandfather had done this long ago.

Little did she know, but a few years from this time in our story, a cousin would attempt to persuade her to join him in going for it. "Aiiyyy, no WAY!" she would shout. "I don't care how beautiful it is. You give money for that?! For them to pop your teeth out of your mouth? Even if *you* pay *me*, I'm not doing that! Nuh-uh!" He went alone and came back delightedly grinning. "So you've done it," she said, as he poked his tongue at her through the little gap. "Ew. Just gross."

Three weeks passed from when Monique had opened her dying eyes to Akuyia's toes. She buzzed around outside, all healthy and bouncing, her head full of short new hair in its usual tight wiry curls. The only signs of what she had been through were small scars forming where the deepest cuts had been made around her waist.

Suddenly she heard a sound she'd not heard for weeks: *voom, voom-voooom.*

She laughed and covered her mouth, her dark almond eyes wide in glee. Papa was back! Wouldn't he be delighted to see her all better and no longer inhabiting the floors? Thanks to wonderful Akuyia! What a surprise this will be! She giggled and waited impatiently in the yard to surprise him, stifling her excitement.

Papa parked, got out with a very worried face, and strode quickly right past her.

"Gosh, Papa!" she exclaimed. "You're walking past me?"

He stopped, turned, and stared. She looked straight at him, grinning.

"I know the eyes and the smile," he said. "It's you? You're kidding!"

He picked her up and threw her in the air, catching her in a big hug. "Oh my gosh! It's really you! You're resurrected from that crazy stuff you had! What happened?"

"Akuyia fixed me!" she declared radiantly.

Immediately Papa's smile turned to a scowl. He set her down. "What did he do?"

Monique explained briefly how Akuyia had treated her, and showed Papa her circumference of little scars.

Papa got very angry. He looked up from Monique, who was dismayed and confused by this turn of events, and glared at Akuyia, who was sitting on the veranda with one hand shading his eyes from the sun to watch. Papa stormed up to him.

"What did you do to her?" Papa yelled. "I said nobody should touch my kid!"

Even knowing his eldest son and his hostile attitude to traditional healing, Akuyia still was shocked. He was receiving not only no thanks, but indeed an actual berating for saving the child. Under his shading hand his eyes said plainly: *Are you insane?! ... You are truly your mother's child. When will you know to say thank you for all I have done for you?*

But Akuyia kept his characteristic calm. He looked away, shook his head, and sighed. In a moment he answered in a normal tone, "Yeah, nobody should touch your kid. There she is. She's alive. I'm ready to go."

He went inside to begin picking up his few things around the house. Monique burst out, "Grandpa, don't go! Don't go! It's so nice to have you here!"

"No, I'll go. I'm not gonna fight with modern people."

Papa was still stunned and attempting to process the situation. "Who did this?" he yelled. "He's gonna get it from me!"

"No," Monique said firmly. "He saved my life. Just leave him alone."

Papa said, "So you don't wanna go? To India?"

"I don't wanna see no doctor no more. I don't believe in doctors anymore. Forget it. Besides, I'm all better now."

Papa's shocked mind was still trying to finish the mental calculus of everything changing so much so unexpectedly. "Okay ... Then life is back to normal?"

"Yeah," she said, "and Grandpa, thanks to Grandpa. He's the one who did that for me. He saved me."

Papa went inside. Monique sat near the door, guarding her grandfather's sandals and walking stick and hat. She could not hear if her father thanked Akuyia and made peace with him or not.

Soon Akuyia came to the door with his few traveling things. Monique immediately assaulted him to try to persuade him to stay longer. Akuyia held up his hand: *stop*. Then he pulled out a small paper-wrapped package.

"Look here, little one. This is the last of your treatment. It is more herbal honeycomb. This one, is for about seven days. You just need to nip the corner of it and chew it. Until there's nothing coming out of it anymore. Like gum. And then that's when you throw it away."

Monique took it, and nodded.

"Seven days!" he said. "I made a calendar for you. See here." He handed her a small piece of paper with seven boxes on it. "Every time you chew a piece, just cross this one out. That you did it. OK? That way I know."

"OK, Akuyia." Monique reflected on Akuyia's excellent, meticulous care for her. He was illiterate: yet he had saved her when no one else could. He had even prepared this further week of honeycomb for once he left, and its calendar.

"Oh my GOSH!" she burst out. "Oh, I wish I had my grandpa every day with me." She began crying.

"Ohhh. I know, honey. But everybody else also ... There are other people that need me, to help them. You know. I'm just here to help a lot of people. ... I want you to know, when I'm here, I'll help you. I'll help you through and through. Until I'm convinced you're OK. And then I'll go. I'll go somewhere else. If you need help, whether your dad wants it or not," he gestured inside with a glance, "I'm gonna do you anyway." Monique laughed. "There's nothing he can do to me. It's not gonna stop me."

"I know. But I don't want you to keep going. When you leave it's no fun anymore. It's so much nicer when you're here! Even the naughty uncles are well-behaved and no one gets into any trouble ..."

"Aw, honey." He gave her a hug. "But now you are OK, and it is time for me to go. Seven days!" he said to her seriously.

And then he took from her his hat and stick, stepped into his tire sandals, smiled a last time, and began walking off, four days north to Baragoi.[17]

---

[17] It is hard to know what exactly Monique was ill with. But regarding her dark blood, low oxygen content significantly darkens blood. Very dark blood indicates critical illness. Her symptoms indicate she may have had visceral leishmaniasis, or kala-azar, a disease caused by parasitic sandflies that is common in the region and has a 95-100% fatality rate if left untreated. Treatments in western medicine were very hard to find at the time she was ill. It's also common in India, which is likely why Papa wanted to send her there. Mayans also experience it, and traditionally treat it with antiparasitic herbs. Akuyia's treatment, administering antiparasitics, and then nursing her back to health was likely an excellent traditional treatment when performed in expert hands, and it was doubtless developed over centuries of local experience with this illness.

21

Never Again

Monique's illness caused her to miss so many months of school that once she was better there was no point sending her back: she was going to have to repeat the grade anyway. So she stayed at home the rest of the year. She still had to do many chores, but was able to continue recovering and strengthening in her own home, with abundant good milk and food, fresh air, and family around. She enjoyed much extra time with the animals, shepherding, visits to Ms. Bridget, and adventures with Jimmy and Papa and her uncles.

Uncle Baba Lkopina often grilled extra meat to help her regain her strength. Extraordinarily, remembering that their culture did not approve of adults spending time with children, especially not girls, he often kindly brought the out-of-school and alone-at-home girl along on his trips collecting honey. They went when the night was brightly lit with a full moon and stars, or in early dawn, so she could see better. As Baba Lkopina worked high up in the tree with his knife to slice the hives free and harvest the honey,[18] Monique watched keenly from below and darted here and there to catch the falling blobs and drizzles of honey on her tongue—or face or hand.

---

[18] Baba Lkopina kindly kept his loincloth on on these trips. Even so, they were never stung. He was very good with bees, just as with livestock and grilling meat.

At home she started experimenting a bit in the kitchen. When the aunts scooped the milk's cream off to make butter and ghee, she poured some into a tin can she had saved. She mixed in brown sugar, and placed it on the back corner of the giant stove, where it was heated indirectly. When she came back to it hours later, she was delighted to discover it had turned into a delicious caramelly toffee. This became a regular treat.

She also tried to replicate the delicious orange juice Ms. Bridget had (and Papa refused to buy), heating water and scraping the innards of a fresh orange into it and adding honey.

"Hm," she said, sipping. "Nope. Not right. Not right at all."

She sighed. She really did love orange juice.

She also experienced for herself the mysterious missing-clothes-and-shoes phenomenon. Because the house had running water, instead of laundry being washed at the river it was generally done on the back veranda, in giant tubs with soap and little cubes of the ubiquitous Reckitt's Blue mixed in for stain removal and whitening. After rinsing and squeezing, the items were hung on clotheslines stretched across the yard.

It had long been known that for some reason smaller items like underwear, children's shirts, or dishrags sometimes went missing. This was accepted as one of life's peculiarities. Now that Monique was home and helping with laundry, she saw that a hung-up t-shirt of hers just blipped out of existence one day. Weeks later a small towel disappeared. And from the veranda, a pair of children's shoes and one adult sandal went missing during her time at home. They watched the dogs, but no one saw them chewing anything. It remained a mystery.

As for her many extra days in the field with the animals, she ended up putting them to unexpected good use.

One afternoon during school break, all the kids—Monique, her sisters, and a dozen-plus visiting children—were having a grand time. The adults had stuck them together at the house and then left somewhere. The kids ran around out front, laughing and shouting.

A white van went down the road, heading away from town.

The children initiated a dodgeball game, hurling the ball viciously and jumping and yelping for a good twenty minutes.

The van passed again, now going towards town.

The kids kept playing.

Ten minutes later the van reappeared, again turned away from town. It pulled up in front of the gate, and a white man got out from the driver's seat.

Monique trotted right up to the gate. "Hello, sir," she said in English. "Do you need help to know where to go?"

Mzungus were always getting lost and asking for directions around Maralal. When they stopped for directions at the home gate, they were usually lost on the way to the Safari Lodge.

"Yes, we're on the way to the Maralal Safari Lodge. Do you know where it is?"

Monique gave him directions. Then prompted by some wild hair, or perhaps echoing her courteous father who would certainly have made the same offer, she asked, "Would you and your passengers like to all come in for tea?"

The driver was delighted. They had been driving for hours, were lost and frustrated and cramped, and it was indeed teatime. "Ah, but they don't speak English."

"What do they speak?"

"French."

"French? How does it sound?" Her flaming ears itched. "OK, this I've got to hear. I'm opening the gate: please drive in and join us for tea."

The entire vanload of tired French tourists that afternoon stretched their legs and took their teatime in the Maralal house, served by a huge gaggle of kids without an adult in sight, instead of at the elegant Safari Lodge. The driver translated as they talked and smiled.

When the guests were refreshed and again ready to attempt their drive, Monique said to the driver, "Tell them if they come next year, promise to stop here first for tea. If they do, I'll be speaking French."

"But you don't have a French school here!" he exclaimed.

"So what? I don't need that to learn it."

"How will you learn then?"

"Leave that to me."

"Well then, we have a deal."

The kids waved goodbye as the tourists climbed back in their van and drove off, and then they closed the gate and resumed their play.

That night at dinner, Monique asked Papa, "Can I borrow your radio when I go out with Jimmy? I promise to bring it back: I won't drop it in the bush or anything."

"What do you want to borrow it for?"

"I'm going to learn French."

"French?! OK, surprise me."

Daily she brought the little battery-powered radio out with her. Remembering how the language sounded she turned the dial through different stations, listening for a match. She quickly found a Kenyan Radio France broadcast that included news and language lessons.

She kept the radio tuned in during her long shepherding days, listening while watching the animals, and chucking practice words and phrases at Jimmy or some little goat. She took her one-year deadline very seriously. Within a couple weeks she was tossing off small, simple French phrases at Papa.

« *Bonjour, Papa ! Comment-allez vous ?* »[19]

"Ah, you don't really know French. You're just bluffing." (Papa had no way to judge this: he did not speak French.)

She wasn't bluffing. She kept learning, out in the fields with her beloved dog and the animals. This time was heaven. She was learning a foreign language at her own pace, no one was bothering her with any nonsense, and all day she got to enjoy shepherding and its delights with Jimmy. He was finally properly-grown, and she had no fear taking out the animals alone with him, despite Lorekesho's earlier visit several months prior. He indeed had not returned. And she had full faith again in her dog, if not her uncles or the police.

Jimmy had learned the scent of the water chestnuts. When he detected them underground, he dug, exposing them for Monique to delightedly uproot and gobble. She adored their crunchy succulence. She also snacked on plump red berries, and incredibly sweet small black ones. As she toted her radio prattling its French and snacked and went deep into the bush with the livestock, she encountered many interesting things.

Wildlife was abundant, especially wild hares and large families of huffing, snuffling small warthogs with tiny waggling tails. Seeing these made Monique salivate. They were particularly delicious. The warthogs mingled fearlessly among the cows, trotting along with them: until Monique yelled, "Hi Jimmy, go catch them!" He darted and dove, chasing the comical little snorting, tail-wagging beasts. They ran helter-skelter away, zigging and zagging and changing directions to suddenly disappear rear-first into their tiny holes in the earth. They reversed in so incredibly fast that even Jimmy looked around confused,

---

[19] "Good morning, Papa! How are you?"

baffled where they had magically gone. Monique rolled in peals of laughter.

Commonly they came across proud, resplendent morans leading livestock or going on their business, and travelers or vagabonds roasting meat and enjoying open-air meals. She regularly encountered Turkana people with their neat twisted mohawk hairstyles: often a woman with a baby on her back, engaged in various bushcraft. *Is there anywhere a Tukana woman without a baby on her back?* she wondered. She spoke enough Turkana to offer a polite greeting, and was welcomed to watch while the animals grazed. Some skillfully twisted rope from long grasses, and others worked in the stages of producing charcoal.

Turkanas were known for making excellent charcoal. Regularly Papa drove to trade with them. The Land Rover left laden with cash, meat, milk and other goods, and returned heaped full of bags of top-quality charcoal, good firewood, beautifully stone-ground grains, and corn remnants for Namada.

The process of making charcoal fascinated Monique. She watched them dig a long shallow trench in the earth and line it with fresh leaves. On this they laid nice thick branches, then lit a fire and covered it over with more leaves and mounded earth. The fire smoldered in there for days. When they deemed it time, they kicked and brushed the dirt aside, revealing fat nuggets of beautiful black charcoal. These they stuffed into sisal bags and sewed them shut, to take to market or a private customer. They could obtain a good price. Charcoal was highly valued as a portable and light fuel that lasted years without spoiling. It also burned wonderfully: strong, long, and without smoke.

One afternoon like all the rest, back from grazing and sight-seeing in the deep bush, Monique sighed, switched off Radio France, collapsed down the long antenna, and put the little radio in her pocket. It was time to bring the livestock home. Jimmy led the animals up the hill to the house, and she stayed back accompanying the baby sheep and goats as they slowly made their way.

She watched Ndurume, a good bit ahead of her but behind the rest of the flock, pant and struggle to get his vast bulk up the hill. Whenever he managed to get his front legs and massive head with its huge heavy horns a few steps further up, the counterweight of his enormous backside with its flopping ten-pound greasy tail dragged him back down. *Poor thing*, she thought, watching him pitifully battle the physics of huge mass versus limited energy, uphill. *He is TIRED.*

"You can do it, Ndurume!" she hollered. "Come on, move that fat butt!"

At that moment she registered a very tall man suddenly streaking along from further down the field. By the time she realized who he was and what was happening, he had leapt *PWAM* straight onto Ndurume's back, like a man riding a horse.

Monique's mouth fell open and her eyes nearly popped out of her head. What madman would try to *ride Ndurume*? No one could even *touch* him! You just could *not* go there with Ndurume. Ndurume would throw you off; and then he would kill you. And then he would pulverize your dead body into mush in the dirt.

Yet, there it was. Monique stood watching, utterly stunned. Ndurume screamed and bucked and struggled, but The Rapist stayed atop, holding fast to his curling horns. Ndurume could not throw him, or ram him. Lorekesho squeezed him tightly with his arms and legs as he held on, suffocating him.

Within a few moments the unfortunate ram passed out and fell over. Lorekesho knelt down. He hoisted poor unmoving Ndurume onto his shoulders—forelegs over one shoulder and back legs over the other—slowly stood, and then, incredibly, started slowly walking off with the 400-plus-pound ram. Again.

"JIMMY!!" Monique finally managed to scream.

But there was no need.

Jimmy had been so far ahead, practically already at the house with the other animals, that he was long out of sight. (Lorekesho had clearly planned this carefully.) But he was not out of hearing distance. This was Lorekesho's mistake. Jimmy heard Ndurume's screams and turned around and ran like lightning. In the ninety seconds of Lorekesho's struggle with the ram Jimmy had closed the entire ten-minute-walk. The moment Monique screamed the dog came rushing down the hill in a fluid black-and-tan streak of growling rage, and dove onto Lorekesho.

Lorekesho let go of Ndurume's legs to use his hands to fight the dog, and the ram dropped. As Jimmy started tearing into Lorekesho and the man fell with the furious dog on top of him, Ndurume woke up, stood, and *ran*—no problem—up the hill and towards the house.

Monique stayed where she was, back with the terrified baby sheep and goats, watching her dog struggle with The Rapist. Lorekesho tried to beat Jimmy off and kick and punch at him: but it just didn't matter. The dog had become the fury of all Lorekesho's victims incarnate. He bit and released, dodged, tore and scratched, and leapt and bit and tore again and again.

Finally Lorekesho landed one good punch and knocked Jimmy off. He stood up and ran for his life, holding tight a ragged tear on his neck that was spurting blood. Monique saw blood seeping from many other gashes on him as he ran staggering away.

Jimmy was satisfied at this point. He came over to Monique, panting and wagging his stump tail, his clear brown eyes beaming. He was covered in blood, and clearly delighted by his victory.

Monique was thrilled. She didn't want to pet the blood-soaked dog and ruffle his fur (*eww, nasty*), so she cheered and clapped and danced. "Good dog! Good dog! Yayyyy! Thank you! Thank you!"

They got the last of the herds up safely into the compound. Again it was teatime. As she hosed Jimmy off at the outdoor faucet and confirmed that he had no wounds and the blood was all Lorekesho's, she relayed to her uncles what had happened.

This time they believed her.

When Papa arrived home and she told him what had happened, and how Lorekesho had again attempted to take one of his favorite animals, he was furious. He declared, "If I find that motherfucker I'm gonna hit him with my car. I'll chase him with my Land Rover *down*."

But there was never a need. From that day on Lorekesho was never seen again.

Never again was a creature stolen and killed by him; never again was a man attacked and robbed by him; and never again was any woman of any age beaten and raped by him. The little girl and her dog had indeed handled what the police and grown men had not.

And nasty, mean Ndurume lived out the rest of his years in peace as the king of the herd, ramming boys and men and flirting with girls and women all that he wished.

22

Namada

Princess Namada continued in her peculiarity and persnicketiness as she aged. "You think you're the Queen," Monique scolded her. "All you need are shoes and earrings. And a very big bra."

The cow was so well conditioned to be milked after Papa arrived with machicha that her teats started flowing just from the sound of the Land Rover gunning up the hill. After days of losing milk in wasted torrents before they were ready, the family learned to station her in advance in front of the machicha trough and pull up their stools and milking cups and prep her teats, so once the sound occurred they could start milking immediately. While they dealt with the initial flow Papa drove in, and with the uncles dumped the sacks for Namada to dig in. The cow was happy, the women could finish milking her out, and all was good. Milking time ran smoothly.

Except for days when Papa was late. She would kick and whip her tail and not let herself be milked until she heard the *voom, voom-voooom*. There were twenty other cows to milk, but the women didn't dare leave Namada to attend to the others, as the sound could occur at any time and then her precious milk would be lost. Everyone was stuck just sitting around waiting.

One day when Papa was running late, Baba Lkopina got an idea. "Eh, watch this, everyone," he said.

He walked to Papa's second car that was sitting on the property. He ran the engine: *Voom, voom-voooom.*

Namada perked up, released her milk, and got happily milked out. The women rejoiced: finally a solution for the crazy cow's obstinance! But Namada looked around perplexed as to why her machicha wasn't there.

The next time Papa was late, Baba Lkopina again ran the spare engine. *Voom, voom-voooom.*

But it was no good. Namada already knew. She was furious. She wouldn't give any milk, and instead kicked and whipped the buckets and stools and all the people she could reach.

In the midst of the women's streams of cursing, Baba Lkopina observed: "Man, she is smart. She can tell the engines apart."

Monique commented, "She's saying, 'Leave me alone. I'm not giving you nothing, because you didn't give me anything.'"

"Yes. This cow, man." Baba Lkopina laughed and shook his head. The women too shook their heads and sat down to wait. Nothing could be done. Namada was a grumpy and unmovable old lady they could do absolutely nothing about. They cursed her in all the shades of the highland sky, but had to let her have her way.

So that was that. From then on they were stuck waiting for the sound of the Land Rover.

Namada's next variation in Being a Difficult Cow was developing issues with grazing properly. She would walk with the herd to the grazing lands for the day, and then suddenly stop. She'd stand, look about a bit, and piteously moo, *Uuoooohhh.* Then she would turn and amble right back to the house. Someone at the gate would let her in and she headed immediately to lick the machicha trough and wander and slurp dishes and leftovers through the kitchen windows.

The aunts and uncles laughed at her. "Look at this idiot cow. She doesn't want to go graze with the other cows. She doesn't want the morning grass. The grass is so good!"

"Because she knows she will not find a piece of ugali out in the bush. She will not find a used cooking pot, with porridge in it. She will not open any window anywhere."

"This cow is just foolish."

And then they fed her plates of porridge and ugali they had secretly been keeping aside for her.

Namada still greedily devoured anything she could reach, her favorites remaining machicha and the household food, and her belly grew even more massive.

"I don't like her stomach," Papa observed, on several occasions. "It looks weird." "It's unusually big." "It's swollen."

The aunts and uncles laughed. "Oh, she's just fat." "She's greedy." "She's eating all this stuff."

"I hope she's not having cancer or something," Papa said. But the cow seemed perfectly content: just bizarre and thoroughly oversized. She pooped normally, and chewed her cud like other cows. The vet was never called.

As she continued further eating and aging, Namada's udder, already prodigious, also grew even larger. When she occasionally deigned to remain in the grazing lands for the day with Monique and Jimmy, her udder often swelled so large and heavy with milk that she got stuck at the bottom of the hill, unable to come up.

Muuh, muuh, muuh she mooed piteously, looking around and dripping milk. Monique heard this as, "Help! Help! Somebody help! I can't go up this hill!" Her malfunctioning enraged Jimmy. He leapt and barked at the laggard cow *Wroo wroo-roorooroo!!*

"Aw, dangnabbit," Monique grumbled. She left the piteously mooing cow with Jimmy angrily guarding her, and got the rest of the livestock up to the house. Then she grabbed two milk buckets, a third with some machicha scraps, and walked the ten minutes back down to the still-stuck distraught cow and pissed-off dog.

"Calm down, Jimmy," she said, and settled down to milk Namada. "You are overfed, girl! That's why you have so much milk! I don't know, your breasts are the size of what?!"

After being milked for nearly an hour, the cow was much relieved and able to climb the hill and walk back. Monique led her with the machicha bucket. But she additionally had to carry the milk buckets back, full of the weight she had relieved Namada of: thirty or more pounds.

This occurred more and more frequently. Monique started leaving the heavy buckets abandoned at the bottom of the hill, muttering "Anybody wants milk, just can *have* it."

After a few weeks of this the uncles and aunts decided unanimously to tie Namada up in the mornings and not let her go down the hill. There was enough grass on the property to sustain one lone cow. And plenty of porridge and ugali.

So Namada continued aging in her best life, the equivalent of a large Samburu family's highly spoiled pet cow. She finally became so old and tired that Papa ordered, "Don't milk her no more! We don't want any more from her. Better let her sleep." Her milk dried up after this.

Watching his favorite old cow Papa frequently muttered, "That poor thing just needs to be put to sleep." But he could never bring himself to make the call to Aunt Leticia.

One afternoon, Namada was hanging out in some shade not far from the house, with Monique nearby. Suddenly her forelegs gave out and she toppled. Monique rushed over. Namada tried to stand, but couldn't. Her neck and head and legs splayed out uselessly like small ridges around the huge mountain of her belly. She looked at Monique. *Wooooooohhhm*, she weakly mooed. And then she closed her eyes and was quiet.

Monique rushed to get Papa. "Ah, I think that was it for her," he said, but sent Uncle Le'e to fetch Aunt Leticia. He and Monique and the remaining family members sat with the cow and patted and stroked her and watched her labored breathing slow.

When Leticia arrived, she examined Namada. "This is it for her," she confirmed.

Monique cried and exclaimed, "Really? This thing is really crazy. It's been eating everything. Are you sure it's the end for her? Maybe there's a calf stuck in there?" She gestured to the huge stomach.

Leticia shook her head. "No, not a calf. Just the end."

Papa said, "Trust me, I won't miss her, but she's a good cow."

That evening, Papa asked Baba Lkopina, "Can you please go and slaughter her? And save everything for me, especially the skin."

Ten minutes later Baba Lkopina cried out, "Eh, PK! Come see what's in your cow!"

Everyone rushed over.

Baba Lkopina was bent double laughing. His head ducked up and down, and his shoulders heaved. His funny laughter was always contagious: this time, instantly. For there, spread out for all to see, were the contents of their favorite crazy cow's stomachs.

"Oh my God! It's my shoe!"

"That's my shoelace!"

"My t-shirt!"

"My sandal! It went missing years ago!"

"What even was this?? A washrag?!"

Namada's prodigious belly had been stuffed with inedible objects she had slyly grazed, for years, from off the clotheslines, inside whatever doors and windows, and off the veranda. The missing shoes-and-objects mystery was solved, and the dogs were absolved.

In their surprise no one took an inventory, but if they had it would have looked something like:

-two matched pairs of children's shoes, whole, and three more unmatched

-two different whole adult sandals, plus two partials

-three t-shirts

-four pieces of various undergarments

-three partially-digested small towels and dishrags

-a leather shoelace

-many completely unrecognizable fabric and leather remnants

-several goopy chewed-up and partially-digested stacks of cardboard and paper

-at least a quart of miscellaneous plastic wrappers and trash

... and more.

After the discovery and laughter subsided, Papa said, "Damn, this cow. No wonder she was so fat in the belly. She was eating all kinds of crap."

"Man, Namada," Monique said. "You were a dumpster. That was walking on four legs."

Indeed her palate had been extraordinarily wide.

Normally when Samburu animals die, if the meat is fresh and undiseased it is joyously butchered up and eaten. Many of Papa's cows had provided a funerary banquet this way. But Papa forbade this with Namada. "No, man. That's my cow. No one's eating her."

The next traditional option with animal carcasses is, if they are unwanted for some reason, they are wrapped and dragged out into the bush to be given back to nature and the hyenas and other scavengers. This Papa also forbade. "I can't even give her to wild animals. No way."

Monique thought of the huge buffalo skull hanging over the door of The Buffalo, and some other cool skulls her father had collected in his study. (After Maama was kicked out he was able to rebuild his collection.) "Can you hang her skull somewhere?" she asked.

Papa replied, "Please. Don't haunt me with that. She's crazy. Maybe every cow I'll get will be like her. No no no no. She's high-maintenance. I can't do it. Just like women are. No no no no. No skull."

And so, after her skin was carefully removed, ultimately Namada's carcass was dragged off a bit and burned, and the ashes and last bits of bones raked into the compost pile. Papa was so upset he could not even watch. Monique stood next to Baba Lkopina watching the flames, and brushing tears from her face. She was sad Namada had died, but that didn't cause her tears. "Look at all this wasted delicious meat!" she cried to Baba Lkopina, gesturing. He too shook his head. It would have been wonderful grilling.

Monique thought of perhaps getting the beautiful golden skin, with its espresso accent stripes, and making it into a nice rug or throw for the sisters' room. This cheered her, and she asked Papa for it. But the skin went to his mother Granny Ears, who was also keening in her grief over the loss of her favorite cow. She made Namada's hide into the top, lovely cover for her bed: the bed which she never let her grandkids—other than Senenkon—share.

And that was the end of the family's beloved weird cow. Only normal ones remained. Monique and the rest of the family were very sad for a few days. Papa, however, was gutted, for weeks.

"This damn cow. This is why she was so fat. I wish I knew."

"She was just an animal, Papa," Monique replied. "And she had a very good life. She lived a really long time for a cow!"

"No, but I have an attachment to this cow. She gave me so many of those cows you see on the farm."

"Yeah, that's true."

"So she just can't go like that."

Baba Lkopina interjected, "PK, you love your cows more than your women."

"That's true," Papa replied. "Because my cows don't let me down."

23

Aunt Antonella

In January Monique returned to St. Mary's to repeat fourth grade after her illness. She was still much younger than her classmates, but the gap had closed by one year. Esther too was one year closer to catching up, and now had a proper circle of friends and her own bed, next to her sister.

It was hard to see Rose much, as she was always running, playing, or goofing around, whether at home or school. She still got in trouble occasionally, had her thumb-sucking habit when she was stressed or not paying attention, and spent all the time outdoors she could. But the beautiful girl saved from dying on the streets seemed to have finally found her place in school, as an athlete. She was very interested in martial arts, and good in many sports. But she absolutely dominated in running. Rose ran like the wind. Just moments after the starting signal rang out, she was disappearing in the distance, the only thing visible the big black cloud of her hair trailing behind her. She ran every chance she got, especially when stressed or bored.

"Why do you like to run so much?" Monique asked her at recess.

"Eh," Rose answered, shrugging her shoulders. "It's fun." And she took off.

Papa had the previous late August begun studies in America, clear across the world. He came back when he could, but this was very infrequent: at most during the December and summer breaks. Again the children were left in the care of the school and the family. Uncle Baba Lkopina was in charge of livestock matters, and Uncle Le'e handled most other things.

Granny Ears, adoring her son as she did, always sent him off with special provisions. When Papa was getting ready to travel abroad, back in the manyatta Nkiyaa would Begin Production.

First she gathered much cooking wood, placed within handy reach. Next she lined up a dozen or more beautiful beaded gourds with their lids and leather rope ties, all along the hut wall. Then she cut fresh meat up into tiny dices, and dry-fried these over the fire for hours and hours until they became weensy dry jerky pieces, flaky and almost crispy. She scooped the precious wee flakes so that not even a speck fell on the ground, and packed them tight into a gourd and covered them with ghee. She firmly tied down the lid with the straps. Like Akuyia's jerky coils, this style of dried meat would last a year or more, and it was Papa's favorite.

Then she roasted more. And more, and more, and more, for many days until all the gourds were full and tightly tied.

The smell was beyond tantalizing. It was a summons. It was a command. *Come and eat me! Eat me now!* If anyone of lesser formidableness had made this delicacy, it would have been ransacked. But everyone was properly terrified of Nkiyaa and her belt, and she was extremely declarative that this was Only For Her Son. If you took even one speck off the top or side, she would perceive the negative space where once there had been meat, and enforce retribution. (Monique had discovered this.) So the entire village had to suffer and salivate uselessly, for days. It was torture. Many tried to make dried meat as well as Nkiyaa; however, somehow no one could match it. Perhaps they were just not mean enough.

After she presented the myriad gourds to her son, Papa smuggled them in to whichever country he was visiting, as "decorative gifts," which they also were. Once ensconced in the foreign land he delightedly munched his way through the stash: it was enough to be his meat rations for a whole year, if he happened to come back only that often. Incredibly, this always worked. He was not once robbed of his meat at any customs crossing.

However, each time after Granny Ears had presented the gourds to him, glared at everyone while fingering her belt, and left, Papa eyed his children and a couple of the aunts. He very stealthily gathered them and said, "Er. You know, this is a bit too much. I may not be able to bring quite this many with me." He passed one or two gourds, wrapped in towels to hide them, to Monique and her sisters and aunts. "You must be very secretive and hide the empty gourds well," he quietly said, "or else all hell will break loose and you will eat the belt."

The girls and young women had wonderful late night silent parties together in their room, sneakily devouring the meat. What a tragedy that no one else made it as delicious as Nkiyaa!

Papa was not the only one gone on new endeavors. Several years earlier his younger sister Aunt Antonella had married. She became the second wife to a politician from the town of Wamba, where she had studied: a seven hour drive on bad roads to the east. Since she moved to her husband's city house, Monique had rarely seen her. She occasionally asked uncles to bring her to stay in Wamba with Antonella during school breaks. Antonella still generally found her young niece irritating, but Monique was clueless to this, and as Antonella was older and further along life's path, she idolized her.

Monique again persuaded an uncle to drive her to Wamba over a school break. By this time Antonella had two young daughters, and Monique enjoyed watching them and helping out around the house.

It had become clear over the visits that the marriage was going sour. Monique often heard the familiar sounds of yelling and fighting. At this time, it was considered normal and acceptable in Samburu society for men to abuse their wives. They did not even need a "reason" to do so.

Once Monique asked Uncle Le'e, "Why are men always beating their wives?"

He chuckled and answered, "That's the way we show them we love them."

She did not find this persuasive.

One day on this visit, Monique had the two kids while Antonella and her husband were in the next room. She was playing with and teasing the girls. Suddenly there was an outburst of terrifying fighting and screaming: truly ferocious and desperate.

Monique threw open the door.

Antonella's husband was slashing at her with an incredibly long thin knife. Monique had never seen a sword before. Antonella jumped back and threw her arm up in defense. The sword grazed her neck and sliced along the underside of her forearm.

Monique was horrified and shocked. *A long knife?! Actual slashing?!*

The sword had been concealed in the husband's cane.[20] He had a limp, from an old leg injury. He picked up the cane, sheathed the sword inside, and stiltedly stomped off.

---

[20] The concealed-sword-in-cane was a popular import from Somalia. Monique had never seen any blade used in domestic disputes: it is far outside the code of settling-things-by-fighting, and beyond even what she witnessed with her parents.

Monique watched her aunt wind and wind her sliced arm with a long piece of white cotton cloth. Then she bent to nonchalantly clean up her own blood from the floor. A small rivulet of blood seeped from the untended smaller gash on the side of her neck as she wiped the floor.

That's it, Monique thought.

She walked to a neighbor's house and asked to use their phone. Her father knew she often visited Antonella and had given her the phone number of a close friend and former classmate of his. Papa said he was a good man, in the army and stationed nearby, and she was to call him if anything came up in that area in Papa's absence.

Her fingers shook as she dialed the numbers. *What if he doesn't believe me? Then there will be no other way ...*

She forced herself to finish dialing. After a few rings he picked up.

She forced herself to speak. "Apaanyiaa[21] Lemanyian?"

"Yes. Who is this?"

"It's Monique Leparleen."

"Ha! Little Monique." She was around seven. "What do you want?"

"You're my dad's friend, right?"

"Yes ..."

"Can you help me?"

He laughed at her seriousness. "What do you want?"

"I need a getaway car."

Silence. "A getaway car? Where do you want to go? You know your dad is not here: he's in America."

---

[21] "Apaanyiaa" is a Maa term of respect used to warmly or endearingly address men of your father's generation. Lemanyian was this man's name: in Maa it means "the one who is blessed." *Manyani* means "blessings."

"I want to take my aunt Antonella somewhere special. Away from this mad man."

More silence. "... When do you want the car?"

"Tomorrow."

"... Listen, what's going on?"

"I'll tell you tomorrow when I see you. Will you help me or not?"

"... OK. Yes. Where do you want the car?"

"Hidden at the river in the morning. Where we do laundry."

"... OK. Tomorrow I'll be in a car near the river. I'll hide behind the bushes. Look for me."

"Thank you, Apaanyiaa."

The next morning Aunt Antonella and Monique spread a big sheet on the floor. They threw all their clothes and Antonella's younger daughter's clothes in it. They tied this up in a huge bundle. Antonella slung it over her shoulder.

"We're going to the river to do laundry," she told her husband's family members at the house. Laundry was an all-day thing: no one would go looking for them until evening. "Monique will watch Naai."

Monique picked up the toddler. The three of them walked right out the door.

Antonella's older daughter Naeku, three or four at the time, was standing at the table where the husband's family was seated. She was extremely, possessively adored by them. They kept her tight with them at all times, including this morning. Antonella and Monique knew Naeku could not leave even to help wash clothes.

Antonella had to look at her wide-eyed beloved young firstborn as she informed everyone she was leaving to do laundry, and then turn and leave her behind.

They walked to the river and found the army jeep parked in the bushes, with Lemanyian waiting inside. As they climbed in, he took in Antonella's gashed neck and wrapped, bloody arm.

"Where to?" he asked.

"Maralal," Monique said. "We need to take my aunt to the hospital."

Lemanyian grunted affirmatively.

"You must all hide," he said. "Your husband is too well known and you could be recognized," he said to Antonella, "and I don't want people asking any questions, seeing an army man driving a gashed-up woman and some children in his vehicle."

Antonella and her young child hid in the back among the laundry, which they opened and scattered out. Monique scrunched up out of sight deep in the passenger seat footwell.

Lemanyian started the jeep and they drove off. They took smaller roads and fueled up and stopped at out-of-the-way places to further eliminate the chances of drawing attention. This stretched the journey to nine hours.

Though she was uncomfortable, Monique was elated. Antonella was going to be safe.

As for Antonella, she was terrified, in pain and bleeding with a long, deep wound, hopeful of escape, wracked with grief over leaving Naeku: and yet she had to hold things together for Naai and keep her calm and quiet. All this as they bumped along hidden under laundry for nine hours.

Lemanyian got them to Maralal safely. Antonella's wounds were treated properly and stitched in the hospital. When she recovered she moved back into the Maralal house. Fortunately every male in the vicinity was terrified of inviting PK Leparleen's rage, so her husband didn't dare come get her, even with Papa overseas.

It turned out Aunt Antonella was pregnant when she escaped. The baby, a third daughter, was born in Maralal. And so yet another life was saved. But Antonella's eldest daughter still remained in Wamba with her father.

When Papa heard what had happened and how his little sister had been treated, he was furious.

"I'll go break his other leg!" he roared.

This did not happen, likely because the situation was too delicate. Samburu traditionally view children as belonging to their fathers, unless they are unwanted when a wife leaves. That Antonella had escaped with one child and her own life was already remarkable: she further hoped that through the courts she could get her eldest back as well.

But despite all her best efforts, it would be years of heartbreak and court battles and more heartbreak and more battles until Antonella could reunite with her lost child, who she had to look in the eyes and tell that she was leaving to wash laundry, and not even be able to say goodbye.

24

Returns

In late May, a few months after Antonella's escape, the headmistress summoned the three sisters. "Girls, you have a special visitor," she said. "Come with me."

She led them out to the school gate. A tall handsome man stood waiting for them. He had a big Afro and was wearing a brown corduroy suit with suede elbow patches.

Monique elbowed Rose. "Who is this dude?" she whispered.

Rose shrugged. "I don't know!" she whispered back.

Then he smiled.

"Oh my God, PAPA!" Monique hollered, and ran to him. The girls squealed and jumped on their father.

"You may take the day off to spend with him," Ms. Mary informed them.

What a delight!

Papa had just gotten out of his university classes for the summer. He was so eager to see his children that after the long flight—across the world and with many transfers—he drove seven hours straight to St. Mary's from the airport, still in his American hairstyle and outfit.

Exhaustion was written all over his face, but the girls couldn't see it due to the enormous distraction of his hair. Monique had never, ever seen him with hair longer than one tight curl—and even that would be shaved immediately. She couldn't take her eyes off the Afro. The clothes were also very different from how he dressed at home.

Oh, Americans must be like this, she thought. *This is so cool!*

"Don't get attached to the hair," he said once they were in the car. "Or the clothes. I am now going straight to the barber shop and then home to change. Then we'll go to the Safari Lodge and for some meat. Like old times. Now that I am back for a few months, I'll be fetching everyone every Sunday, until you're on break too. And then we will all be together for a while."

"Yayyyy!" the girls sang out, and boogied in their seats.

After their goat meat, he went with the girls to the manyatta to greet his grandmother Nkooko and spend time with his mother Granny Ears. Nkiyaa had a long list of people to complain about at him, beginning with his daughters.

Later at home the girls discovered an unexpected surprise. Three immaculately lovely clamshell-style suitcases sat on their beds. The hard sides were a beautiful light blue, and a rim of silver metal ran around where the halves met. They had never seen such pretty suitcases. Just sitting around closed they were a delight to look at, and to run hands over.

After a few moments' admiration, the girls inspected the silver metal latches, and discovered when they turned them the cases sprang open. More delights! The insides too were gorgeous, with wonderfully-sewn satin linings and pockets, glossy and delightfully smooth to touch.

And the contents! Not empty gourds of smuggled meat, but a great many beautiful, well-made girls' clothes, suitable for their climate, in designs they hadn't seen before. And at the bottom were many various pairs of shoes!

The girls squealed in delight as they gently inspected all the items. Papa watched from the doorway, his silver eyes alight.

"Thank you, Papa!" they sang. Rose and Esther took out what they wished, and Monique took a couple pieces. She had devised a plan: she quickly whispered it to her sisters, who nodded in happy approval. They packed the rest of the items back neatly, and carefully placed the beautiful suitcases under their beds.

It was wonderful having Papa home. He had several matters to attend to while he was back: his official job (it was they who sponsored his studies), his businesses, the livestock, and all the relatives' concerns.

Another matter Papa quickly attended to involved Monique's French. Shortly after she had started learning it, he was seized by dread: she might want to go to France, and perhaps even marry a French man. "I forbid it!" he had declared. "I hate the French!"

"Monique! Are you still learning French?" he asked now.

« Oui, Papa ! » she answered. « Je trouve ça très intéressant et dans quelques mois les touristes seront de retour. »[22]

Papa grunted. He still couldn't tell if she was learning it, but he had clearly best execute his plan. While in America he had devised a scheme to both advance his career and keep an eye on his daughter. Now that he was back, he enrolled in the Alliance Française Kenya to start his own studies in French, so that he could jump ahead of her in learning it.

When he brought his books and tapes and battery-powered cassette player home, he recognized phrases his daughter had been using. *Holy crap, she really has been learning French!*

Papa studied hard during his free time to pass her abilities. He was determined to keep her out of France and away from French men. Monique was delighted with this turn of events:

---

[22] "Yes, Papa! I find it very interesting and in a few more months the tourists will return."

now there were French books in the house! She snuck looks and studied from them when he was out. And she could practice with Papa!

Each Sunday Papa brought them home and Monique practiced her French and smuggled back goat meat for her friends. One time when Papa brought them back to school, he also brought in the suitcases, still full of clothes and shoes. Normally such items could absolutely not come into the school, but he persuaded the headmistress to make an exception. They would of course not be able to wear any of the items in school. But because he would soon be leaving and they had no mother at home to watch things safely, the girls would be allowed to store the cases there, shut properly under their beds, as long as they did not cause any disruption.

This fed perfectly into Monique's plan.

One evening, when things were calm and the matron was in a relatively good mood, Monique approached her.

The matron was a huge, powerful, six-foot Kalenjin woman. Monique had never seen such a strong woman. When stirring the school's ugali she effortlessly worked the oar-sized mwiko paddle through the huge pot, and could casually flip the entire dozens-of-gallons contents as she wished. She was also strict and often terrifying; no-nonsense and with no respect for personal space or privacy. Unpredictably in the middle of the night she would abruptly thrust her huge hand under the children—who were naked under their thin blankets—to check if their beds were still dry. When she discovered a child had peed the bed, she would with one hand whip the unfortunate youth up in the air by the ankles, and with the other immediately be smacking the little butt. (The matron had to wash all the bed linens, boiling them in a vast cauldron on the lawn, mixing in Reckitt's Blue, and then hanging them all to dry. This doubtless fueled her zeal in the war against bedwetting.) Her accent cracked Monique up: when she nightly recited the Lord's Prayer in Swahili for all the children before bed, Monique got in trouble countless times for giggling.

This woman had been the matron for all the girls in the family, from Aunt Antonella down through baby Esther. Monique had somehow discovered that she, despite her formidableness, also actually had a kind heart.

"Please," she asked the matron quietly so the others could not hear. "We have in these cases many clothes and shoes my father brought from America. You know many of the girls won't have good clothes and shoes when they go home. I need to share these out. Can I lock the door?"

The matron must have been keenly familiar with the need—remembering that indeed some of the children had arrived naked. She stepped out from the room, and Monique locked the door behind. She and Esther quickly opened the suitcases and spread out the items across several beds, while the children watched. She put her finger to her lips, pointed to the clothes, and said quietly but clearly: "Come! Take what you can use. There's enough for everyone."

The girls' eyes lit up and huge smiles broke out across their faces.

They wandered and looked and lifted and quickly tried on buttoned cardigans, spaghetti strap tops, shorts, skirts, pants, nice long socks, tons of shoes ... All the items were new and high-quality. Papa had chosen many with spangles, huge American flags, large hearts, "God Bless America" emblazoned across the back, and so on. The girls were delighted. They quickly chose items and placed them in their boxes for when they went home.

When all was tidied away, Monique went and opened the door. To her surprise the matron, standing outside, was crying. "Oh no, what's wrong?" she asked.

"You're too young to know how to be this kind."

"Oh ..." Monique looked down. She replied quietly, "How can anyone not have compassion? I don't feel like I should have everything I have when other kids have nothing. ... I can't stand it."

The matron wiped her tears. "Your life is already set. God will always have opportunities for you."

They went back in the room.

Everyone acted like absolutely nothing had happened. Except there were perhaps a few more tiny, sneaky smiles than usual.

But somehow Papa found out. He was both pleased and angry, as he often found himself with his daughter. The next Sunday he had a brief discussion with her.

"If I come back again and you have no clothes ..." he looked at her sternly. "I want you to know. I am not Mother Teresa. I am not the one to fix all the world's problems. I work *hard*. And I work hard so that I can take care of my own. You should at least have some things for yourself."

Monique looked down. "Yes, Papa."

But that was the most recrimination she got. From then on Papa always made sure a few extra items for Monique were stashed somewhere, in case she had given the rest away.

A few weeks later, while the girls were home on break and out playing with cousins in the afternoon, a white van pulled up. The mzungu driver got out and came to the gate.

Monique was thrilled. It was this same break last year when the van had first appeared. She dashed to the gate.

« *Bon après-midi ! Bienvenue ! S'il vous plaît, venez prendre du thé !* »[23]

The driver laughed and burst into a delighted grin.

The tourists were back. They kept their promise to stop for tea on the way to the Safari Lodge, and Monique kept her promise to be speaking French. Again they enjoyed their tea-time with over a dozen happy, goggling children and absolutely no adults at home. They had a splendid time. To Monique's delight they had kindly brought French learning materials: textbooks, a verb conjugation book, and a dictionary. She was over the moon, and bid them adieu with much thanks and a promise to keep learning.

At this time Monique did feel like perhaps things in her life might be set. Maybe God was indeed going to help her keep learning and escape the traditional fate of girls. She felt hope: that she could eventually attain her freedom and career, and the same for her sisters, and perhaps they could keep helping some others along the way.

But it was all to come unexpectedly, spectacularly crashing down.

---

[23] "Good afternoon! Welcome! Please come in for some tea!"

25

Maama

In late August Papa again departed for his studies in America, and the sisters and aunts enjoyed another sneaky, delicious late-night gourd meat party.

When January arrived, the girls began their last year together at St. Mary's. Rose was now in the highest year of instruction they offered, and Monique was starting fifth grade. But shortly after school began the sisters were summoned to the headmistress's office, with the instruction to bring their small tin boxes of personal items. She escorted them out to the gate.

There stood Uncle Le'e, leaning against one of Papa's cars. One of Le's's friends was in the driver's seat. For some reason he always got someone else to drive him everywhere.

"Thank you, Madam Headmistress," he said. She nodded and cast a glance at the children, then went back in. Uncle Le'e opened the car back door. "Get in," he commanded.

"Where are we going?" Monique asked once they were driving.

"We're going where I say, because I'm the boss."

"Whose boss are you?" she retorted.

He turned and glared at her. Rose elbowed her, to be sensible and not irk him.

Le'e's friend drove the girls on the same terrible roads to the southeast as going to Wamba. They slowly descended the highlands as they drove: the lushness they were used to dried up and the land desiccated and harshened. After six hours, an hour or two short of reaching Wamba, the car stopped. They were in front of a house in a very small town, in the middle of nowhere. Scrubby, rocky, nearly barren land surrounded them.

"OK girls, this is where you will be living now," Le'e said. "This is your mother's house, and we are in Lodungokwe. She is pregnant: it is not right that she does not have her daughters to help take care of her. That will be your job. I will be staying for a few days to see that things are settled correctly."

Monique could not believe her ears. "What?! But we have school tomorrow! And Papa said we are never to see that woman!"

Le'e replied, "I am the boss now with your father gone, and this is what I have decided. You will be enrolled in school here."

"Here?!" The girls looked around in shock. The evening light showed only about twelve houses along one street, and a few small shops. A few more small structures sat atop distant hills. "Is there even a school here?!"

"Enough discussion! Get inside: it is time to rest. Tomorrow will be a busy day."

It quickly became apparent that Maama, through an unknown channel, had somehow persuaded Uncle Le'e to do this. He did everything she asked, like a puppet, and seemed to be under a spell to please her. Monique could not believe his constant fawning and praise. *Gag. Gross.*

Maama spent her days dolling herself up and going out, or sitting around the house and entertaining a constant stream of family and friends. She showed off Esther and Rose, collected rent from the properties Papa had set her up with, and sold out bottles of contraband liquor. Monique was ordered to do the cleaning, the water fetching, the firewood gathering, the cooking: all the housework.

There was indeed a small school down the street, although it was much worse than St. Mary's, and the girls were enrolled there. However, Maama's demands often caused Monique to miss school. Maama didn't care. Le'e remained for days further, to "oversee" matters. Monique additionally had to wait on him.

I cannot believe this, she thought. *Papa would never agree to this! After his clear instructions, and paying our school fees?! And now I'm a servant not to an old husband, but to horrible Maama! And Le'e!*

Maama made it clear that solely Monique was to slave, be beaten, and be spurned. She fawned over Rose and Esther; they did no work and she made sure they attended school daily. She directed them to sleep together on a bed with blankets and eat first and at the table, and she never laid a hand on them.

Monique, however, had to sit in a separate chair across the room at mealtimes. She was only fed any last scraps. She had to do the cooking, cleaning, and water- and firewood-fetching, late into the night. She became a servant even to her sisters, which horrified them. She could only attend school sporadically. All day Maama yelled at her and smacked her. When her crying sisters attempted to intervene, Maama threatened them with death.

Every night Rose cried, and whispered, "This is bad. This is a bad idea. This is very bad."

Every night Monique replied, "I'm gonna make sure we all get the hell out."

The tin boxes they had brought from school held a few spare clothes, and Monique's box included her Sunday best, a lovely yellow dress. Once she arrived in Maama's imprisonment, she hid it, rolled up tightly in a paper bag underneath the girls' mattress. She decided it was going to be her escape outfit. When she found a way out, she would put on that dress and her St. Mary's white socks and black shoes, and run, swim, or fly to freedom.

Very soon it was clear to her that her mother was not only using her as a servant and punching bag, but was actually trying to kill her, again. The worst were the beatings. In addition to smacks or horrific ear-pulling all day, her mother had taken to severely abusing her behind a closed door.

The next worst were the freezing nights. The temperatures plunged at night, and the house had no heat, as well as no electricity. Her sisters were warm snuggled up together up on their bed, with their blankets. Monique too could easily have fit in with them. But Maama forced Monique to sleep only in her clothes on the freezing cement floor, with no pillow or blanket: like a dog. She quickly learned to use someone's shoes in lieu of a pillow, and to stick any spare clothes she could find anywhere on her body. She put her feet into the biggest shoes she could find, to try to keep a bit of warmth. But despite these strategies the cold cement sucked her body heat away and made it nearly impossible to sleep.

Night after night, underfed, beaten, freezing and miserable, she wracked her brain.

What I can do. To get away.

Either I escape and survive, or I'm dead meat.

She was eight years old.

One might wonder why Monique did not simply run away.

Aside from not wanting to leave her sisters, she was deeply aware of the peril of her situation. Maama had planned it well.

They were in the middle of nowhere, and she knew if she ran without seeking assistance, she would perish in any number of terrible ways. Seeking assistance seemed nearly impossible, as Maama was clearly liked or feared by most of the villagers, and Monique had already learned she could not rely on the police. And ultimately, if she did somehow escape, Uncle Le'e would speak "as her father's representative"—Papa would be overseas for many more months—and get her sent back. She shuddered at what would likely happen then.

She realized she only had one hope.

When the girls were growing up, normal writing was done with pencils or black or blue pens. Red pens signaled danger, SOS, extremity. The girls were scared to even handle a red pen.

Monique found a red pen, and paper and an envelope. She began her letter in all caps to further underscore the urgency.

> DAD, THIS IS WHAT THIS LETTER IS ALL ABOUT. IT'S AN EMERGENCY, YOU NEED TO ATTEND TO.
>
> Hi Dad, how are you? We're all good. I hope you're doing OK. HOWEVER, we're NOT REALLY GOOD, I just wanted to tell you, that we're in Lodungokwe, we've been kidnapped by Le'e!! And I don't understand why we were supposed to be taken out of the school you put us in to come here and get really treated like slaves!
>
> I don't want to live with this crazy woman! I get a beating every day. I fetch water every day. I get punched for everybody's mistakes.

And then she told him about the water thief and the Sudanese raiders.

26

The Water Thief

M onique arrived near the end of the dry season. There was actually a public water pipe in town, and when it was working water was easily fetched. However, it wasn't working when she arrived: likely because the water table had dropped too far. Each day she had to walk to the river, either alone or with other kids to get water. Each day they found the water lower and lower.

Just a few days after her arrival she and a gaggle of the village's younger boys and girls discovered the river was finally dried up. "Do you know where the waterhole is?" she asked the children. They nodded and after an hour's walk they arrived at a subterranean hole similar to the one outside Maralal.

Monique did not like the look of the hole, but she had no choice: as the eldest and toughest she would have to descend and do the scooping. She stationed the kids at the top with the jerry cans and told them to keep lookout: there was a woman she didn't recognize wandering nearby. Then she said a prayer, crossed herself, and began climbing down the unfamiliar hole, feeling her way and carrying the two big water cups. She discovered the waterhole was deeper than the one she knew, pitch black and with sheer walls and handholds and footholds she had to feel for in the dark. It was terrifying.

When she reached the bottom and felt for water she found there was only a trickle. She slowly filled a cup, and then felt in the dark for the handholds. She carefully climbed back halfway to where she could pass it up to the children's outstretched hands. She said another prayer, crossed herself, and re-descended into the terrifying blackness.

She repeated this again and again. It took hours. As the last containers began to fill, the trickle reduced further and further, just as the river had. Finally there was only a slow dribble. She stayed at the bottom on the final trip for quite a while, gathering the last precious drops and poking around to see if any more could be enticed. But it was useless. The waterhole was drained.

When she emerged into the light, blinking, with the last scant cup of water, the kids looked at her and burst into wails of despair.

"What?!" she asked, in a sudden panic. They gestured: the water jugs that had taken so many hours to fill sat there empty.

"WHAT HAPPENED?!"

"That woman came and took all the water! She emptied it into her own containers and left with it!"

"Dammit! That took us hours! And there's no more water now!" Monique looked at the group of kids. She was astounded that they hadn't stopped the woman, or at least raised an alarm. "There are so many of you! Why didn't you hold her down, punch her, fight her off?!"

The kids burst into louder wails. "We were scared of her!"

Monique seethed. *Will adults never stop bullying children?!* She flew into a rage.

"'Scared of her'? Really? Why?! She has two hands, just like you! She comes next time, jump on her! Beat her! I don't care, MAKE her sit down, tie her hands. Lemme come. And I'll do the rest. She'll be sorry. She'll never have to do it again."

The children calmed somewhat as they contemplated swarming the woman. Fighting back using their numbers was apparently a new concept. But Monique realized, *Oh my gosh, today we're going to be whooped. They'll think we were playing in the river, we didn't bring the water home.*

She looked at the crying kids. There was only one good way out of this situation, and even that was not good: it was already afternoon.

"OK guys. Look. It's going to be OK. Let's just go find another waterhole. Does anyone know where one is?"

One sniffling child said she thought she knew. They loaded their empty containers and followed her. The whole walk Monique was furious. How could an able-bodied adult steal water from a bunch of small children? Without even an apology or excuse! And then take *all* of it!

If I see that woman, I'll kill her with my bare hands! she seethed.

After an hour of wandering, they indeed found a waterhole. It was easier to access and had more water than the first, and they were able to re-fill the containers. But by the time they strapped the heavier containers on the larger kids, and placed lighter ones in the hands of the smaller children, it was getting dark. They started trying to make their way home.

Maama had not provided Monique with even tire sandals to go fetch water in. All she had were cheap flimsy house sandals. *The land here is all teeth*, she thought: the ground was full of jagged bedrock and sharp thorns. Her sandals had started shredding once they left the fairly-smooth river path. Now they turned completely to ribbons. As the evening changed from violet to black and they kept walking, her shredded shoe remnants fell off completely.

Her soles were still tough from a lifetime of going barefoot: even so they were no match for this land. She felt a thorn pierce; and then sharp rock slice. She had to keep walking. The familiar faint silver light of the night sky was completely absent: thick clouds obscured the moon and stars. It was soon pitch black, a darkness she had never experienced. She and the children tried to sense in the blackness where the trail was.

Noises from animals unseen in the bushes rose around them. The land continued biting her feet. Soon each step was sticky with blood.

We're lost, she realized, through the pain. *I have to get these kids home. I have to get us all home. I can't lose even one of these children. What can we do.* Several children had already begun sniffling and crying and complaining of the cold. They were all only in light daytime clothes, and with the sun's disappearance the temperature had plummeted.

Suddenly she perceived the light of a fire in the distance. *If we can make it to the fire,* she thought, *we can get back home. Let's just make it there.*

She rallied the sagging children and encouraged them: she told them stories and had them share their own, while they picked their way towards the faint red glow.

She did not let the children know what was happening to her feet.

Soon they were able to follow a cow that was also making its way to the fire. As they drew nearer, she saw there were many, many cows there: hundreds of them. She had never seen so many cows in one location. As they approached more closely through the herd, she could make out figures of men sitting around the fire.

Warning sirens began sounding in her mind, but she saw no other way. They slowly stepped past the last cattle and into the firelight.

Monique had suspected what type of group they had stumbled across in the wilderness. Now that there was light, it was manifest. The men looked up sharply with fierce faces, hands to knives and guns. Long bandoliers of bullets crossed their chests.

She had led the children to raiders.

Mostly from Sudan but some local, raiding bandits every year without consequence killed villagers, rustled cattle, and trafficked people. She remembered an uncle saying, *They light fires when they're out, to alert the locals they are there and not to mess with them.* Aunts had shared horrors: *They take the older village girls along with them and use them. They don't want any hassle. When the girls fall pregnant, they kill them and throw their bodies aside for animals to eat.*

They were called the *shiftas*.[24]

The men paused in surprise, seeing a group of small children toting water suddenly appear, with a tall skinny eight-year-old leading them.

Monique was in front, and the smaller children hid behind her. They were all freezing from wandering lost in the cold night: the warmth of the fire on her skin felt wonderful, and gave her courage.

She spoke, trying Maa first. "Do you speak our language?" she asked.

A dark, exceptionally handsome bandit stood up. He was very tall, and Monique noted the belts of bullets across his chest,

[24] Swahili for outlaw or bandit.

and the long-strapped sandals he wore laced up his calves.

"I speak your language, and I speak Swahili, too. Do you speak both?"

"Yeah."

"Who are you?"

"Oh, I'm just the oldest kid. We went to get water, but we don't know how to get back home. We're lost. It's so dark!"

"And so you came over here to ask us for directions." He raised his eyebrows. "Man, you have some bloody guts." He grinned approvingly, and then turned and translated in Swahili for his companions. They laughed and nodded.

"Eh, you look like someone I should know. I think I've seen you before," he said.

"Well, you guys go all over the place, you could have seen me anywhere."

"No, not from *that*. I think I've seen you with people I know. Who is your father?"

Oh my goodness, she realized. *That's why he's so handsome and tall. He's Samburu, from our area!*

It was true. He knew Papa from the community somehow, well enough to recognize Monique. This delighted him and his companions.

What the hell are you doing being a bandit? she thought. *You're healthy. You're good looking. You should have many opportunities!* But for once she kept her mouth shut.

After the men had a good laugh, the Samburu shifta said, "I know exactly where you guys came from. You must be living in those houses in the little city place over there."

"Yeah."

"OK. This group of cows here, they will be walking back that way. Follow them." He gestured to something unseen in the darkness.

"What cows? I can't even see them. It's too dark!"

"OK. Uhhmm ..." He thought a moment and regarded the cold, terrified, lost children. "You need me to walk you guys? Are you scared?"

"I quit being scared a long time ago. My feet are bleeding: from stepping on the thorns..."

He looked at her feet and whistled. "Why are your feet bleeding *so much?*"

"Because I only had sandals to wear and they got torn to ribbons and destroyed."

"Why do you not have good shoes? Your father has money!"

"My dad's not here. He's overseas."

"Yes, I know. That man never gets enough of education. OK, that's it. I'm escorting you back."

He informed his companions and brought a flashlight. It was wonderfully powerful, and lit the whole way in front of them. Beyond seeing the cows and path clearly, they could even see details in the bushes.

This bandit, who had likely committed innumerable horrific crimes, escorted the lost children all the way back to their homes. He picked up the two weakest children and carried them on his back. They held on gripping his bandolier straps.

I don't understand why you joined the shiftas, Monique thought. *But tonight you're our angel. Thank you Jesus for leading us to this man.*

When they arrived back, the whole town was out uselessly shining their flashlights and lanterns into the nearby bushes and yelling the children's names. "Oh my gosh, they're right there!" someone cried as they approached, and everyone came running. In moments mothers were taking their children, crying and hugging them. They relayed what had happened, and the parents profusely thanked Monique and the man for keeping the kids safe and bringing them back.

Esther and Rose sprinted over and held tight onto their sister. Rose frantically alternated crying, hugging Monique, and sucking her thumb to try to calm down; Esther simply non-stop cried and held tight to her sister.

The other children had all dropped their water containers along the way. Only Monique returned with her heavy load still strapped on, as she knew she'd get a beating otherwise. But before she could even get the water off, Maama was there with a big stick, shining a flashlight in her face. She dragged Monique away from her sisters, who wailed and followed, towards the house, and began beating her with the stick and yelling about playing at the river and wasting time.

She did not listen about what really happened. She did not care.

At the house she shoved her into a room and closed the door behind them. She picked up the belt she kept there for this purpose, seized it by the end with the holes, and beat her daughter viciously. The buckle struck hard all across her face and neck, and then everywhere else. Monique was still numb from the cold and from blood loss, and was so spent she couldn't even cry any more, much less resist.

As Maama continued beating her, she thought, *That's it. If she's going to kill me, let her kill me.*

Finally Maama tired and ordered Monique out of the room. She tottered out, covered in fresh bruises and cuts and her feet still bleeding and full of gouges, rocks and thorns. Her shifta rescuer was at the table with a kerosene pump lantern before him, having a drink of water before returning to his camp. "Wow," he said. "Watching how this went, now I know you are being just the maid here."

"That's right. You see how it is. But thank you. So much. You saved all of us." She weakly shrugged off the heavy water containers—at least they had protected her back from the beating—then turned the corner and practically fell into her room.

Rose came in quietly with a basin of warm water and another lantern. "Let's take care of you," she said between gasps of tears. "I heated this at the fire and added some salt. And I found some old socks we can use for rags."

Monique put her tattered feet in the water, and winced and bit her lip and then her hand while her sister gently worked out the rocks and thorns and cleaned her wounds the best she could. Esther too came in, still crying, and brought some old rags. They tied up Monique's feet with these, and they all tried to sleep.

Far too soon the sun rose and brought a new day. Maama forced Monique to still do all the housework, on her torn, swollen, and bleeding feet. She also again had to go fetch water.

And then again the next day, and the next.

27

The Safari Rally

When Monique had relayed her brief summary of these events, she shifted her throbbing feet (this was just a few days later) and continued her letter:

And thank God really for those raiders, because they were sympathetic to our situation.

I don't like the school I'm in, because there are boys. They smell, I don't like them, they're stupid. And the school is too easy. I don't like it. I should go to a school that I feel I'm challenged. And I think St Mary's was a really great place for me to start.

Please, please, please, if you can take off some time from school, to save me, I'll never ask for another favor from you again.

I'm giving this letter to one of your friends to mail it for me. Because I know it'll never get to you if I give it to anyone else.
Respectfully,
Your daughter,
Monique

She capped the red pen, and folded the letter and put it in the envelope. She hid it as if her life depended on it.

She started asking a few people if they knew a Mr. Lemanyian, who was with the army near Wamba. Incredibly, the fourth or fifth person she asked did know him, and wrote down his telephone number. One of the friends she had managed to make had a telephone. She snuck to her friend's house and called the good man, again to aid in a rescue: this time her own.

When he met her at the river—it had started flowing again: the thick clouds the night they got lost had been the heralds of the rains beginning to return—he was surprised to receive just the envelope and her simple request.

"Oh, you want me to mail this for you?"

"Yes, please, Apaanyiaa. It's very important."

"Hmmm ..." Lemanyian considered. Ensuring international mail would arrive safely was tricky at this time. "It'll take me *a while*, OK? I have to wait until I go to Nairobi to put it in the mail, because I'll be sure it will go properly from there. If I send it from Wamba or Maralal or wherever, it may never make it to your dad."

"Okay. Can you find his address in America and put it here correctly?"

"Absolutely. Don't worry. And I'll be very careful with your letter. Just remember though, this is going to take *a while*."

Monique thanked Lemanyian, and then hustled to finish getting the water. She did not want any more beating than she was already going to get.

From then on, each morning she desperately prayed that Papa would get her letter, and come soon and take them away.

When Lemanyian had taken her envelope, it felt as if he had also removed some kind of heavy weight from deep in her chest, and left with it. In all her horrific difficulties, the worry somehow had lifted. She now could feel her freedom on the horizon, and see and even taste it: if only she could hold on long enough.

The rainy season arrived properly, and with it water fetching became faster and easier, other than slipping and sliding. The pump at the street even started working again. And Monique didn't know it, but the season was also to bring a small true delight.

The local kids began excitedly whispering that it was time for the Safari Rally.

Monique had been obsessed with engines and cars and speed her whole brief life. She had heard of the Safari Rally: a very long-distance, multi-day auto race mostly competed by mzungus and Indians in rally cars. It was part of some kind of worldwide competition. Near the cities the cars raced on paved roads, but the rally rapidly changed to rugged unfinished-road racing as the cars tore around the Great Rift Valley, traversing the varied terrains at great speed. She had never had the opportunity to see such a thing: Maralal was too far up the highlands for the race courses to reach. The possibility thrilled her.

The day that the rally was scheduled to pass their area, the cars started racing near the safari resorts, giving the tourists great daytime views. They would pass by Lodungokwe at night.

In the afternoon, despite intermittent rain, the town burst into festivity. Vehicles parked everywhere with people hanging out and eating and laughing. Arms and legs dangled off hoods and roofs and from open doors and truck beds. Men barbecued meat and shared or sold it; adults sat around chewing *miraa*[25] and drinking beer; children raced up to abandoned cups and food and stole what they could. As evening fell everyone waited out on the hills and lining the road. Maama was out with friends

---

[25] Miraa is also known as *khat*. A stimulant leaf native to east Africa and the Red Sea region, it is chewed widely in Kenya, especially by men. Monique's mother and relatives on that side chewed miraa.

somewhere: Monique stood excitedly with her sisters among the other children near the road, to watch as closely as possible and scramble out of the way as necessary.

Soon the first roars of an engine echoed through the hills. Then headlights flashed and a small rugged two-door sports car came zooming by at 50-60 mph. More cars shortly followed, engines roaring and lights beaming: like brief, hurtling chariots of thunder and lightning.

The rain picked up: now the maram roads were churned into thick, nasty mud. The remaining cars careened and skidded dramatically through the muck, making the kids scream and jump in excitement (and terror, when the car was near). Many of the drivers took a few moments to ham it up for the excited crowds: they spun around and performed and threw mud up on the cheering and clapping audience.

Several cars stopped for quick tire changes. Monique had never seen such a thing and watched intently, in awe. The teams swapped out all four tires in just moments, and then the cars thundered off again, the rear tires spinning fountains of sticky mud all over the screaming children eagerly watching behind.

Incredible!

This was another very dangerous moment for Monique. With all the speed and roaring and her intense desire to escape and all the mzungu drivers, something snapped in her mind. It was idiotically asking, *Can I jump in it? Can I go in one? Can I be taken by one? Can they save me?*

She found herself pulled toward the cars as if by magnets.

Rose noticed and held her back. "No, don't go near it! It's dark: they can't even see us! You'll get hit!"

Her sister's touch yanked Monique back to her senses. They enjoyed the rest of the evening, watching the filthy rally cars come through every several minutes and tear hell for leather through the road.

When they returned home at midnight happy and mud-covered there was again a beating waiting for Monique: but her mind escaped to fast cars, to freedom, and to zooming away.

28

Do You Want a Rock?

Months passed. Monique's yellow dress remained where she had hid it.

Every day she was overworked and starved. She became seriously malnourished. She was still forced to sleep on the cold floor. And every day she was hurt or beaten.

Her feet never had a chance to properly heal: their many wounds fell into and out of infection. Maama pulled her ears so hard that she expected to see them remaining in her hand. Mere breezes stung and brought tears to her eyes, so raw was her face from smacks. Maama forced Monique to carry extremely hot items for male guests, like tin cups of scalding tea, and when she dropped them from her burnt hands, Maama made scathing sexual insults to the guests about her daughter's hands: things the innocent young girl had no comprehension of. She found little respite outside: she knew that if Maama saw her chatting for a moment with a friend there would be a stick or belt or shoe waiting at home, thirsty for her blood.

After Maama was satisfied each day, Monique often lay around on the floors, in such pain that she was unable to get up. She didn't know it at the time, but she had developed fractures in many bones from Maama's abuse. Maama also tormented her psychologically, telling her—and guests—that she was troubled and losing her mind.

This is all either of us can bear to say about her state at this time.

Her sisters knew she was in pain. They often saw her on the floor whimpering, but as Maama hid the worst abuse behind the closed door, they didn't know what exactly was happening. They could not figure out much to help their sister: Maama made it clear that any interventions would not only jeopardize their safety, but also make it worse for Monique. So they cried for her, and tried to sneak her little comforts where they could.

Monique cried every day. She called up the faces and memories of those near to her and who loved her—Papa, Akuyia, Nkooko, Ms. Bridget, her school friends—to remember better times and conjure in her heart a wisp of their encouragement and love. Prayer became her respite, and her lifeline.

If her chores took too long and she couldn't go to school, or if she found a few spare minutes, often after beatings, she sat in a little spot in the red dirt behind the house, facing the sunset. The tiny spot was peaceful and had a nice simple view. She liked to pray there. But often pain, emotional and physical, blocked her heart, and she couldn't pray. At those times she wrote her questions and despairs and prayers in the dust.

How can the sun be so nice and bright and happy, and everything I have experienced under the sun is agony and pain?

Why does God let me suffer? What did I do wrong?

Am I really losing my mind? Am I really troubled?

How come God takes care of so many kids, but not me?

Please let my dad come home so he can save me from this monster.

Many days in these moments, it seemed to her that the sun paused its setting, and just hung there in the sky. For a few minutes it took a little break and accompanied her in her grief.

Then, her heart momentarily lightened, she wiped her words from the dust and returned to her duties and her sisters.

Much later Monique came to understand that she was, in Maama's mind, a proxy for her father. She looked like him; she spoke like him; she had his ways. Everything about her was Papa. And Papa had believed her, every time she reported Maama's mischief, including when she tried to poison them. She had ruined her plans. And Papa loved Monique.

So Maama intended to slowly touch on Papa's closest child, who was a small girl version of him, until she dropped off the earth. That was her goal. If she managed to gradually hurt and kill her, she would feel she had achieved something.

She would likely get away with it. The community wouldn't blame her. Maama could persuade anyone, except Papa, that she was innocent and the kid just fell mysteriously sicker and sicker. She had already been paving the way for this, for months, making comments to guests about her troublesome second daughter's dysfunction and ill health.

One Sunday early morning as the sun was rising, Monique heard a long, long unheard sound.

Voom. Voom-voooom.

It was the Land Rover. Unmistakable.

And then she heard, *click,* her mother lock them in the bedroom from outside.

Oh, that's definitely it then, she thought. *Here's my salvation. My letter was actually received.*

She slid her hand under her sleeping sisters' mattress and pulled out the paper bag. As quickly as she could in her weakness and pain (she had just gotten a fresh beating the night before), she dropped off the clothes she had been sleeping in and dropped on her yellow dress. She gingerly pulled on her white socks and black shoes that had come with her from St. Mary's. Then she went to the large, low window.

In the dawn light she saw the car park and Papa get out. *He was really there!* The clouds parted and sunlight streamed down and angels sang.

An instinct came to her hand. She turned the window latch, and it opened. *All this time,* Monique laughed to herself, *of Maama locking us in here and this thing opens?*

She opened the window and tripped out.

Papa yelled, "Oh my God! Don't fall!"

"'Don't fall?' I don't care, let me fall. You're here now. I can go."

Papa came and picked her up. "Oh my God. I can't even recognize you. You look *awful.*"

Monique cried out, "Don't touch me, don't touch me, my back hurts. Everything hurts."

Papa's eyes teared up. He gingerly wrapped her in a hug. In her father's arms, Monique felt her fears and worry evaporate. He was here. All of the earth's problems were resolved: everything else could go to smoke. She had really made it. The letter had worked.

Thank you God. Thank you Jesus. Thank you Lemanyian. Thank you mail people, she thought. *Thank you Papa.*

After a minute or so, Papa said, "It's OK. Now you're safe. Let's go. Where's everybody?"

"They're sleeping. Maama locked us in." Monique's calm transformed to ecstatic excitement. "Papa!" she exclaimed. "Do you want a rock? I'll give you a rock!"

She had, all these months, been watching a good-sized rock that was outside the kitchen door. She had been waiting for if the time would come that she would decide to bring it smashing down upon Maama's head.

Papa said, "No, I'm not here to fight. I'm just getting all my kids. Wait out here."

Monique climbed gingerly into the Land Rover and waited in the front seat while Papa strode in the house.

She heard him kick open the locked bedroom door. *BAM!* In a few moments he came out. Little Esther was slung over his shoulder, still sleeping and sucking her thumb. Rose walked alongside holding his hand, blinking her long lashes furiously, dropping down tears and processing her relief.

Monique bounced up and down on the seat, gesturing *Let's go, let's go!*

Papa did not say a word to Maama. He simply took the two sisters, loaded them in the back seat, and drove away.

As he drove, Monique flipped between joy and pain.

"I am so glad that you got my letter. I'll never ask you to do for me anything in my life."

"Monique, you never asked me for anything. So if this is the only thing I had to save, so be it. ... And all these motherfuckers who did this, they're gonna pay for it."

She started crying. Watching the passing landscape and thinking about how Maama had treated her, and Maama's accusations, she said, "You know, Papa, I'm not the troubled person here."

Papa grunted in agreement. *That bitch*, he muttered.

After a few more minutes, Monique said, "Papa, I want to join the police force. So I can stop this terrible stuff happening to other people."

"No, you can't join. You're dangerous."

Rose piped up, "No, that is for me, because I am more calm."

"Yeah, that's more like you, because you have a calm nature. But Monique? I would not let her. She'll kill everybody I know."

"Yeah, payback time, man," Monique chuckled. *I would indeed kill every one of those motherfuckers*, she thought.

After a few more minutes passed and Papa sensed the children's swell of emotions had settled, he cleared his throat. "Er, so girls. If you look around the car, you will see there are a few things stashed here and there. You should explore and help yourselves. This ride will be a bit long."

The girls squealed and set to investigating. They found a cooler. Inside were bottles of cold water, and cans of sweet mango and orange juices, and small packs of yummy milk with little straws. They exclaimed and shared these out and happily sipped and boogied.

Next they found snacks. There was a bag with all kinds of delicious fruits, and then there were crackers and some low-sugar chocolates. (Papa liked to minimize sugar intake.) There were also some small crinkly dark brown paper bags: tearing into them, they discovered they held many little round colorful candies. They looked like Cadbury Smarties to Monique, which she had tried a few times and adored. The bags said in big bold letters "M&Ms."

"Papa, are these from America?" Monique asked.

Papa grunted, and the girls cheered and tried them.

"It's chocolate! American chocolate!" Rose declared, wide-eyed.

The girls had only been exposed to British chocolates. Trying chocolate from the actual other side of the world was magical. Esther bobbled her curly head around in delight.

After munching, the girls sipped more water and juice and milk. "There's still more to find," Papa said. "Look further. You're going to need this stuff where we're going."

The girls hadn't asked or cared where they were driving. This was Papa, and they just knew things were going to be good.

In the back, tucked up where it wasn't easily seen, Rose discovered a large suitcase. They all clambered back and opened it up.

Inside were wonderful new clothes: jeans and t-shirts, underwear and thick long socks, and three pairs of excellent, sturdy safari-style boots in their different sizes. Papa grinned ear to ear as the girls' happy commotion wafted forward: yips and oohs and ahhs as they pulled out more delights. Toothpaste! Toothbrushes! Nine of them! ("Three for each of you," Papa said.) They had only ever used mswaki before: toothbrushes were quite exotic.

At the bottom they discovered absolute treasure for girls their age: small storybooks, and three beautiful complete large stationery sets. The girls burst into an excited ruckus, clapping and exclaiming. There were notebooks and drawing pads and pens in the colors of the rainbow.

"*What?!*" Monique hollered. "You're telling me colored pens come in other than *red?!* Can have green? And orange and purple?!"

There were nifty little pencil sharpeners, and separate erasers, and many beautiful yellow pencils with soft pink erasers on top. Most wonderful of all, there were three colored pencil sets. The girls all whooped and clapped again. They loved drawing and making art. Even just receiving regular pencils was great: once you got your one pencil at the beginning of the quarter at St.

Mary's, you wouldn't see another until the next quarter! Actual *colored* pencil sets were like legendary pirate gold.

Explorations finally complete, the sisters settled back in their seats.

Her spirit restored and back up front, Monique took on her customary role of bouncing up and down and egging her father to drive faster, just as she did during bush hunting.

"Faster! Go faster!" she demanded.

Papa's silver eyes gleamed in delight and he complied.

"Faster!" The car started skidding all over the maram roads.

"No more!" Papa said. "You'll kill us!"

"No! Faster!" the girl chortled. Papa was her first rally driver.

To distract his mini speed demon from her demands, Papa started telling stories about life in America: the weather, what children's lives were like, the schools, food, and so on. The girls peppered him with questions. Just hearing his voice was delightful. Beyond having missed him and the drama of their rescue and it being generally wonderful to hear him and talk with him, he sounded different. He now spoke perfect Oxford English with an American accent. Soon they were asking any old silly questions just to get him to talk more and say different words.

He shifted to lecturing and encouraging them. "If you want to go to university anywhere in the world, the sky is the limit."

"OK, that's it," he said, and abruptly stopped the car.

"What?!" the girls exclaimed. "We're here? Already?!"

"Yep. Time for fun. Let's go."

Papa had driven them a usually-eight-hour-drive from Lodung-okwe not back to Maralal, but instead further away, past Wamba and then much further, to the highly-prestigious and relaxing Samburu Lodge resort in the Samburu National Reserve, at the edge of Isiolo County. In their joy and interest the journey had flown by: it seemed like only an hour had passed. (Papa did also speed enough to cover the journey in just over six hours: it was only late lunchtime when they arrived.)

When the girls saw where they were, they were gobsmacked. Going to the Samburu Lodge was every kid's dream. It was Disneyland. Not in what you did there, but in the mystique, the joy, the prestige. It was truly special, and very, very far from Maralal, and they had never been there. No one had remotely contemplated this possibility.

"OH MY GODDDDD!" the girls all screamed. They grabbed their new toothbrushes and toothpaste and changes of clothes, and socks and safari boots, and dashed to the bathroom to wash up and change.

The bathroom alone was a revelation. It was spacious and lovely and clean, with the legendary flush toilets—Monique flushed one several times just for fun—and the taps miraculously emitted wonderful warm water, not frigid as they were used to. Bright white, plush towels sat out, which the girls were scared to touch lest they sully them.

"Can you believe this?!" Monique trilled. Rose and Esther beamed and boogied. They figured out their toothbrushes, giggled and spat, and then washed their faces and hands and smoothed their hair. They dried their hands on the plush towels, and, radiantly happy, traipsed out to join Papa.

The family strolled to a beautiful outdoor dining area. Superbly professional, cheerful, impeccably dressed local staff were everywhere. A smiling receptionist had greeted them on arrival; here in the dining area cooks strode by wearing tall white chef hats and white jackets, and black pants with long white aprons at the waist. Similarly well-dressed waitstaff walked elegantly here and there. A long buffet with many chafing dishes sat to the side: at its end stood a large meat-carving station with many roasted meats, and an attendant pleasantly serving them out. The girls drank everything in with wide eyes. The contrast from the tiny scrubby village and abuse they had escaped could not have been greater.

Papa settled Rose and Esther at a table and told them to order anything they wanted. A server appeared and courteously took their order, and placed four sets of binoculars on the table, to better enjoy the wonderful views of the rolling hillsides and distant animals. Once her sisters were settled, Papa brought Monique to the nearby nurse's station.

Papa clearly had chosen to bring the girls to the Lodge to delight and restore them, and for his own restoration as well. But he also somehow knew, trusted, and was friends with the European nurse there. She warmly welcomed Papa and Monique into the treatment room, closed the door, and asked Monique to remove her boots and clothes and socks, leaving on her underwear. She passed Monique a cute woven vase-shaped container that was filled with small candies. "Please enjoy some of these love, while I take a look at you. OK?" Monique nodded.

"PK, this is *bad*," the nurse murmured, sadly shaking her head, as she assessed Monique's malnutrition and surveyed her mosaic of bruises and cuts. She began to clean and treat her many wounds as gently as she could. "This is extremely serious. ... I want to make a police report on your ex-wife, for child abuse and attempted murder."

"No, it doesn't work here." Papa said, frowning. "It never works in this country. So let's leave that alone. I just need her to get a medical ... some medical attention. Give her some antibiotics or whatever she needs."

"But PK, look. This is far too terrible." To Monique she asked, "When did she beat you?"

"Oh. I get this every day. This is an everyday thing for me."

"For months?!"

"Yes." Monique popped another candy in her mouth, and focused on savoring it.

The nurse burst into quiet tears and kept treating the wounds. Then she said, "Listen, Monique. ... If you survived this, it's because God really wants you to stay alive."

And the girl cried and the nurse cried, while the nurse kept working and the girl flinching, and the man considered what to do with the white-hot fury in his heart.

Later, assessment and treatment complete, the nurse released them with instructions for restoring Monique's overall health and further treating her wounds over the next weeks, especially her poor feet. These were finally properly cleaned and treated and bandaged, and were far more comfortable. The nurse handed them a bag with many bandages, rolls of gauze and medical tape, GV solution, and ointments. She refused to take back the little woven container of candies, and asked Monique to please keep it as a gift.

They joined the others at the table. "What do you want to order?" Papa asked.

"Fish and chips!"

She had tried this once with relatives and now it was all she wanted. When the huge plate arrived she could only finish half, as the past months had damaged her appetite. Rose and Esther, long done eating, called for more cold orange Fanta for everyone. They packed their leftovers in tidy boxes and set them aside, and then spent the afternoon drinking their Fantas, exploring the resort, and watching wildlife through their binoculars. (Papa had brought his own from the car, and left the fourth set untouched on the table.)

Even for girls who were relatively used to seeing wildlife, the experience here in the national reserve was incredible. The animals were different, and far more numerous and completely wild.

Through their binoculars they watched a herd of enormous elephants slowly lumber and wave their trunks. Several had fantastically long curving tusks. Over in another area of the rolling landscape many tall giraffes grazed the tops of the acacia trees. Large dazzles of zebras cantered to and fro, noisily huffing and braying. Further along roamed herds of buffalo, and tiny adorable dik-diks and klipspringers, and elegant gazelles.

Monique was fascinated by the gazelles' black stripes, so vivid and precise against their white bellies. "It's like someone took a brush and painted them all *so accurately*," she exclaimed to her sisters. The graceful creatures whisked their tails and pranced about, shaking their heads and their long, curving horns.

Papa gestured and told them the mighty Ewaso Ng'iro, the "dirty river," fed by the glaciers of Mount Kenya, was just a bit further past the thickening belt of clustered trees in the distance. He described how it never dried out, and that at night they could see hippos and many other creatures there.

"Hippos I don't need, but can I bring one of these gazelles home?" Monique asked, grinning.

"Absolutely not."

And just like that, the girls all suddenly became sleepy. "Come, let's go," Papa said. They gathered the leftovers and medical supplies, and returned the binoculars. The girls waved goodbye to the pleasant staff and climbed into the Land Rover.

Nearly immediately they were asleep. They slept the entire very, very long journey, as Papa drove them safely back, past Wamba and Lodungokwe and all the way back to the manyatta.

The day had begun with Monique imprisoned, hearing an engine and the click of a lock, and ended in serenity and peaceful dreams of beautiful animals roaming wild and free.

Papa never spoke to Uncle Le'e again. He had to find other work, as he was no longer trusted with Papa's affairs.

As for Maama, Papa said, "I'm not going anywhere near her ever again. If I do I'll kill her, and I don't want that. I got things to do."

He got emergency court orders that she was never to be near his children. He passed copies of these and a letter he wrote to Monique, saying, "When I leave, let Ms. Mary read these. I don't want to explain anything. I'm tired of explaining things to people who can't understand. So tell her she has a copy, you have a copy, and I have a copy. I have to go back to school. 'Cause I had to take a week off. To come get you. Literally."

Before Papa left to catch his flight, he escorted the girls back in to St. Mary's. He instructed them that in future absolutely no one was allowed to come visit or even see them.

"Do you see this latticework brick wall here, with all the holes where people can look through?" he asked. The girls nodded: everyone went there to talk to people outside the grounds. "You're to even stay away from this area. OK? It's for your protection. Now you understand why you should be here. This is a more secure place."

Papa brought them in to the headmistress and then said goodbye.

After reading the letter and scanning the court order, Ms. Mary looked at them soberly. They had been gone for months.

"Girls," she quietly said, "you will not need to repeat the grade. You may pick up with the rest of the classes and complete the year. Esther and Rose, you may proceed to your dormitories and the matrons will take care of you."

After they left, Ms. Mary looked at Monique. "My dear, I am so sorry for what you endured." She blinked tears away and continued, "Come, let's get you to the infirmary. You still need some attention."

Monique rested and recuperated several more days at the school infirmary before resuming classes. She received further care for her healing wounds, and extra nutrition for her emaciation. Her feet gradually healed, and miraculously they healed well: but they remained covered in dark scars, spotted like a leopard's skin. Slowly, her pain and bruises also cleared.

And then bit by bit life went back to normal.

She delightedly resumed her studies in fifth grade. Her education was returned to her along with her life, and she was determined to make the most of it. St. Mary's really was a far better school than the one in Lodungokwe, and in the higher grades more opportunities became available, for clubs, competitions, and extra challenge and service. Monique drank all these in like delicious, clear cold water. After the heinous, truly murderous cruelty she had escaped from her own mother, bearing the difficulties inherent in school life was nothing. She was even more determined to achieve her goals of education and freedom, and to help others on the way if she could. Her compassion, already strong, was now ironclad.

Her emotional pain and anger at what she had been through also gradually faded. But like the lines of her fractures from Maama's abuse, and the scars on her feet from the brutal path she had been forced to walk, they never completely went away.

They lay hidden, usually invisible, but in the right conditions could still be seen.

29

The Cut

There are still many stories to share, involving a leopard, elephants, camel races, stolen brides, Jimmy and a lion, snakes, many cakes, running away twice, several diplomatic bags, and more. However, we have been informed that one book cannot fit all these things, and so as when portioning out a jam-packed fruitcake, we had to choose a place, close our eyes, and just make a cut to yield a manageable first serving. This is the cut. On this side are these stories, leaving Monique and her sisters returned to their primary school, in their last year together. On the other side are their many further adventures, together and separately.

We will not say anything to spoil your future reading, but are happy to share that nothing quite as horrific as her experiences in Lodungokwe happened again to Monique. Papa will indeed return from America, both over breaks and then permanently. And if you are familiar with the region, he eventually became credited with driving an enormous amount of development, including innumerable children educated thanks to his help, and starting many families in businesses. With men, that is.

If you are wondering how Monique and her sisters will fare, in a society that was far more heavily patriarchal than this book perhaps lets on, reflect on the outcome from her bicycle request.

But also reflect on the determination of the little girl who descended abysses to fetch water; who dragged herself, near death, across the house and yard to use the restroom; who on torn and bleeding feet brought lost children out of the wilderness; and who escaped her own mother's repeated attempts to kill her. How will such a girl fare?

You can probably guess.

Glossary

These words and names are defined as what they meant to Monique at the time she used them, in her family and context. Many of these words are shared across multiple languages, and have variant spellings. Note that the Maa sound represented by "ny" is not a standard English "ny," but something like a "soft ny," with the "n"s inaudible to new listeners.

Akuyia *Maa*: "grandfather": in this book, specifically Monique's paternal grandfather.

Apaanyiaa *Maa*: a respectful and endearing term of address used for men of your father's generation.

Apiyio *Maa*: "uncle": in this book, used by Monique to refer to one particular uncle, her grandfather's favorite son who was his companion and apprentice.

Baba *Maa, many other languages*: name appellate meaning "father of." Monique had two uncles known as Baba Lkopina, "father of Lkopina," and Baba Senenkon, "father of Senenkon."

busaa *Swahili*: a homebrew beer popular in Kenya, made from millet and corn.

chai *Swahili, from Indian languages*: tea, whether made in the classic Indian style or otherwise. In Swahili it also can mean "a bribe."

chang'aa *Swahili*: literally "kill me quickly," a very potent illegal alcohol brew, or moonshine.

chapati *Swahili, from Indian languages*: a popular simple flatbread made from flour, water, and salt, cooked with oil or ghee. Kenya adopted chapatis from its Indian residents, and commonly has both the simple flat chapati and a multilayered one similar to an Indian *paratha*.

ghee *Indian languages*: clarified butter: the oil portion of milk. In Swahili, called *samli*.

hodi *Swahili*: A greeting called out to seek permission to enter: used to enter homes and to cross rivers. Roughly, "Hello, may I enter/pass?"

jiko *Swahili*: a small portable cookstove made from metal and ceramic. It commonly burns charcoal but can also burn wood, and has supports on top to hold a pot.

Kuuliza si ujinga *Swahili*: literally, "Asking is not stupidity." Similar to the English "There are no stupid questions."

Lemanyian *Maa*: the name of Papa's kind friend who saved Monique and her aunt. It means "he who is blessed," derived from *manyani*, "blessings."

Lorekesho *Maa*: "the rapist." Refers to the local bandit who terrorized the Maralal area.

machicha *Swahili*: residue from straining a liquid. Here, specifically the spent grain remnants from making busaa. Papa fed this to his cows, and Namada was especially appreciative.

Madaraka Day, Jamhuri Day *Swahili/English*: Kenya's two national holidays celebrating its independence and establishment. *Madaraka* means authority or power, especially to rule; *jamhuri* means republic.

mandazi *Swahili*: delicious Kenyan deep-fried small sweetbreads, similar to doughnuts or frybread.

manyatta *Maa*: a village or settlement, traditionally simple huts surrounded by a thorn fence.

maram *Maa*: also spelled *murram*: unfinished dirt roads.

miraa *Swahili*: also known as *khat*: the leaves from the local bush *Catha edulis*, chewed as a sociable stimulant.

moran *Maa*: the life stage for young Samburu men when they serve as "warriors": expected to manage the livestock and defense. They have many prerogatives and restrictions during this period, which lasts about fourteen years, from adolescence through early adulthood.

mswaki *Swahili, from Arabic*: toothbrush, or the common stick cut from the "toothbrush tree," *Salvadora persica*, chewed on to clean the teeth and gums.

mwiko *Swahili*: a strong wooden cooking paddle: used to stir and turn ugali. Mwikos range in size from a large cooking spoon to a small oar, depending on the quantity of food being cooked.

mzungu *Swahili, from Bantu*: literally meaning "wanderer," refers to foreigners, commonly white people or those from Europe.

Nailukiaa *Maa*: Baba Senenkon's nickname for Monique: "ears on fire."

Namada *Maa*: literally meaning "foolish": the name of Monique's favorite cow.

Ndurume *Kikuyu*: "the ram": the huge "king" ram of the family's flock of sheep.

Nkai *Maa*: God, the Creator.

Nkiyaa *Maa*: "Granny Ears": Monique's paternal grandmother, so called because of her ability to hear anything going on.

Nkooko *Maa*: "grandmother": Monique used this to refer to her beloved great-grandmother.

ntotoi *Maa*: the Samburu version of the ancient game known as *bau* ("board" in Swahili) or mancala, played on a wooden board on a piece of cloth, or an impromptu "board" dug from the earth. Players move stones around two rows of cups, trying to "capture" the most stones. In Samburu culture this game is extremely strictly reserved for men: women are not even properly permitted to watch or approach it.

rumba *Swahili*: a dance move like a boogie version of the twist, where the hips and shoulders twist and shimmy opposite each other.

rungu *Maa and Swahili*: a throwing/threatening/whapping stick commonly carried by Samburu men. About a forearm's length, with a knob or bend on the end, and worn in the belt.

shifta *Swahili*: bandit or outlaw.

shuka *Maa*: a traditional thin cotton shawl/blanket, worn many ways but usually draped over the back and shoulders. Generally plaid or striped, often in bright colors, favoring orange, red, yellow, blue, and purple.

sukuma wiki *Swahili*: literally, "push the week": a popular Kenyan and regional dish of braised collard greens, often with a small amount of meat. The name refers to the greens' excellent nutrition helping to "stretch" the supply of meat and food.

terere *Kikuyu*: a wild amaranth with highly-nutritious leaves that Monique found unbearably slimy once cooked up. It also features in many Asian cuisines.

ugali *Swahili*: an extremely-widespread cornmeal dish, made from boiling fine cornmeal in water or milk and then cooking it further and turning it until it becomes dough-like and pillowy. This dish is known by many names throughout many African countries.

Preview of the Sequel

It was still early morning in the manyatta, but the dawn's cool had already scattered and it was hot, dusty, and dry. Nine year old Monique grabbed some rest in the shade outside Second Granny's hut. Granny Ears was in a fury, gesturing wildly and yelling about something one of the uncles had done. She finished her tirade, and her flinty eyes turned towards Monique. Her fingers went to her belt. *Whoa, uh oh,* Monique thought. *Time to get out of the manyatta.*

Before Nkiyaa's mouth could open, Monique stood up. "I'll go get water and wood. For everyone. Where are the girls?"

"They're busy. Helping with beads for the wedding." Granny Ears's glare clearly added that *they* were not useless at this task, unlike her granddaughter.

"That's OK. I'll go alone. I'll get it for everyone."

Seven hours later, Monique slowly staggered across the dusty red path towards the line of the manyatta fence. She had been going all day. Each long trip to the river had seen her return with over five gallons of muddy water in jerry cans on her back and a pile of firewood tied atop. This was her fifth, last trip. It was mid-afternoon.

A haze of heat and exhaustion kept rising and blurring out her view. She knew she was almost home: she was coming up on the huge, magnificent mahogany tree that stood right outside the manyatta main gate. It was known as the Goat Tree, because the village goats liked to clamber around in its branches and happily brag and bleat away. Though Monique didn't hear any goats now.

"Hoh. I'm so tired."

Her steps faltered and she squinted. She was only about twenty steps from the manyatta gate.

Hoh. I'm done, she thought. *I can't even go home.*

She tottered sideways a few steps into the inviting shade of the tree. *Let me just lean on this tree because I really ... I am so tired. I can't even move from here.*

She plopped down and leaned back, banging her load of water and firewood against the huge trunk. Her head fell back on the pile of sticks. *Man, this is actually a great pillow*, she thought: and then she was out.

After minutes or hours, not knowing she had fallen deep, deep asleep, suddenly

POOM!

A stunning jolt—something massive suddenly hitting the ground *right there*—shook through the earth and her body and her load and the tree. Her eyes flew open, but she couldn't see anything.

She was inexplicably in a thick cloud of dust.

The heck is that!? Her hands fanned the air. The dust swirled and began drifting.

Spots slowly materialized through the dust. They were in her face.

Dang!

Whiskers. Right in front of her nose.

She just blinked and looked, her consciousness creakingly pulling itself together like a very old man slowly standing up, except he is looking around first to see where he has put his walking stick.

Man, this thing is cute. WOW.

She was looking into large, beautiful amber eyes, inches from hers. A multitude of silver whiskers quivered underneath, clean and crispy. Lovely golden skin all over; many, many dark brown spots. The creature coming into focus as the dust continued to clear was just incredibly fresh and nice and pretty.

Wow. Gorgeous. I like the spots!

Monique's consciousness still hadn't found its cane. She pulled her arms out of her load-straps as she admired the creature. They were eye to eye, its whiskers almost touching her face. It regarded her in her calm interest, like it was wondering, *Unafraid creature, who are you?* It didn't snarl or even lick its lips: just looked into her eyes calmly.

Dang! This is CUTE! Monique was able now to make out more of the huge body behind. *Oh, you're a boy!* she thought.

His breath was hitting her face. The breath smelled fresh.

Notes on the Collaboration

by Ann

Monique and I met seemingly through blind luck.

In 2011 I had just moved back to America after a decade living overseas in Southeast Asia, where my husband is from. We settled in a completely new region, the Pacific Northwest: we'd never been anywhere near the place and knew no one. At one of my kids' first events at their new school, I was reeling from reverse culture-shock, and my shyness and awkwardness were fully up to ten, when they're natural to me at about a six or seven anyway. Yet I love people and love to chat and make friends. What to do?

In the loose crowd of parents I spotted an elegant woman who was unmistakably African. And she looked like she was nice! I had only seen one African woman in ten years[26] and it was obvious that this lovely woman was now far from home, just as I had been far from home myself all those years in Asia. Remembering how much I appreciated people befriending me when I was abroad, I walked up to her and said hello. That is

---

[26] African women are quite rare in Southeast Asia. The only one I met was the Cameroonian wife of an imported soccer player, who had moved into our Malaysian small-city condo complex. She had a strong, active, fierce four-year-old son, which did not lend for good mixes with the local kids. The highlight of our brief friendship was me trying to help defuse the situation when her son had pushed an older Chinese-Malaysian kid, who ran home crying, and the local kid's mom came out with a frying pan. She ran and chased the little Cameroonian boy around and around our complex's swimming pool, waving the pan and shouting, "You hit my son! You hit my son, ah! I hit you, ah!" This

how I met Monique, and those were some of the best few steps I ever took. Monique was not new to America at this time, but she, like I, was indeed new to the area, and it was a great time for us to begin our friendship.[27]

As luck would have it, I had decided to pause my usual career of teaching English, reading, and writing, to focus on settling my family at our new home and raising our three school-age and younger kids. With the spare time I stupidly thought I'd have I had determined to work on some unfinished writing projects. Those projects are still unfinished, because as I got to know Monique over the years it became clear that this remarkable woman's great stories were languishing away mostly unheard as she busted her butt providing for her kids, working in first hospitality and then elder care. She is great at that work, too, and it is highly important work! But I felt her stories needed to get out, and she had no time to write, working far overtime to raise her two daughters in our city and give them all the opportunities she could.

Few are the stories I could think of that could compete with her extraordinary life. And her stories needed to be told for her daughters. Further, they offered valuable insights into a culture's vanishing ancient ways and the lessons from them, and from a too-rarely-heard girl's and woman's perspective. They also resonate for any of us caught in struggles between

---

prompted several more alarmed adults to come out, including the Cameroonian mother. That family left soon after. Funnily, a few years later on a visit back to Malaysia it was my young son who got fed up with a smaller local kid punching him at a dinner and casually tripped him. This alarmed the adults, and they sprang up and were angry and scowled at us. Play among children, especially from different cultures, can be very hard to navigate successfully.

[27] The forces of our lives brought us together from over 10,000 miles to become friends and collaborate. I flew 8000-plus miles from Malaysia: she traveled over 2000 miles from Atlanta. If you count her being long-ago rustled out of Kenya, our total is over 18,000 miles: across most of Earth.

what our society says we should do, and what we feel we *must* do to survive and thrive. And her life came at a particularly interesting time, when her culture was just beginning to face modernity and wrangle with it. So getting her stories told was an obvious, urgent matter. But as often as I urged Monique to write them herself, or submit a query somewhere, it never happened. (Of course not: what time did she have for this?) She, with characteristic fierce loyalty, declared I'd have to be the one to help her. Which was great, except that I was also a too-busy mom, myself.

So over more than ten years, between her working double shifts and whenever I had rare moments free, we collaborated on this work: two well-traveled women, both adjusting to a new home and both completely overstretched. We often could only find time to meet over her lunch breaks, out together on errands or grabbing coffee, or literally while driving her from one shift to another. When the Covid-19 epidemic hit, it slowed us even further as she was slammed at work in elder care and I was stuck with my entire family at home on remote learning and work. That year was a writing loss for both of us. The year after knocked me specifically out, as my teen daughter came down with a horrifically debilitating illness, eventually diagnosed as ME/CFS, which required me full-time as her carer while she was suddenly bedbound for months. (She fortunately got much better after nearly a year of intensive, at-home care, and was able to go to university.)

A collaboration on a memoir is inherently time-consuming. Monique and I recorded several interviews together, and then I typed full transcripts, to use her own words as much as possible, especially in dialogue. This was slow. I never learned to type properly, and type with one hand, like an idiot. One minute of recording took on average ten minutes to transcribe.

But this labor was preciously important: most of the dialogue in this book—both inner dialogue and spoken—is verbatim from her storytelling. Then we had to sort which stories, details, and dialogue went where in her life, both physically and temporally. I also did hundreds of hours of research into the land, people, and history relevant to her stories, to help convey things well and reduce bugging her. Then we collaborated on what would be included. As I wrote she read over and checked and corrected everything: which led to her remembering more stories and information that often set the process back to transcribing/ frenzied note taking and rewriting all over again. All this was done in those tiny windows of time we had over the years.

We're delighted we finally got this first book through her young childhood completed. The followup book is underway. (A series of her stories adapted suitably for children is also planned.) The extra years provided more time for the friendship and collaboration to deepen. I suspect this may be a better work due to having developed over such a long and sincere friendship, than if she had indeed found a "professional" partner.

Here are a few of the funnier moments from our collaboration.

The meeting, #2

After meeting Monique at school, I again saw her, with her younger daughter this time, at a park. My youngest son had a kite, and her daughter was interested in it. Both kids were not yet school aged, but her daughter was at that time definitely bigger and tougher. I'm not clear what happened next: I remember offering it to the girl to play with or possibly keep. But Monique remembers her daughter actively snatching the kite from my son and running away with it, making him cry. About six years later this son would be the one to get in trouble for tripping the Malaysian kid who was pestering him, continuing the cycle.

As we're shopping in Warehouse Club #1

Me: Monique. Those ears. The Samburu ears with the big holes. (Samburu often train holes in their ear lobes that can reach inches long, making their ears resemble looped handles.)

Monique: (Picking up a set of glassware to examine) Uh huh?

Me: My kids are wondering. Don't they get caught on stuff?

Monique: Pfft. NO. (In an "Are you stupid" tone.)

Monique at that moment gets a tiny loop of thread on her infinity shawl caught on her keychain and it rips out a good six inches. I couldn't believe it.

Me: See, like that. No, they never get caught? Not on branches or anything?

Monique: Pfft. NO. (Still untangling her scarf thread.)

Me: Huh. OK.

In the car in front of Warehouse Club #2

Me: So, Monique, the kids are wondering about Samburu kids going around naked so much. Don't they get ... cut up? Or injured?

Monique: Pfft. NO.

Me: Ehhh ... , and look. (I show her a picture from Nigel Pavitt's fabulous book *Samburu*. A small mob of butt-naked kids are excitedly running up and sliding down a slick mud hill on their bare tooshes.) Don't they get mud or something up in there?

Monique: No. Well, yes they do, and if anything goes up in there, it comes on out and it's all OK.

Me: Huh. OK.

A last note: It was surprising to both me and Monique how often my lived experience in Malaysia, another ex-British colony at a somewhat similar developmental point to Kenya, related to aspects of culture and history she described. Both countries are equatorial with tropical highlands, received independence not long from each other, share many characteristics, and even use similar slang for the local bribes: *duit kopi*, "coffee money," in Malaysia and *chai*, "tea," in Kenya! My Malaysian husband was also the product of his country after independence, and went to a similar Catholic public (boys') school. It will be interesting to see how many other residents or children of Commonwealth countries recognize echoes from her story.

Resources on the Samburu

We are grateful to the many authors, photographers, and researchers who shared their insights on Samburu history and culture. These helped us check and "round out" our descriptions of Monique's experiences. Here is a non-alphabetical list of some resources that we used and others may find helpful.

Pavitt, Nigel. *Samburu.* Henry Holt & Co., 1992.
Chock full of gorgeous photos and excellent information from a long-term Kenyan resident and friend of the Samburu: the very best resource on what traditional life was like near the time of Monique's childhood. Unfortunately this book covers very little of the lives of women and girls, but there is a bit there, and there is a great deal on the lives of boys and men, and overall cultural and historic information. It is also unfortunately currently hard to find!

Lesogorol, Carolyn K. *Contesting the Commons: Privatizing Pastoral Land in Kenya.* University of Michigan Press, 2008.
Scholarly work by a highly-esteemed professor and researcher who also spent much time in Kenya.

Samburu Women Trust. *The Unspoken Vice in Samburu Community.* SWT Research Report, April 2016. Available in multiple places as a PDF download.
An excellent research report into the Samburu practice of "beading" young girls and the social and practical circumstances around it.

Holtzman, Jon D. "In a Cup of Tea: Commodities and History among Samburu Pastoralists in Northern Kenya." *American Ethnologist*, vol. 30, no. 1, 2003, pp. 136–55. JSTOR, http://www.jstor.org/stable/3805213. Accessed 10 Dec. 2023.

Holtzman, Jon. "The Food of Elders, the 'Ration' of Women: Brewing, Gender, and Domestic Processes among the Samburu of Northern Kenya." *American Anthropologist*, vol. 103, no. 4, 2001, pp. 1041–58. JSTOR, http://www.jstor.org/stable/684128. Accessed 19 Dec 2023.

Iannotti, Lora, and Carolyn Lesorogol. "Dietary Intakes and Micronutrient Adequacy Related to the Changing Livelihoods of Two Pastoralist Communities in Samburu, Kenya." *Current Anthropology*, vol. 55, no. 4, 2014, pp. 475–82. JSTOR, https://doi.org/10.1086/677107. Accessed 7 Jan. 2024.

Almasi, Oswald, et al. *Swahili Grammar for Introductory and Intermediate Levels*. UPA, 2014.

Image Credits

We're grateful to the following artists: your works, shared via generous copyrights, wonderfully illustrated Monique's surroundings and culture.

If you would like to see more, visit Kenya and Samburu County: or, alternatively, the artists' home pages, or daughteroftheleopard.com .

<u>Front Cover</u>

Leopard cropped and faded from "Leopard looking through the grass at Queen Elizabeth National Park" by Giles Laurent, at Wikimedia Commons, used under CC BY-SA 4.0

Girl's eyes cropped from purchased royalty image "African child" by poco_bw, at iStock Photo

Ripped paper vector reworked from "Ripped Transparent Paper Texture Free PNG" by sayhellonan graphics at Vecteezy.com

Background Maralal topo map adapted from public domain map at the Library of Congress

Beads cropped and darkened from "Samburu Girls necklaces" by Redemption93, at Wikimedia Commons, used under CC BY-SA 4.0

Ewaso Ng'iro river cropped and darkened from "Ewaso Ngiro River" by Panegyrics of Granovetter, at Wikimedia Commons, used under CC BY-SA 2.0

Vehicle (reminiscent of Papa's Land Rover) cropped and darkened from "Photograph of a Car with Yellow Lights" by Vishva Patel, at Pexels

Young morans cropped and darkened from "Young Samburu male" by Sankara Subramanian, at Wikimedia Commons, used under CC BY 2.0

Filmstrip frame (also on spine and back cover), numbers changed, from Joseph_alban at Pixabay

<u>Spine</u>

Maram road and blue sky cropped from unnamed image by Vishva Patel, at Pexels

Feather adapted by Ann from public domain image

<u>Back Cover</u>

Background pawprint and vehicle tread: cropped, darkened, and faded from "Samburu - march 2019 -52" by Weldon Kennedy, at Wikimedia Commons, used under CC BY 2.0

Zebra cropped from "Zebra" by Gabriele Brancati, at Pexels

Water buffalo cropped from "African buffalo and yellow-billed oxpeckers, Maasai Mara, Kenya" by . Ray in Manila, at Wikimedia Commons, used under CC BY 2.0

Women building a hut cropped from "The Samburu women are building a new hut," Dr. Ondřej Havelka (cestovatel), at Wikimedia Commons, used under CC BY-SA 4.0

Vervet monkey cropped from "Vervet Monkey (Chlorocebus pygerythrus)" by Thomas Shahan, at Wikimedia Commons, used under CC BY 2.0

Young Maasai shepherd cropped from "Young Masai herder" by Andreas Lederer, at Wikimedia Commons, used under CC BY 2.0

Elephants cropped from "Samburu National Reserve" by Panegyrics of Granovetter, at Wikimedia Commons, used under CC BY-SA 2.0

Superb starling cropped from "Close-Up Shot of a Common Redstart Bird Perched on a Tree Branch" by Vishva Patel, at Pexels

<u>Interior maps</u>

Large Africa map: adapted from public domain CIA map.

Kenya/Samburu County map: built by Ann on a base map of Kenya's counties and rivers, grayscaled, rivers faded, and then details and labels added. Base map: "Location Map of Kenya" by NordNordWest, at Wikimedia Commons, used under CC BY-SA 3.0 DE

To see copyright deeds, visit:

CC BY 2.0: https://creativecommons.org/licenses/by/2.0/deed.en

CC BY-SA 2.0: https://creativecommons.org/licenses/by-sa/2.0/deed.en

CC BY-SA 3.0 DE: https://creativecommons.org/licenses/by-sa/3.0/de/legalcode

CC BY-SA 4.0: https://creativecommons.org/licenses/by-sa/4.0/deed.en

Childhood Photos

Unfortunately Hurricane Katrina swallowed most of Monique's childhood photos, along with many other prized possessions. She does, however, have these from this time in her life.

Both of these are on our website as well, in wonderful vintage 1970s-80s photo color.

Monique and other girls from her kindergarten class, in a tiny photo snapped by one of the nuns and dated on the back. Monique is in the upper right, making the demonic face.
(personal photo)

Papa asked someone at the Samburu Lodge to snap this photo of him and Monique after the nurse treated her. Note her yellow dress and the woven candy basket.
(personal photo)

About the Authors

Monique N. Leparleen

Monique has led one of the world's most interesting lives. She went from manyatta life to enterprising in Nairobi, traveling Europe and Israel alone, moving to America for study and marriage, fleeing Hurricane Katrina with her kids, and ultimately whisking her children to the furthest corner of America she could find: the tip of the Pacific Northwest. Here she now keeps her elegant, multilingual Samburu self, cosmopolitan and yet very down-to-earth, in a gleaming small city among huge lakes and soggy, chilly evergreen forests. Utterly out of place, but utterly at home.

If you wish to book Monique for a reading or sharing her stories, visit daughteroftheleopard.com.

Ann Hendricks

Ann lives with her husband and children in the same Pacific Northwest city. She is grateful for her faith and her family, especially her parents, and for all those who showed her friendship and life lessons—and encouragement to write—here and back in Illinois, Kentucky, Singapore, and Malaysia. In addition to writing, Ann is an ESL and reading/writing/critical thinking teacher, and had a brilliant time teaching at both the National University of Singapore and in her own private classroom in Malaysia.